D0998850

Electronic Elsewheres

For more books in this series, see page 281.

CHRIS BERRY, SOYOUNG KIM,
AND LYNN SPIGEL, EDITORS

Electronic

Elsewheres

Media, Technology, and the

Experience of Social Space

PUBLIC WORLDS, VOLUME 17

UNIVERSITY OF MINNESOTA PRESS

MINNEAPOLIS LONDON

A shorter version of chapter 4 was published in *European Journal of Cultural Studies* 8, no. 4 (2005): 403–26. Portions of chapter 10 were previously published in "A Fine and Private Place: The Cinematic Spaces of the London Underground," *Screen* 47, no.1 (2006): 1–17. Chapter 11 is derived from portions of *Tourists of History: Memory, Kitsch, and Consumerism from Oklahoma City to Ground Zero* (Durham, N.C.: Duke University Press, 2007).

Copyright 2010 by the Regents of the University of Minnesota

All rights reserved. No part of this publication may be reproduced, stored in a retrieval system, or transmitted, in any form or by any means, electronic, mechanical, photocopying, recording, or otherwise, without the prior written permission of the publisher.

Published by the University of Minnesota Press
111 Third Avenue South, Suite 290
Minneapolis, MN 55401–2520
http://www.upress.umn.edu

Library of Congress Cataloging-in-Publication Data

Electronic elsewheres : media, technology, and the experience of social space / Chris Berry ... [et al.].
    p. cm.—(Public worlds ; v. 17)
    Includes bibliographical references and index.
    ISBN 978-0-8166-4736-1 (hc : alk. paper)
    ISBN 978-0-8166-4737-8 (pb : alk. paper)
1. Mass media and culture.   2. Mass media—Social aspects.   I. Berry, Chris.
   P94.6.E43 2010
   302.23—dc22

2009034204

Printed in the United States of America on acid-free paper

The University of Minnesota is an equal-opportunity educator and employer.

16 15 14 13 12 11 10   10 9 8 7 6 5 4 3 2 1

Contents

Chris Berry, Soyoung Kim, and Lynn Spigel

Introduction: Here, There, and Elsewhere

What is an "electronic elsewhere"? With this term we emphasize the idea that the media do not just represent—accurately or inaccurately—a place that is already there. Rather, as numerous essays in this book suggest, places are conjured up, experienced, and in that sense produced through media. This anthology explores how different world populations experience place through media technologies. Drawing on a long tradition of scholarship in media studies, we ask how media technologies (from the analog to the digital) have contributed to the spatial relations of modern/postmodern life, in its various global contexts. *Electronic Elsewheres: Media, Technology, and the Experience of Social Space* explores how media technologies both construct and transform the meaning of home, community, work, nation, and citizenship.

Media help to reconfigure the taken-for-granted environmental boundaries between public and private, and global and local, to create electronic elsewheres. While media technologies never on their own determine social change, they do work in concert with larger sociohistorical, industrial, political, and geographic shifts (such as shifts in migration or travel) to create new social configurations and meanings. The essays in this book investigate the convergence of media and the physical space of built environments (for example, the media-saturated home); but the authors are also just as interested in the way media help us imagine places like homeland, nation, or city. For example, how have media (from radio to film, television, and digital billboards) shaped the places of everyday life from the street to the mall to the airport to the classroom? How will "smart" technologies and telerobotics change our domestic and public environments? How have media constructed a sense of imaginary transport, cultural contact, and/or transnational community among distant populations? To what extent does the Internet provide opportunities for new alternative publics and public spaces to form? In what ways do media provide diasporic populations with a new sense of home and/or community?

By asking questions like these, *Electronic Elsewheres* inscribes and investigates the interdisciplinary field that is emerging at the point where Film and Media Studies meets Cultural and Social Geography. Not long ago, there was relatively little research on the intersection between geography and media. And when it did occur, it focused more often on how places were represented in the media than the role of the media in the production of place. However, the currency of concepts like "transnational" and "globalization" has put a spotlight on the spatialization of media distribution, production, and consumption as well as the ways in which media are transforming our apprehension and negotiation of space. Other volumes—in many cases by authors included in this collection—have considered particular aspects or single media, but this volume seeks to mark the emergence of the interdisciplinary field by encompassing a range of questions and media that have mostly been treated separately so far.

Therefore, before outlining the structure of the book and introducing the individual chapters, this introduction traces the gradual shift toward a focus on how the media shape space in a number of different fields: the media and the home; the media and migration, diaspora, and ethnicity; the media, the nation, and the region; general theories of space and place; and the mapping of globalization and the city. *Electronic Elsewheres* recognizes the common forces behind these developments, and seeks to generate synergy between them in order to highlight their coalescence as an interdisciplinary field.

One vector through which the emergence of this interdisciplinary field can be traced is the shift of focus between David Morley's two seminal works on the relationship between media and the home—*Family Television: Cultural Power and Domestic Leisure* from 1986, and *Home Territories: Media, Mobility and Identity* from 2000.[1] In his introduction to the first volume, Morley describes home as a physical and social site that shapes how television is used and interpreted. In regard to other work on media and the home, this idea of varied consumption of television in different homes also underlies James Lull's anthology, *World Families Watch Television*, which ranges from Venezuela to China.[2] However, in some of the material Morley covers in *Family Television*, he also notes, "Television can be used as a controlling mechanism. It can regulate the environment by providing background noise, punctuating time, or scheduling other activities."[3] And with *Home Territories*, this dialogic and transformative relationship between media and the domestic sphere is the full focus of the work, in aspects ranging from the role of media in articulating the domestic family to the nation-as-family to the haunting of the domestic by distant events introduced by the media.[4]

This transformative interaction between media and the space of the home—and the media as part of the space of the home—has been increasingly important to other scholars, too.[5] In the 1990s media scholars such as Ann Gray, Odina Fachel Leal, Lynn Spigel, Roger Silverstone, David Gauntlett and Annette Hill, and Shaun Moores explored television and video's relationship to everyday life (as well as to issues of family, generation, class, gender, and/or the spatial logics of home). More recent books by Barbara Klinger and William Boddy further develop issues of media and domestic space, looking, for example, at the introduction of cinema/DVDs into the home and at the convergence among television, cinema, and new media.[6] New forms of "smart" domestic technologies (from computers to DVRs to interactive stoves to fully digital homes) are explored by a range of media scholars, sociologists, ethnographers, and historians including Joseph Turrow and Andrea L. Kavanaugh, Elaine Lally, Fiona Allon, Derek Heckman, and Spigel (whose 2005 essay is reprinted in a longer form here).[7] The historical convergence of media and home has also created interdisciplinary dialogues between media scholars and people working in the field of architecture (both practice and theory). Writing from the field of architecture, in the 1990s Beatriz Colomina traced utopian visions for the "media house" across the twentieth century (as conceived by architects such as Le Corbusier and Buckminster Fuller). More recently, in her book *Domesticity at War* Colomina traces the influence of military technologies (as well as media such as cinema and television) on visionary architects of the postwar United States.[8] Finally, a range of work has emerged on the deployment of home as both metaphor and construction in cyberspace, from personal homepages to the "home" page anchoring all multipage Web sites.[9]

Scholars have also focused on the way film and media relate to social practices and subjectivity in public space (and how the media help define what is public and what is private). This scholarship often highlights the contradictory ways in which media work to create systems of control and surveillance, but also how the media can help open up possibilities for human agency and new forms of sociality in specific historical contexts. Work on silent cinema, for example, has explored this contradiction in relation to new modes of sexuality and female agency in the early part of the twentieth century. Miriam Hansen's influential book *Babel in Babylon: Spectatorship in American Silent Film* demonstrates how the public space of the movie theater and the development of classical film style required new modes of bourgeois spectatorship and interaction among patrons. Yet, at the same time, she considers early female film fans in relation to Oskar Negt's and Alexander Kluge's theory of proletarian counterpublics, and she shows how women transformed the space of the urban movie theater (and its environs) into a place for communal female experiences at a time when public spaces were dominated by men.[10] Also interested in counterpublics, Mary Carbine and Jacqueline Stewart have separately explored how African Americans—many of whom migrated from the South—experienced a shared sense of culture and community in movie districts and theaters located in major metropolises like Chicago (places marked by racial segregation).[11] Similar historical work on urban space, race, class, and gender continues to form a significant wing of film and media studies.[12]

The mediated environments of postwar television (and now the Internet) have sparked even greater debate about the degree to which the media work as instruments of surveillance versus the degree to which human agency exists in mediated landscapes. Some of this work draws (as does the silent film scholarship) on early Frankfurt school thinkers. So too, the work of Canadian scholars Harold Innis and Marshall McLuhan (especially McLuhan's oft-cited concept of the "global village") has been inaugural to concerns with media and the spatial dynamics of communication. And scholars often draw on a range of continental theorists including Michel Foucault (particularly his concept of the "pantopticon" and surveillance); Michel de Certeau (especially his interests in space and cities in *The Practice of Everyday Life*); Henri Lefebvre (whose interests in the "production of space" and book of that title have been central for critical geographers like Edward Soja, and more recently to media scholars); Jean Baudrillard (especially his theory of "simulation" and his famous exploration of Disneyland as place that makes the rest of Los Angeles look real); and Paul Virilio (especially his arguments about the way "speed" has erased space in a world where digital information flows and nuclear weapons change time–space relations).[13] Dealing more specifically with broadcasting, Raymond Williams's theory of "mobile privatization" has been particularly important for television scholars. Williams argued that by connecting the home to the world outside, telecommunications, and especially broadcasting, negotiated a central paradox of modern life in the industrial West: the rise of the private family home on the one hand and increasing mobility in the industrial city on the other. [14]

More generally, concerns with the dynamic and mutually influencing relations between the private and the public—and the media's constructions and negotiations of each—have been central to radio and television scholars. Paddy Scannell's *Television, Radio and Modern Life* demonstrates that the rise of broadcasting in Britain was occasioned by new relations between public and private places. For example, when television broadcast live events to the nation it brought the public world closer to the world of everyday citizens and created a double articulation of space (the power, through live broadcasting, of being in two places at once). This in turn entailed new ways of addressing citizens as participants in public life and, most importantly, new attitudes towards public/national life for everyday citizens. For example, someone physically at the coronation of Queen Elizabeth II in 1953 might behave and respond very differently in public than would a TV watcher at home (who might do all sort of things at home that one would not do in public when witnessing the event).[15] Writing about the U.S. context, Margaret Morse's influential essay "The Ontology of Everyday Distraction: The Freeway, the Mall, and Television" drew upon the work of Walter Benjamin, Michel deCerteau, Raymond Williams, and Jean Baudrillard to consider how the historical coincidence of television, malls, and freeways in the United States of the 1950s created new kinds of "derealized spaces" that encourage distraction and create simulated modes of public life. For Morse, the concluding problematic lies in the degree to which community and social action can exist in a world where people are never where they are (for example, the freeway cuts through surrounding neighborhoods so drivers never experience those places, and television's aesthetic of "liveness" and presence encourages viewers to feel part of a crowd even while they are actually alone at home watching a world in miniature).[16] Anna McCarthy's *Ambient Television: Visual Culture and Public Space* takes up these questions of media, space, and place by focusing on the less spectacular mediated environments of ordinary everyday life. Her chapters about site-specific media demonstrate how the placement of television sets in restaurants, bars, and stores both express and construct gender and class relations, and she also shows how media orchestrate social relations in those environments.[17]

The increasing use of mobile technologies and DVRs also helps to reformulate conceptions about what is public and what is private. Working in connection with broader patterns of media globalization, as well as broader patterns of social life (such as changes in family, work, travel, and migration), these new mobile technologies are encouraging modes of media timeshifting and placeshifting in which people receive and send (and sometimes produce) previous forms of home-based media (like TV programs) or work-related data while on the go. The advent of these technologies has numerous scholars and industry people predicting not only the future or end of TV as we knew it, but also, more broadly, the future or end of the broadcast era's articulations and ideologies of private and public. Work on the Internet and cyberspace develops political issues regarding virtual publics as scholars consider the possibilities that electronic places (like chat rooms) hold out for new forms of community and democracy. Although authors such as William Mitchell have high-lighted the prosocial potential of cyberspaces, others (such as Morley, Kevin Robins, Steven Jones, and Lisa Nakamura) question the degree to which the old problems of physical realities—racism, sexism, class divides, and other traditional social struggles in cities, suburbs, and other built environments—are transported and reconfigured (but not solved) in cyberspace.[18] In this volume, Lisa Nakamura considers how the virtual and seemingly disembodied spaces of chat rooms are affected never-theless by the physical marks of embodiment (she deals with a literal example of female bodies by looking at chat rooms and home pages for pregnant women).

Another strand of scholarship explores the media's intersection with migration, diaspora, and ethnicity. Whereas some scholars examine how people are represented in the media, others question how people use the media to transform both the societies they leave and those they enter. In his influential 1993 monograph on Iranian community television in Los Angeles, Hamid Naficy noted that "exile media . . . 'speak for' exiles. They also do more than that. They are a force in shaping the experience of exile."[19] A number of different focuses have developed in the examina-tion of this shaping process. Naficy himself has concentrated on television programs and film production by diasporic communities, showing how the process of production builds exilic and diasporic cultures and iden-tities.[20] Other ethnographic studies focus, for example, on generational differences among diasporic populations. Marie Gillespie's work on British–Asian youth culture in Southall, (the East End of London) shows how young people use television creatively and critically in intergenerational negotiations; for example, they use media (such as soap operas or news) both to create new traditions and to criticize existing ones of their heritage (as well as their host) countries.[21]

In addition to demonstrating how population flows relate to media flows, these and other authors highlight the forms of cultural hybridity common to people living in the diaspora. For example, Vicky Mayer explores how Mexican–American girls acquire a sense of cultural hybridity through their viewing of Mexican telenovelas and her book *Producing Dreams, Consuming Youth* also considers the way Mexican Americans living in the border city of San Antonio, Texas produce media and shape a sense of national/cultural identity through this.[22] In their scholarship on migration, Kevin Robins and Asu Aksoy have examined patterns of both consumption and production on the part of the Turkish communities in Europe, showing that the intersection of imported Turkish media, European transnational Turkish television, and European media shapes a distinctively transnational and abstract European Turkish cultural space.[23] Whereas some authors look at diasporic communities that already exist, others emphasize the role of the media in guiding future migration patterns. Much earlier work focused on the media's (often very biased and discriminatory) representation of migrants. But this newer work examines how media representations of other countries are taken up in source countries as inspiration for would-migrants. For example, Nick Mai's work looks at how the electronic elsewheres conjured up by Italian media images mobilize and direct Albanian emigration.[24]

Just as the relationship between migration and the media is no longer seen only in terms of how migrants are represented in the media, so the understanding of the relationship between the nations they move between and the media has also changed. The rhetoric of individual nation–states and their advocates claims primordial origins and eternal life, but scholars such as Benedict Anderson and many others have shown that the nation–state is a modern invention with distinctive characteristics of its own, and to be distinguished from other polities such as monarchies and empires, as well as from peoples who may develop a cultural identity without a corresponding polity. Anderson's term "imagined communities" refers to the formation of communities that are too big for all the members to know each other and which therefore are sustained through the imagination. Although Anderson specifies the importance of the printing press in producing national imagined communities, where language markets correspond increasingly to national borders, since the twentieth century various media that use electricity have become more and more important, reconstituting these print imagined communities as electronic elsewheres.[25]

These insights have transformed work on the relationship between media and nation. Writing about film studies, Mitsuhiro Yoshimoto observed already in 1993, "Writing about national cinemas used to be an easy task: film critics believed all they had to do was to construct a linear historical narrative describing a development of a cinema within a particular national boundary whose unity and coherence seemed to be beyond all doubt."[26] Yoshimoto's statement signaled the implosion of that assumption. Tom O'Regan's study of Australian cinema and Susan Hayward's book on French cinema are included in a "national cinemas" series. Nevertheless, they are among the earliest examples of writing that take this insight on board and examine the relationship between cinema and the national as a contingent one.[27] More recently, Chris Berry and Mary Farquhar argue in *China on Screen* for the transformation of the field of national cinemas, which assumed nation–states, into the study of cinema and the national as a problematic. Here the media do not express the nation but work to construct and, in many cases, to trouble it.[28] This rethinking of the relationship of media to nation has not been confined to the cinema, as demonstrated by David Morley and Kevin Robins's pioneering investigation of electronic media, *Spaces of Identity: Global Media, Electronic Landscapes, and Cultural Boundaries.*[29]

If the nation–state was a historical development within the contradictions of European culture as monarchy struggled with an emergent bourgeoisie, for the rest of the world it arrived on a gunboat, along with the other concepts and practices constituting "modernity." Postcolonial theory has highlighted the resultant ambivalence and instability that animates the imagination of the national in much of the world, and this is manifested in the growing range of work on the role of the media in producing postcolonial nations as very different electronic elsewheres. In *China on Screen*, Berry and Farquhar examine how a variety of often competing Chinese national formations and identities from the Republican to the Communist and the ethnic to the class-based are configured in the cinema. In Egypt, the cinema serves the entire Arab language region, and Lila Abu-Lughod has shown that television has been at least as important in producing the national community. In particular, she examines the contradictions inherent in modernization projects of Egyptian television producers who create serial programming aimed at rural populations, and she demonstrates, for example, how rural audiences often reject the modernization ethos in the serials.[30]

The regional plays out in a different way in India compared with Egypt. Whereas the regional exceeds the national in Egypt, India exceeds the regional. As a result, in India, different regional cinemas marked by regional languages serve specific areas of the nation. As Arvind Rajagopal in *Politics after Television: Hindu Nationalism and the Reshaping of the Public in India* and Purnima Mankekar in *Vision: Screening Culture, Viewing Politics: An Ethnography of Television, Womanhood, and Nation in Postcolonial India* have shown, the introduction of the state-owned national television network Doordarshan and its booming popularity since the 1980s has been closely tied both to the production of a stronger and new sense of national identity, and to the opening of the Indian economy to global capital and the development of a consumer economy. Both of these tendencies are grounded in and driven by the burgeoning middle-class. Mankekar has emphasized the gendered dimension of this phenomenon, with television helping to link domestic and public spaces and mobilize middle-class women.[31] Rajagopal has also emphasized the link of television to the rise of right-wing Hindi nationalism,[32] which he pursues further in his essay here, undermining common assumptions that democracy and modernity are necessarily opposed to religion and sectarianism.

In *Feeling Asian Modernities: Transnational Consumption of Japanese TV Dramas*, Koichi Iwabuchi similarly explores the varied experiences of modernity, in this case by highlighting the situated and local meanings of television programs as they traverse different nations and regions in Asia. In their essay in that volume, Elizabeth MacLachlan and Geok-lian Chua conduct audience research to demonstrate generational differences among women of Chinese ethnicity who watch a Japanese "(post)-trendy" serial aired in Singapore. The authors find that whereas married older women tend to see the sexual liberalism in the (post-trendy) drama as an affront to traditional Asian values and as proof of the loose mores associated with postindustrial Western societies, younger women see sexual content (for example, plots about adultery or premarital sex) as a welcome aspect of globalization, even while they still believe in traditional values of marriage. MacLachlan and Chua argue that we need to consider transnational media in the context of Joseph Straubhaar's concept of "cultural proximity" (or shared identities, gestures, fashions, lifestyles, etcetera) and they explore how the younger women share a sense of "real time" resonance with other non-Western modernities, even as they also recognize differences.[33] Similarly, in her epigraph to the same book, media scholar and cultural theorist Ien Ang considers the transnational East Asian success of the (post-) trendy Japanese drama *Tokyo Love Story* (which aired in the early 1990s), arguing that rather than thinking about globalization as a worldwide phenomenon with homogeneous effects, we should explore how cultural proximity among audience formations accounts for both program popularity and the transnational flow of meanings across national boundaries.[34] Such research suggests that even if media products circulate on a global market, formats (such as serial dramas) take on local inflections, and interpretations among audiences are in no way uniform. In such accounts the concept of "glocalization" undermines previous notions of cultural homogeneity through globalization, even if a few multinational global corporations (such as Rupert Murdoch's News Corporation or Viacom) are still the dominant producers on the global market.

The movement away from thinking about globalization in terms of homogeneous effects, as well as the movement away from thinking of nations and regions as pre-given static entities (untouched by transnational flows), is key to much of the contemporary scholarship on place and space. Scholars often now think about nations and regions as being hybrid, relational, variable, and mediated—concepts that are also more generally linked to the transformation of the discipline of geography. The ideas of "space" as abstract and "place" as concrete and specific have been widely debated in geographical theory since well before even Yi-Fu Tuan's 1977 volume, *Space and Place*, which attempted to pull together many of the debates around the issues.[35] But since then, there has been a growing tendency against thinking of space as the generalized and inert field in which human culture produces place, somewhat in the manner of older thinking about biological sex and gender. Instead, just as Judith Butler has argued both sex and gender are concepts and therefore culturally produced, Doreen Massey has argued influentially that space and place are both dynamic and historical, shaped and formed by all manner of social power relations. This leads her to think (along with Harvey) about "space–time." Furthermore, contrary to the older assumptions, places may be more anchored and fixed than space, insofar as places are "attempts to stabilize the particular envelopes of space-time . . . attempts to get to grips with the unutterable mobility and contingency of space–time."[36]

The arguments about space and place are part of geography's shift in English-speaking countries from a positivist and functionalist-dominated discipline to a much more theoretical and critical one that no longer understands its objects in a positivist manner as unproblematic givens but as critically produced by thought and discourse. Possibly most prominent among the geographers who have followed this path is David Harvey, whose *The Condition of Postmodernity: An Enquiry into the Origins of Cultural Change* both looked beyond the traditional concerns of geography and demonstrated the relevance of geography to other critical disciplines in the humanities.[37] A more recent collection of his essays is titled *Spaces of Capital: Towards a Critical Geography*.[38] His personal role in the development of this critical geography is traced in a fascinating opening interview, "Reinventing Geography." Here, as well as the significance of Marx, the crucial role of the encounter with continental thinkers about space such as Henri Lefebvre is underlined.

In connection with this focus on geographies of modernity and post-modernity, the mapping of globalized space has been pioneered by books such as Arjun Appadurai's *Modernity at Large: Cultural Dimensions of Globalization*[39] and Fredric Jameson and Masao Miyoshi's *The Cultures of Globalization*.[40] A number of scholars have also drawn on insights from geographic theories to interrogate the construction of the global city. Edward Soja's *Thirdspace: Journeys to Los Angeles and Other Real-and-Imagined Places*[41] and Saskia Sassen's *The Global City: New York, London, Tokyo*[42] are exemplary in this respect.

One of the central vexations for media scholars is the degree to which the mediated city negates human agency with predetermined "scripts" (a la Disneyland) versus the degree to which media cities allow people any ability to shape the environment. In this respect, Michel deCertau's oft-cited essay "Walking in the City" has become a tool for thinking through agency and power in a highly mediated society. In that essay, de Certeau thinks about the city as a semiotic space, and he uses speech act theory to argue that although the city is a language system of sorts, residents can still determine their own uses of urban space (just as a speaker can use the language system to perform her own utterances). Nevertheless, de Certeau does not see this as a mere free-for-all. Even while insisting that scholars attend to human agency and what he calls the "tactics of the weak," he still acknowledges that the dominant institutions in a society consolidate power in part by strategically occupying and consolidating space.[43]

In recent years, a number of disciplines (from architecture to media studies to literary studies to visual anthropology to science and technology studies) have investigated questions of the role that media play in urban landscapes and what this means for community, publicness, privacy, identity, desire, social life, and the visual culture of urban and New Urban environments. In film studies, one of the inaugural works is

Giuliana Bruno's essay on *Blade Runner* (directed by Ridley Scott), a film that inspired her (and many other scholars) to think about Los Angeles as the quintessential postmodern/postindustrial city.[44] Books such as Christine Boyer's *Cybercities: Visual Perception in the Age of Electronic Communication*,[45] Mark Shiel and Tony Fitzmaurice's (eds.) *Cinema and the City: Film and Urban Societies in a Global Context*,[46] David B. Clarke's (ed.) *The Cinematic City*,[47] and Linda Krause and Patrice Petro's (eds.) *Global Cities: Cinema, Architecture, and Urbanism in a Digital Age* all continue to consider intersections between media and city space.[48] Some of these authors (such as Boyer) consider the visual culture of cities, the production of urban subjectivities, and issues of social power and human agency. Also concerned with power, scholars such as Stephan Graham, Simon Marvin, and Jennifer Light focus on the use of media technologies in urban planning and/or the deployment of media (from telephone networks to closed circuit TV to satellites to robots) as systems of control and surveillance.[49] Others, such as John Caldwell or Andrew Ross consider the consolidation of workers in the media and computer industries in Hollywood, San Francisco, and other urban locales.[50] Some of this work speaks in dialogue with scholarship on the history of women and early cinema. For example, Anne Friedberg has considered the history of urban visual pleasures (shopping, cinema, etcetera) with respect to women's place in the city and the mobile female figure of the *"flaneuse."*[51] More generally, the work on media and cities reflects a movement from looking at how cities are represented in the media to understanding the media both as part of the city and as active in constructing the contemporary urban experience. It is this direction that the authors working on the city in *Electronic Elsewheres* develop further.

These tendencies in these different areas of writing come together to form the foundations for this anthology on the transformative relationship between media and space. We designate this work on media and space with the term "electronic elsewheres," a phrase that Jeffrey Sconce first coined in his book *Haunted Media*, and which he extends in his essay in this volume.[52] In our view, this term serves as a compelling way to conceptualize the emergent interdisciplinary field of scholarship on media and the production of space. It signals both the material sense of lived environments constructed through media, but also an imaginary "third space" open to alterity and reinvention. Following some of the largest concentrations of existing scholarship, we have divided the volume into three sections: the reconfigured home; electronic publics; and the mediated city.

In the first section, the reconfiguration of the literal home by new technologies links David Morley's and Lynn Spigel's essays—which bookend the section—whereas Lisa Nakamura's and Jeffrey Sconce's essays find mediated homes in the realm of the virtual and the imaginary, respectively. In "Domesticating Dis-Location in a World of 'New' Technology," David Morley traces the role of media technologies in breaching the boundary between the public and the private. "New" media technologies of the past and the present have not only brought the "elsewhere" into the domestic sphere but also enabled the creation of homelike spaces in the world outside the physical home. As indicated by those quote marks around "new," Morley is skeptical about the utopian discourse of newness that surrounds media technology at the same time as he is deeply interested in how these technologies are actually being used. Lynn Spigel shares Morley's skepticism about the deeply interested production and circulation of utopian discourses around "new" media technologies in her essay, "Designing the Smart Home: Posthuman Domesticity and Conspicious Production." As well as tracing the production of these discourses, she also analyzes the smart home as a space where media technology is connecting the human and the artifact, turning the home into a form of artificial life with whom humans form affective bonds, or integrating the inhabitant as a component of a kind of domestic machine.

Spigel's essay also pays particular attention to how gendered domestic labor is—or is not—reconfigured in the discourse of the smart home. Lisa Nakamura also focuses on the gender deficit in the world of media technology. But although she acknowledges that women have been relatively slow to build their homes in cyberspace, her essay "Avatars and the Visual Culture of Reproduction on the Web," examines how the avatars that women are creating at pregnancy sites and homepages challenge established imaginaries of the female body. These established imaginaries are not just the exaggerated female bodies of cyber fantasy but also the erasure of the female body in medical imagery that reduces women to containers for unborn babies. Jeffrey Sconce's essay in this section joins Nakamura's interest in the use of media technology to produce virtual and imagined homes and bodies with Morley's and Spigel's commitment to revealing the long history of the "new" in "new media." However, the particular electronic elsewhere he examines was made famous by radio in the 1930s, and concerns the peculiar case of Gef, "The Talking Weasel of Doarlish Cashen." Sconce shows Gef to be a cross between a poltergeist and a simulacrum of the radio, missing from the household Gef invades. Invisible but very audible, Gef transformed the domestic space in which he manifested himself, bringing the world into it and it to the world—courtesy of coverage on the BBC. Interesting though this case is as an oddity, Sconce uses its intersection of new technology and older spectral discourses to challenge the idea that new media technologies directly produce or express new subjectivities. He argues that instead of understanding electronic elsewheres as manifestations of new ways of Being, we should analyze them as new but historically specific and variable ways of doing with media.

One way of doing things with the media that has consistently engaged the interest of a wide range of scholars is the use of the media in the production of the public. This forms the basis for our second section, "Electronic Publics." The first two essays share a common interest in how publics should be theorized. Both Chris Berry in "New Documentary in China: Public Space, Public Television" and "The Undecidable and the Irreversible: Satellite Television in the Algerian Public Arena" by Ratiba Hadj-Moussa eschew the Habermasian concept of the "public sphere" as overly idealized, preferring to use less loaded terms like "public space" and "public arena." Berry's essay traces the emergence of new documentary practices and forms in China, both on state-owned television and in the independent film world, and their connection to the formation of more active publics than the "masses" waiting to be mobilized in the socialist heyday. He uses these examples to rethink the concept of public space and argue against the usefulness of ideas like the "public sphere" and "civil society," which have dominated discussion of such changes in Chinese society to date. Hadj-Moussa's essay focuses on satellite television in Algeria, and its integration into and transformation of the neighborhood, or *houma*. Much as many of the writers in the first section demonstrate how media technologies breach the boundaries of the public and the private, Hadj-Moussa also researches the politicization of both the neighborhood and the home and their constitution as spaces of participation in the public by the arrival of the satellite television dish and the new programming it brings. Like Spigel, she also pays particular attention to the transformation of gendered patterns of behavior and interaction made possible by the dish.

Implicit in Hadj-Moussa's chapter is a relationship to the national public of Algeria and its processes of political participation. The constitution of the national public as and by electronic elsewheres is explicit in the next two essays. In "The Voice of Jacob: Radio's Role in Reviving a Nation," Tamar Liebes-Plesner joins those authors concerned with the history of media technologies and electronic elsewheres to investigate the special role of radio in the production of the national public space of the state of Israel. Starting from the observation that, unlike Greek culture, Jewish cultures privilege the voice over the image, Liebes-Plesner shows the intimate and integrative role of radio in the early days of Israel. According to Liebes-Plesner, television was not as important as radio in constructing a national public in Israel. In contrast, Arvind Rajagopal's "Violence, Publicity, and Secularism: Hindu–Muslim Riots in Gujarat" is premised on the primary role of national television in India in the renewed sense of Indian national cultural and public space. However, the primary thrust of Rajagopal's argument is against the common assumption that media play a key role in the production of a secular and rational national culture (allied to the notion of the "public sphere" discussed in Berry and Hadj-Moussa's essays). Using the example of the riots in Gujarat in 2002, he reminds us how the media can be deployed in the production of the electronic elsewhere of an alternative modernity that is nationalist, religious, and violent.

Finally in this section, Asu Aksoy and Kevin Robins also look at satellite television. However, their focus in not on national public spaces, but on the transnational. Or, to put it another way, they are interested in the tension between the national as culture and the national as territory. Examining the development of Turkish satellite television in Europe from a practice originally aimed back at audiences within Turkey to a practice that not only encompasses European Turkish audiences but also addresses and constitutes European Turkish audiences as a public.

If transnational publics are a relatively new formation associated with globalization and increased transborder flows that, as Aksoy and Robins argue, challenge the national "imagined community" theorized by Anderson, then our final section focuses on the role of media in another formation closely associated with globalization—the global city. In "The Mediated City," Marita Sturken, Charlotte Brunsdon, and Shunya Yoshimi examine mediated New York, London, and Tokyo respectively. Each of them is interested in locally specific mediations that produce electronic elsewheres of the physical city.

In "The Elsewhere of the London Underground," Brunsdon traces the representations and imaginations of a literal elsewhere—the famous "Tube" system of subway trains that run underneath London. Ranging from maps, art, and book covers to feature films and documentaries, she shows how the Tube has come to be synonymous with the city and an iconic—if difficult to represent—landmark. However, Brunsdon chooses to end her essay with documentaries that reveal the gendered labor of the Underground system, so often occluded in entertainment discourse.

Brunsdon's essay was already drafted before the 7/7 bombings, but Marita Sturken's essay is squarely focused on the aftermath of 9/11 in "The Image at Ground Zero: Mediating the Memory of Terrorism." She examines the emergence of an electronic elsewhere as a web of mediations of Ground Zero from television coverage to home videos, and how they have been taken up in a movement from spectacle to narratives of redemption of the city and the nation.

Finally, in a majestically ambitious essay, Shunya Yoshimi responds to a very specific event—the election of a right-wing nationalist governor of Tokyo who used fear of immigrants and "outsiders" to win votes—with a very broad yet precise historical sweep over the different imaginings of Tokyo as world and global city. He demonstrates how the mediation of the city is deeply imbricated with economic development and political transformation as Japan's leaders have sought to integrate their country with the world capitalist system. In this light, globalization has not only led to outward expansion but also to inward flows that have transformed the city from within and are challenging conventional definitions of what a global city is or should be.

In the volume as a whole, we have worked hard to include work from a wide range of countries and cultures, such as Yoshimi's. We believe this is important not only because the issues we are dealing with here are global, but also that these issues are experienced in different ways around the world according to the different historical trajectories and cultural conditions in which they take place. As a result, the development of an appropriate body of knowledge and conceptual tools cannot be confined to the usual Euro–American focus that bedevils so much of media studies and has led to calls for "de-Westernization."[53]

This volume has come together after two conferences. In 2002, Kim Soyoung spent a term as Visiting Professor at UC Berkeley, during which the "Look Who's Talking Now: Globalization, Film, Media, & the Public Sphere" symposium was held. Lynn Spigel and Chris Berry also spoke at this event, and it led to the "Electronic Elsewheres: Media, Technology, and Social Space" conference at Northwestern University in 2003. Most of the essays included in this volume had their initial outings at the Northwestern conference, and we would like to thank both Northwestern and UC Berkeley for supporting those events. We would also like to take this opportunity to thank all the contributors for their contributions to this volume and for working so patiently through the painstaking publication process. We would also like to thank each for sticking out the editing process, even during a temporary illness on Kim

Soyoung's part, which made it impossible for her to contribute a paper to the volume as originally intended. Finally, we would also like to thank Dilip Goankar of Northwestern for helping us to bring this volume to press in its early stages.

Notes

1 David Morley, *Family Television: Cultural Power and Domestic Leisure* (London: Comedia, 1986); Morley, *Home Territories*.

2 James Lull, ed., *World Families Watch Television*, (Thousand Oaks, CA: Sage, 1988).

3 Morley, *Family Television*, 25–26.

4 Morley, *Home Territories*, 3, 9 of the introduction and corresponding chapters.

5 Ann Gray, *Video Playtime: The Gendering of a Leisure Technology* (London: Routledge, 1992); Odina Fachel Leal, "Popular Taste and Erudite Repitore: The Place and Space of Television in Brazil," *Cultural Studies* 4, no. 1 (1990): 19–29; Lynn Spigel, *Make Room for TV: Television and the Family Ideal in Postwar America* (Chicago: University of Chicago Press, 1992); Roger Silverstone, *Television and Everyday Life* (London: Routledge, 1994); David Gauntlett and Annette Hill, *TV Living: Television, Culture and Everyday Life* (London: BFI, 1999); Shaun Moores, "Satellite Television and Everyday Life," Academia Research Monograph 18 (Luton: University of Luton Press, 1996).

6 Barbara Klinger, *Beyond the Multiplex: Cinema, New Technologies, and the Home* (Berkeley: University of California Press, 2006); William Boddy, *New Media and Popular Imagination: Launching Radio, Television, and New Media in the United States* (London: Oxford, 2004).

7 Joseph Turow and Andrea L. Kavanaugh, eds., *The Wired Homestead: An MIT Press Sourcebook on the Internet and the Family* (Cambridge, Mass.: MIT Press, 2003); Elaine Lally, *At Home with Computers* (Oxford: Berg, 2002); Fiona Allon, "An Ontology of Everyday Control: Space, Media Flows and 'Smart' Living in the Absolute Present," in *Media Space: Place, Scale and Culture in a Media Age*, ed. Nick Couldry and Anna McCarthy, 253–74 (London: Routledge, 2004); Derek Heckman, *A Small World: Smart Houses and the Dream of the Perfect Day* (Durham, NC: Duke University Press, 2008); Lynn Spigel, "Designing the Smart House: Posthuman Domesticity and Conspicuous Consumption," *European Journal of Cultural Studies* 8, no. 4 (November 2005): 403–27; and additional citations in Spigel's essay in this volume.

8 Beatriz Colomina, "The Media House," *Assemblage* 27 (1995): 55–66. See also, "Media Homes, Then and Now," *International Journal of Cultural Studies* (Winter 2002): 385–411; David Morley, *Media, Modernity, Technology: The Geography of the New* (London: Routledge, 2007). Beatriz Colomina, *Domesticity at War* (Cambridge: MIT Press, 2007).

9 For example, Joseph R. Dominick, "Who Do You Think You Are? Personal Home Pages and Self-Presentation on the World Wide Web," *Journalism and Mass Communication Quarterly*, 76, no. 4 (1999): 646–58; and Charles Cheung, "A Home on the Web: Presentation of Self on Personal Home Pages," in *Web Studies: Rewriting Media Studies for the Digital Age*, ed. David Gauntlett, 43–51 (London: Oxford University Press, 2000).

10 Miriam Hansen, *Babel and Babylon: Spectatorship in American Silent Film* (Cambridge, Mass.: Harvard University Press, 1991), 114–25; Hansen is drawing on Oskar Negt and Alexander Kluge, *The Public Sphere and Experience: Toward an Analysis of the Bourgeois and Proletarian Public Sphere*, trans. Peter Labanyi, Jamie Owen Daniel, and Assenka Oksiloff (Minneapolis: University of Minnesota Press, 1993).

11 Mary Carbine, "The Finest Outside the Loop: Motion Picture Exhibition in Chicago's Black Metropolis, 1905–1928," *Camera Obscura* 23 (1990): 8–41. Jacqueline Stewart, *Migrating to the Movies: Cinema and Black Urban Modernity* (Berkeley: University of California Press, 2005).

12 See, for example, Shelley Stamp, *Movie Struck Girls: Women and Motion Picture Culture after the Nickelodeon* (Princeton, N.J.: Princeton University Press, 2000); Gregory Waller, *Mainstreet Amusements* (Washington, D.C.: Smithsonian Press, 1995); James Forcher, *The Community of Cinema: How Cinema and Spectacle Transformed the American Downtown* (New York: Praeger, 2003); Janna Jones, *The Southern Movie Palace: Rise, Fall, and Resurrection* (Tampa: University Press of Florida, 2003).

13 See, for example, Harold Innis, *The Bias of Communication* (Toronto: University of Toronto Press, 1951); Marshall McLuhan, *Understanding Media: The Extensions of Man* (1964; Cambridge, MIT Press, 2001) and Marshall McLuhan and Quentin Fiore, *War and Peace in the Global Village* (New York: Bantam, 1968); Michel Foucault, *Discipline and Punish: The Birth of the Prison*, trans. Alan —Sheridan (New York: Vintage, 1979); Michel de Certeau, *The Practice of Everyday Life*, trans. Steven Rendall (Berkeley: University of California Press, 1984); Henri Lefabvre, *The Production of Space*, trans. Donald Nicholson-Smith (1974 reprint; London: Blackwell, 1991); Edward W. Soja, *Thirdspace: Journeys to Los Angeles and Other Real-and-Imagined Places* (Oxford: Basil Blackwell, 1996); Jean Baudrillard, *Simulations*, trans. Paul Foss, Paul Patton, and Philip Beitchman (New York: Semiotext(e), Inc. 1983); Paul Virilio, *Speed and Politics: An Essay on Dromology*, trans. Mark Polizzotti (1977; New York: Semiotext(e), 1986); Paul Virilio, *Open Skies*, trans. Julie Rose (London: Verso, 1997); and Jean Baudrillard.

14 Raymond Williams, *Television, Technology and Cultural Form* (1974 reprint; Hanover: N.H: Weslyan University Press, 1992). In addition to the concept of "mobile privitization" Williams's concept of "flow" in this same book has been key for TV scholars.

15 Paddy Scannell, *Radio, Television, and Public Life: A Phenomenal Approach* (London: Blackwell, 1996).

16 Margaret Morse, "An Ontology of Everyday Distraction: The Freeway, the Mall, and Television," in *Logics of Television: Essays in Cultural Criticism*, ed. Patricia Mellencamp, 193–221 (Bloomington: Indiana University Press, 1990).

17 Anna McCarthy, *Ambient Television: Visual Culture and Public Space* (Durham, N.C.: Duke University Press, 2001). See also Nick Couldry and Anna McCarthy, eds., *Mediaspace: Place, Scale and Culture in a Media Age* (London: Routledge, 2004). See also her anthology with Nick Couldry, *Mediaspace*. See, for example, Michael Sorkin, ed. *Variations on a Theme Park: The American City and the End of Public Space* (New York: Noonday Press, 1992); John Hannigan, *Fantasy City: Pleasure and Profit in the Postmodern Metropolis* (London: Routledge, 1998); John M. Findlay, *Magic Lands: Western Cityscapes and American Culture After 1940* (Berkeley: University of California Press, 1992); Andrew Ross, *The Celebration Chronicles: Life, Liberty, and the Pursuit of Property Value in Disney's New Town* (New York: Ballentine, 1999).

18 William J. Mitchell, *City of Bits: Space, Place and the Infobahn* (Cambridge, Mass.: MIT Press, 1995); Morley, *Home Territories* and *Media, Modernity, Technology*; Kevin Robins, *Into the Image: Culture and Politics in the Field of Vision* (London: Routledge, 1996); Steven G. Jones, ed. *Virtual Culture: Identity and Communication in Cybersociety* (London: Sage, 1997); Lisa Nakamura, *Cybertypes: Race, Ethnicity, and Identity on the Internet* (London: Routledge, 2002). Also see Alondra Nelson and Thuy Linh N. Tu, eds., *Technicolor: Race, Technology, and Everyday Life* (New York: NYU Press, 2001); Ella Shohat; "By the Bitstream of Babylon: Cyberfrontiers and Diasporic Vistas," in ed. Hamid Naficy, *Home, Exile, Homeland: Film, Media, and the Politics of Place*, 213–32 (New York: Routledge, 1999); Chris Berry, Fran Martin, and Audrey Yue, eds., *Mobile Cultures: New Media in Queer Asia* (Durham, N.C.: Duke University Press, 2003); Beth E. Kolko, Lisa Nakamura, and Gilbert B. Rodman, eds., *Race and Cyberspace* (New York: Routledge, 2000); Jeffrey Sconce, "Tulip Theory," in *New Media: Theories and Practices of Digitextuality*, ed. Anna Everett and John T. Caldwell, 179–93 (New York: Routledge, 2003).

19 Hamid Naficy, *The Making of Exile Cultures: Iranian Television in Los Angeles* (Minneapolis: University of Minnesota Press, 1993), xvi.

20 As well as *The Making of Exile Cultures*, see Hamid Naficy, *An Accented Cinema: Exilic and Diasporic Filmmaking* (Princeton, N.J.: Princeton University Press, 2001), and also his anthology, *Home, Exile, Homeland: Film, Media, and the Politics of Place* (Los Angeles: American Film Institute, 1998).

21 Marie Gillespie, *Television, Ethnicity, and Cultural Change* (London: Routledge, 1995).

22 Vicki Mayer, "Living Telenovelas/Telenovelizing Life: Mexican American Girls' Identities and Transnational Telenovelas," *Journal of Communication* (September 2003): 479–95; Vicki Mayer, Producing Dreams/Consuming

Youth: Mexican Americans and Mass Media (New Brunswick, NJ: Rutgers University Press, 2003).

23 Asu Aksoy and Kevin Robins, "Thinking Across Spaces: Transnational Turkish Television from Turkey," *European Journal of Cultural Studies* 3, no. 3, (2000): 343–65; Asu Aksoy, "Implications of Transnational Turkish Television for the European Cultural Space," in *Zwischen Abgrenzung und Integration: Turkische Medienkultur in Deutschland*, ed. Jorg Becker and Reinhardt Behnisch, 63–85 (Rehburg-Loccum: Evangelische Akademie, 2000).

24 Nicola Mai, "'Italy is Beautiful': The Role of Italian Television in the Albanian Migratory Flow to Italy," in *Media and Migration: Constructions of Mobility and Difference*, ed. Russell King and Nancy Wood, 95–109 (London: Routledge, 2001); Nicola Mai, "'Looking for a More Modern Life': The Role of Italian Television in the Albanian Migration to Italy," *Westminster Papers in Communication and Culture* 1, no. 1 (2005), http://www.wmin.ac.uk/mad/pdf/Mai.pdf (4 August 2005).

25 Benedict Anderson, *Imagined Communities: Reflections on the Origin and Spread of Nationalism* (London: Verso, 1983, rev. ed. 1991).

26 Mitsuhiro Yoshimoto, "The Difficulty of Being Radical: The Discipline of Film Studies and the Postcolonial World Order," in, *Japan in the World*, ed. Masao Miyoshi and H.D. Harootunian, 338 (Durham: Duke University Press, 1993).

27 Tom O'Regan, *Australian National Cinema* (London: Routledge, 1996); Susan Hayward, *French National Cinema* (London: Routledge, 1993).

28 Chris Berry and Mary Farquhar, *China on Screen: Cinema and Nation* (New York: Columbia University Press, and Hong Kong: Hong Kong University Press, 2006). From the perspective of media distribution and economic flows, Michael Curtin uses insights from cultural geography to map the historical development of media across the PRC, Singapore, Hong Kong, and the United States, and he shows how distribution patterns and economic conditions of transnational production relate to the cultural styles and creative workforce in various "media capitals." Michael Curtin, *Playing to the World's Biggest Audience: The Globalization of Chinese Film and TV* (Berkeley: University of California Press, 2007); see also his essay, "Media Capitals: Cultural Geographies of Global TV," in *Television after TV: Essays on a Medium in Transition*, ed. Lynn Spigel and Jan Olsson, 270–302 (Durham, N.C.: Duke University Press, 2004).

29 David Morley and Kevin Robins, *Spaces of Identity: Global Media, Electronic Landscapes and Cultural Boundaries* (London: Routledge, 1995).

30 Lila Abu-Lughod, *Dramas of Nationhood: The Politics of Television in Egypt* (Chicago: University of Chicago Press, 2005).

31 Purnima Mankekar, *Screening Culture, Viewing Politics: An Ethnography of Television, Womanhood, and Nation in Postcolonial India* (Durham, N.C.: Duke University Press, 1999).

32 Arvind Rajagopal, *Politics After Television: Hindu Nationalism and the Reshaping of the Public in India* (New York: Cambridge University Press 2001).

33 Elizabeth Maclachlan and Geok-lian Chua, "Defining Asian Femininity: Chinese Viewers of Japanese TV Dramas in Singapore," in *Feeling Asian Modernities: Transnational Consumption of Japanese TV Dramas,* ed. Koichi Iwabuchi, 155–75 (Hong Kong: Hong Kong University Press, 2004). The authors are referencing Joseph D. Straubhaar, "Distinguishing the Global, Regional and National Levels of World Television," in *Media in Global Context: A Reader,* ed. Annabelle Sreberny-Mohammadi, Dwayne Winseck, Jim McKenna, and Oliver Boyd-Barrett (New York: Edward Arnold, 1997); Koichi Iwabuchi, *Recentering Globalization: Popular Culture and Japanese Transnationalism* (Durham, N.C.: Duke University Press, 2002); Koichi Iwabuchi, "Becoming Culturally Proximate: The A/Scent of Japanese Edo Dramas in Taiwan," in *Asian Media Productions,* ed. Brian Moeran, 121–57 (Honolulu: University of Hawaii Press, 2001).

34 Ien Ang, "The Cultural Intimacy of TV Drama," in Iwabuchi, *Feeling Asian Modernities,* 303–10.

35 Yi-Fu Tuan, *Space and Place: The Perspective of Experience* (Minneapolis: University of Minnesota Press, 1977).

36 Doreen Massey, *Space, Place, and Gender* (Minneapolis: University of Minnesota Press, 1994), 5.

37 David Harvey, *The Condition of Postmodernity: An Enquiry into the Origins of Cultural Change* (Oxford: Basil Blackwell, 1989).

38 David Harvey, *Spaces of Capital: Towards a Critical Geography* (London: Routledge, 2001).

39 Arjun Appadurai, *Modernity at Large: Cultural Dimensions of Globalization* (Minneapolis: University of Minnesota Press, 1996).

40 Fredric Jameson and Masao Miyoshi, ed., *The Cultures of Globalization* (Durham, N.C.: Duke University Press, 1998).

41 Soja, *Thirdspace.*

42 Saskia Sassen, *The Global City: New York, London, Tokyo* (Princeton, N.J.: Princeton University Press, 2001).

43 Michel de Certeau, "Walking in the City," in his *The Practice of Everyday Life,* 91–110.

44 Guilianna Bruno, "Ramble City: Postmodernism and Blade Runner," *October* 41 (1987): 61–74.

45 M. Christine Boyer, *Cybercities: Visual Perception in the Age of Electronic Communication* (Princeton, N.J.: Princeton Architectural Press, 1996).

46 Mark Shiel and Tony Fitzmaurice, ed., *Cinema and the City: Film and Urban Societies in a Global Context* (Oxford: Basil Blackwell, 2001).

47 David B. Clarke, ed., *The Cinematic City* (New York: Routledge, 1997).

48 Linda Krause and Patrice Petro, ed., *Global Cities: Cinema, Architecture, and Urbanism in a Digital Age* (New Brunswick, N.J.: Rutgers University Press, 2004).

49 Stephan Graham and Simon Marvin, *Telecommunications and the City: Electronic Spaces, Urban Places* (London: Routledge, 1996); Jennifer S. Light, *From Warfare*

to *Welfare: Defense Intellectuals and Urban Problems in Coldwar America* (Baltimore: John Hopkins University Press, 2003).

50 John T. Caldwell, *Production Cultures* (Durham, N.C.: Duke University Press, forthcoming 2008); Andrew Ross, "Dot.com Urbanism," in Couldry and McCarthy, *Mediaspace*, 145–62.

51 Anne Friedberg, *Window Shopping: Cinema and the Postmodern* (Berkeley: University of California Press, 1994).

52 Jeffrey Sconce, *Haunted Media: Electronic Presence from Telegraphy to Television* (Durham, N.C.: Duke University Press, 2000).

53 James Curran and Myung-Jin Park, ed., *De-Westernizing Media Studies* (London: Routledge, 2000).

PART I

The Reconfigured Home

David Morley

1

Domesticating Dislocation in a

World of "New" Technology

It is now a commonplace that the networks of electronic communication in which we live are transforming our senses of locality and community—and in this context it has been argued that we need to develop a "politics of dislocation" that is concerned with the new modalities of belonging that are emerging around us.[1] The issue I focus on, in this connection, is what all this does to the relation between the media and the domestic sphere—conventionally the place of belonging, par excellence.

Now the home is less and less a self-enclosed space, and more and more, as Zygmunt Bauman has argued, a "phantasmagoric" place—as electronic means of communication allow the radical intrusion of "the realm of the far" into the "realm of the near."[2] The media thus produce a psychic effect that we might describe as that of the "domestication of elsewhere"—a process whereby Hollywood brings images of the streets of the global cities to everyone, without their ever having been there. The media certainly provide us all with a secondhand sense of the "global familiar," but we should remember that, whatever range of imagery they may be familiar with, for most viewers their "horizons of action," as well as their actual experience of geographical mobility, may still be very limited (here we might think of the very low statistics for internal mobility within the United Kingdom or, on a larger scale, of the very low percentage of U.S. citizens who have ever left the United States).

Following the lead provided by Franco Moretti's work on the geographical determination of narrative possibilities in literary fiction,[3] I am concerned with the ways in which particular geographies systematically produce different types of events; returning to Foucault's insistence that our analyses must be sensitive to both the "grand strategies of geopolitics" and the "little tactics of the habitat," I want to address how the processes of globalization and domestication are intertwined, in these respects.[4]

In pursuing these questions, I want to return, via Lynn Spigel's work, to Raymond Williams's concept of "mobile privatization," as a way of understanding what she calls the "simultaneous rise of the mass produced suburb" and the place called "televisionland."[5] Spigel notes that, in the North American context at least, we can usefully understand the genealogy of ideas about domesticity, in a media-saturated world, as developing through various phases, in the postwar period—to the point where we now see the model of the digitalized "smart house" (of which, more later) offering a "sentient space" which, we are told, so thoroughly transcends the divisions of the public and the private as to make it unnecessary to actually go anywhere any more. In its digitalized form, the home itself can thus be seen, in Virilio's terms, as the "last vehicle," where comfort, safety, and stability can happily coexist with the possibility of instantaneous, digitalized flight to elsewhere.[6]

Developments such as these all readily lend themselves to a techno-utopian narrative. As domestic and private spaces are increasingly connected and overlapping with public spaces around the world, it is all too easy to believe that geography and history are being transcended. Yet, in what follows, I hope to demonstrate that it is both true that huge changes are happening—reconfiguring the domestic and the public and their relations at galloping speed and in a huge variety of ways—and that the particular dislocations and deterritorializations involved are still deeply enmeshed with the complexities and vicissitudes of geography and history. In these circumstances, only further attention to specific instances can enable us to map the precise nature of these phenomena.

The End of Geography?

In relation to the claims made by many about the transformative effects of the new technologies of our time, we would be wise to exercise what Ulf Hannerz once called some "unexciting caution."[7] The contrast between the old world of what has come to be known, in some quarters as the "slouchback media," and the exciting new world in which we all sit upright, busily doing things with our mouses and remote controls, is surely overdrawn. We know full well that media consumers of the past were never simply passive—and that much of the activity of the users of the new media is often of a relatively trivial nature.

Among their other effects, the new digital technologies have been trumpeted as heralding the ultimate "death" of geography. One striking example of this is the growth of the telephone call centers—based in India—which, because of their combination of a low-wage economy and a high level of indigenous English language skills, now handle a lot of the customer services calls for a variety of British businesses. The workers in these call centers are carefully trained to present to their callers a highly developed form of virtual Britishness. This involves them operating on British time, for the convenience of their callers; and keeping up to date with British news programs, soap operas, and weather reports, the better to engage their callers in sympathetic conversation about "local" conditions, and to disguise the cultural differences between the two geographical locations. However, it would be quite wrong to interpret these call centers as instances of the deterritorialization of culture. They may not be on British soil, but they are not just anywhere—they are located where they are because of the history of the British empire, which left behind in India the particular combination of a low-wage economy and high indigenous English language skills. The supposedly "deterritorialized" geography of our postmodern era is, I want to suggest, much more legible if one reads it as a set of secondary (or "shadow") geographies created through the history of imperialism.

Despite dissimulations of the kind practiced in these call centers, even cyberspace still has a very real geography—as can readily be seen by consulting a map showing the density of net connections per square mile in different parts of the world. Moreover, as research in the "Globalized Society" project, based in Copenhagen, has shown, "Where are you?" is (still) one of the most insistent questions in Internet "chat rooms," and questions like "Where do you live?"—or, more technically, "Where are you Mooing from?"—are posed so frequently as to suggest a continuing desire to "reterritorialize" the uncertainty of location inherent in online worlds.[8] In parallel with my comments earlier on Indian call centers operating on British time, the Copenhagen researchers found many examples of what they call the "taken-for-grantedness of America, as place and culture, on the Net" so that, in effect, America (and American time) still provides the perceptual horizon of the "online real." Despite arguments that the advent of broadcast TV means that "we" (whoever that is) now live in a "Generalized Elsewhere" where we have, according to McKenzie Wark, neither roots nor origins, only aerials and terminals,[9] I want to argue that the geographical locations that we inhabit still have very real consequences for our possibilities of knowledge and action.

Futurology, Periodization, and History

Let me now turn to questions of futurology. There is a long history of visions of how technical advances in communications—from the telegraph, to the telephone, to the Internet—will somehow lead to "better understanding." The telegraph—or the "Victorian Internet," as it as recently been redescribed[10]—was heralded as ushering in an era of world peace, for this very reason. Such utopian visions not only mistake technical improvements in modes of communication for the growth of understanding in human affairs, but can also be seen to represent backward-looking forms of nostalgia, for technological fixes for the loss of the idealized communities of a lamented Golden Age.

If we are to avoid the twin dangers of utopianism and nostalgia here, we need some way of placing these debates in historical perspective—which brings us to the question of periodization. We certainly have some guidelines to work with here. John Ellis rightly pointed to the necessity of distinguishing, in the realm of television broadcasting, between what he calls the "age of scarcity," the "age of availability," and the current "age of plenty and uncertainty" (as we move into a multichannel broadcast environment, replete with remote controls, time shift videos, and audience fragmentation).[11]

To take the case of the domestication of television, alongside Spigel's work on the United States, Tim O'Sullivan in the United Kingdom, and Shunya Yoshimi in Japan, have investigated the symbolic role played by the acquisition of TV in the development of postwar consumer cultures.[12] Just as Yoshimi points to the significance of the TV—along with the washing machine and the refrigerator as the "Three Sacred Things" in the symbolic repertoire of Japanese consumer culture in this period, one of O'Sullivan's respondents, looking back on the United Kingdom in the 1950s, remembers that "when a house had got a TV aerial and a car—then you could say they would have really 'arrived.'"

However, the dynamics in play, in the entry of TV and other media to the home, are complicated, as we know. Moreover, even the very latest technologies can always be domesticated—to suit traditional purposes.

The most popular Web site in the United Kingdom is now "Friends Re-United," which allows people to find friends from their schooldays, and Turkish migrants in Europe have now set up Web sites for the purpose of facilitating arranged marriages. Clearly any conception of a static realm of "tradition," which is then transformed by new technologies, will be unhelpful here. What we need, rather, is a conception of how "mobile" traditions incorporate new technologies, as they develop.

Some time ago now Maud Lavin argued that we needed to develop what she called the "intimate histories" of living with a medium such as broadcast television. This she described as involving "how the TV set (has been) gradually incorporated into the home . . . and . . . how we design our spaces, habits and even (our) emotions, around the TV."[13] This is also a question of how our personal memories are formulated around media experiences. In this respect we might usefully draw a parallel with Gaston Bachelard's analysis of how the material structure of the house provides the "trellis" on which childhood memory is woven—but perhaps we now need to extend the analogy, to think of how that "trellis" now has a mediated, as much as a material, structure.[14]

The long history of television's domestication—and of its journey from its initial position as a singular "stranger," allowed only into the most public/ formal space of the living room, and [the story of] its gradual multiplication and penetration of the more intimate spaces of our homes—has now to be complemented by the story of the latest personal media delivery systems, which, in their portable and miniaturized forms, might more properly be conceptualized as "body parts." The domestic history of TV is by no means singular, in this respect. Eliseo Veron and his colleagues in France have detailed the similar pathway traced by the journey of the phone in the household, as it gradually multiplied and moved from the public space of hallway, into the other rooms of the house.[15] To jump forward for a moment, when we come to the era of the mobile (or "cell") phone, not only is the phone entirely personalized—and often understood by its users as just as much a "body part" as their wristwatch—but it often becomes, in effect, its user's virtual address, the new embodiment of their sense of home.

In an earlier moment, Simon Frith rightly pointed to the historical role of broadcasting technologies, in enhancing what he called the "pleasures of the hearth."[16] He describes this process as having led to the "rediscovery of the home" as a site for domestic leisure activities. The contemporary issue is what the emergence of both the new forms of public media and the personalized communications technologies now do, to correspondingly destabilize the centrality of the domestic home. The problem here is to understand how new and old media now coexist in symbiotic forms, and how to better grasp the ways in which we live with them.

The Mediated Forms of Fetishism

Clearly, in trying to understand how we live and work with technologies, the last thing we should do is to imagine they are desired, and used simply for their functional purposes. Everything that the anthropology of material consumption tells us points to the fact that, beyond their practical uses, communications technologies also function as powerful totems and fetishes for their users. This is to insist on the importance of the symbolic meanings, as much as the practical functions, of technology. Here we might do well to remember Ondina Leal's work on the symbolic meanings of the TV set as a signifier of modernity in the Brazilian *favelas*.[17] Conversely, we might recall the firm grasp of this point displayed by the Taliban government in Afghanistan, when they hung TVs from the trees, as a potent symbol of the unwanted Westernization of their country. However, this is by no means only a matter of strange cultural practices in "exotic" places. The purchase of one of the High Definition TV sets advertised in the United Kingdom under the slogan "the less you watch, the higher your standards," signifies, whether or not it is switched on, key things about its owner, as a discriminating consumer.

In the same way, the mobile/cell phone's particular style (plain, silver, unadorned and business-like; or with customized fascia and David Beckham pendant)—or its personalized electronic "ringtone"—already communicates the particular cultural identity that its owner has chosen for him or herself, and also functions as a powerful signifier of its owner's degree of social "connexity." Zygmunt Bauman argues that, in the symbolic logic of the current period of "Liquid Modernity," "fluidity is (now) the principal source of strength . . . it is now the smaller, the lighter, the more portable that signifies improvement and 'progress.'"[18] One good example of this would be the British TV advertisement about the "sad" mobile phone, which cannot be taken out any more, because it embarrasses its owner by being too big and clumsy in appearance.

New Mobilities

Mobilities, of various sorts, are clearly central to our analysis here. In this context, the extended family has now sometimes to be seen as stretched out across the long distance phone wires, especially for migrants, who often spend a high proportion of their wages on phone calls home. These new international phone networks now allow people not just to keep in touch, but to contribute to decision making processes and to actively participate in the familial life of multisite households, from a distance.[19]

All of this points to the ways in which people have adapted to the capacities that new technologies offer them to effectively "be" in two places at once. As Kevin Robins and Asu Aksoy argue, in their study of Turkish migrants in London, this ability to oscillate between places is now, for many migrants, no more than a banal fact of their everyday lives—as they routinely move back and forward, at different points in the same day, between British and Turkish TV channels, local, face to face conversations and long distance phone calls to distant friends or relatives. Thus, twisting Raymond Williams's phrase, Aksoy and Robins insist that we must recognize that, for many people, it is now transnational culture that is "ordinary," at least in its mediated forms.[20]

However, new technologies are not only relevant to the lives of migrant families. The research of Jan English-Lueck and James Freeman, on "doing family in Silicon Valley" offers a picture of a situation where the new modes of electronic communication have become the very infrastructure of family life.[21] This, they argue, is especially so among busy, middle-class "dual career" families, living tightly scheduled lives, in which parents have to balance the continually conflicting demands of work and family. In this situation, the issue of which parent is to pick up which child from which place at what time, from their after-school activity club, is negotiated daily by the participants, on the move, by mobile phone, pager, and email. When they get home, the children may reel off their activities for the next day, while the parents dutifully enter them in their palm pilots, checking problems with the scheduling of their other appointments as they go, and promising their children to page them confirmation of their "pick up" point and time by midafternoon of the next day. This is a world in which virtual parenting now has to carry some part of the burden of childcare—and where being in electronic contact with a child (welcoming them home with a text message, hoping that they have "had a good day") is what good parenting is now about.

As we know, for all its continuing ideological centrality, the nuclear family household is declining rapidly in the West, under the impact of demographic change. It may not be possible (or even, ultimately, important) to work out which is the chicken and which is the egg here, but we have to develop a mode of analysis that can articulate these changes in household demographics with the rapid growth of "personalized" media delivery systems. Certainly, in the United Kingdom, the "multiscreen" household is now the norm, and this does affect household life in profound ways. Many people have pointed toward evidence of the internal fragmentation of the home—such as the trend towards the serial "grazing" of microwave meals by individual family members, which has replaced the shared "family meal" in many households. One might also argue that a technology such as the Walkman is intrinsically solipsistic—or, in Stephen Bayley's phrase, a "sod-you" machine, for switching off unwanted interaction with others.[22]

The question of the contemporary fragmentation—and individualization—of both audiences and the media technologies that service them, is evidently central here.

Domesticating the Future

Let me now turn back to the question of the future, which is now defined so much in technological terms. If the future represents, for many people, a troublesome realm, much of this "trouble" comes to be symbolized by—and in—technological forms. The issue then, is how this realm comes to be "naturalized" and domesticated, so as to make it more manageable for its inhabitants. Many years ago Herman Bausinger spoke of how the everyday was coming to be characterized by what he called the "inconspicuous omnipresence of the technical."[23] If an increasing array of technologies has now become naturalized, to the point of literal—or psychological—invisibility in the domestic sphere, we need to understand the process of how that has come about.

However, it is not just a question of how people come to feel "at home" with the technologies in their houses. In the case of the Californians I referred to earlier, I argued that the technologies they used to coordinate their activities had, in effect, become the infrastructure of their lives. With the advent of the "Electronic Dreamhouse"—whether in the earlier versions that Spigel has described in the 1950s and 60s, or in Bill Gates's own "fully-wired" domestic paradise, as described by Fiona Allon, we arrive at a new situation where, rather than electronic technologies being domesticated, the domestic realm itself is now thoroughly mediated. In this vision of the household, the technologies are no longer merely supplementary to, but rather, constitutive of what the home now is.[24]

From Domestication to Dislocation?

Thus far, in my narrative, I have focused on the story of the gradual domestication of the media, and I have taken the "smart house" as the culmination of this story, where the home itself is then defined by the technologies that constitute it. However, perhaps we now face the beginning of a quite different story, where the narrative drive runs in the opposite direction, toward the dedomestication of the media and the dislocation of domesticity.

As Yoshimi has demonstrated, in relation to Japan, in many countries, TV began as a public medium, which only gradually moved into the home.[25] However, increasingly, TV has now reescaped from the confines of domesticity. Nowadays, we find TV everywhere—in bars, in restaurants, in laundromats, in shops and airports, as Anna McCarthy, has documented in her study of "ambient television."[26] Public space is increasingly colonized by advertising discourses and commercial messages. In this context, the old distinction between those who are part of the media audience and those who are not, may be quite outmoded—we are all now, in effect, audiences to some kind of media, almost everywhere, almost all the time.

However, there is yet another dimension to this problem. If, as I argued earlier, the Walkman is a technology that allows its users to "privatize" public space, then the mobile/cell phone is perhaps the privatizing or "individualizing" technology, par excellence. Evidently, one of the things that this technology does is to "dislocate" the idea of home, enabling the user, in the words of one advertising campaign, to "take your network with you, wherever you go." However, like the Walkman, it also insulates its users from the geographical place where they actually are. Often the user is paying no attention to those who are physically close to them, while speaking to others who are far away. To that extent, it might also be argued that the mobile/cell phone often functions not only as a psychic cocoon for its user, but even as a kind of mobile "gated community."

It is usually taken for granted that these phones are principally devices for transcending spatial distance, but just as we know that a large percentage of the world's e-mail is sent between people working in the same building, the mobile/cell phone is also often used in counterintuitive ways—not so much to transcend space as to establish parallel communications networks in the same space (for instance, as in the use of clandestine text messaging by UK school pupils). As we know, the mobile/cell phone call disrupts the public sphere, in a variety of ways and it has been fascinating to see the ways in which this issue has given rise to a whole new set of debates about the "etiquette" of communications. However, more is at stake here than just a question of etiquette.

The mobile/cell phone has also been described as enabling the emergence of an even more "mobile" descendent of the *flaneur*—the *"phoneur."*[27] But just as I noted earlier, in relation to internet chat rooms, the first question in many mobile conversations is often "Where are you?" (Answer: "I'm on the train/stuck in a traffic jam. . . I'll be a bit late"). It seems that geography is not, in fact dead at all—and that one of the things that this technology delivers is, in fact, endless anxious commentary on our geographical locations and trajectories. Perhaps we might even say that these phones are, among other things, devices for dealing with the problems of distance created by our newly mobile lifestyles—and with the emotional "disconnectedness" that that geographical distance often symbolizes for us.[28]

In this connection Timo Kopomaa argues that the mobile phone has now acquired a particularly important place in contemporary culture, as, for many people, their portable magic charm—the device that "makes everything alright."[29] To take one banal—but nonetheless significant—measure of the mobile phone's symbolic significance in contemporary British culture, it is worth noting that by 1999 the mobile phone had replaced the umbrella, as the single item most frequently left behind on London Underground trains. This is particularly interesting, as there was certainly, at that time, no effective network connection on most of the Underground—so these phones were lost by people who had felt compelled to have them to hand, even when they could not actually use them for any practical purpose, save perhaps, playing rudimentary games.[30]

To pose matters more theoretically, the geographer Yi Fu-Tuan distinguishes between "conversation" (the substantive discussion of events and issues—a discourse of the "cosmos") and "talk" (the phatic exchange of gossip, principally designed to maintain group solidarity, which Tuan calls a "discourse of the hearth").[31] Drawing on Tuan's distinction, John Tomlinson argues that the discourse of most "mobile conversation" can be characterized as a form of phatic—or gestural—communication,[32] which is principally concerned with the maintenance of networks of interpersonal contact, rather than with the exchange of significant dialogue. In these terms, one of the things that the mobile/cell phone does is to fill the space of the public sphere with the discourse of the hearth, allowing us to take our symbolic homes with us wherever we go, just like a tortoise in its shell. To this extent, Tomlinson argues, we would be mistaken to regard these new technologies as tools for the extending of cultural horizons.

Rather, he claims, we should see them as "imperfect instruments, by which people try . . . to maintain some sense of security (and) . . . location, amidst a culture of flow and deterritorialization."[33] We now find ourselves in a world where we are all audiences to one or another medium, almost all of the time, and where, after the long process of its "domestication," TV and other media have now escaped the home—to (re)colonize the public sphere, in new ways. And if the domestic home is now becoming an increasingly technological artifact, it also seems that domesticity itself has now been "dislocated"—or perhaps, as I suggested earlier, "embodied" in a range of newly mobile technologies. In this context, as we wander the public realm, protected by the carapaces of our Walkmen and mobile phones, it may be a good moment to re-pose Heidegger's question about what it means to live in a culture of "distancelessness" and to ask again, where we are now, and where are we going?[34]

Notes

1 Larry Grossberg, "The Space of Culture: The Power of Space," in *The Post-Colonial Question: Common Skies, Divided Horizons*, ed. Ian Chambers and Lidia Curti, 169–88 (London: Routledge, 1995).

2 Zygmunt Bauman, *Community* (Cambridge: Polity Press, 2001).

3 Franco Moretti, *Atlas of the European Novel* (London: Verso, 1998).

4 Michel Foucault, "Questions on Geography," in *Power/Knowledge: Selected Interviews and Other Writings, 1972–1977*, ed. Colin Gordon, 63–77 (New York: Pantheon, 1980).

5 Lynn Spigel, "Media Homes: Now and Then," *International Journal of Cultural Studies* 4, no. 4 (2001): 385–411; Raymond Williams, *Television, Technology and Cultural Form*, (London: Fontana, 1974).

6 Paul Virilio, *Lost Dimension* (New York: Semiotext(e), 1991).

7 Ulf Hannerz, "Flows, Borderers and Hybrids—Keywords in Transnational Anthropology," paper presented at *Workshop on Flows, Borders and Hybrids*, Department of Social Anthropology, Stockholm University, October 1996.

8 Jenny Sunden, "The Virtually Global," University of Copenhagen Global Cultures Working Paper no. 8 (2001).

9 Mackenzie Wark, *Virtual Geography* (Bloomington: Indiana University Press, 1994).

10 Tom Standage, *The Victorian Internet* (Boston, Mass.: Phoenix Books, 1999).

11 John Ellis, *Seeing Things* (London: I. B. Tauris, 2000).

12 Lynn Spigel, *Make Room for TV* (Chicago: University of Chicago Press, 1992); Tim O'Sullivan, "Television Memories and Cultures of Viewing," in *Popular Television in Britain: Studies in Cultural History*, ed. John Corner, 159–81 (London: British Film Institute, 1991); Shunya Yoshimi, "Made in Japan: The Cultural

Politics of Home Electrification in Post-War Japan," *Media Culture and Society* 21, no. 2 (1999): 149–71.

13 Maud Lavin, "TV Design," in *From Receiver to Remote Control: The TV Set*, ed. Matthew Geller, 85–94 (New York: New Museum of Contemporary Art, 1990).

14 Gaston Bachelard, *The Poetics of Space* (Boston: Beacon Press, 1969).

15 Eliseo Veron, *Analyses pour Centre d'Etudes des Telecommunications* (Paris: Causa Rerum, 1991).

16 Simon Frith, "The Pleasures of the Hearth," in *Formations of Pleasure*, ed. James Donald, 101–123 (London: Routledge, 1983).

17 Ondina Fachel Leal, "Popular Taste and Erudite Repertoire: The Place and Space of TV in Brazil," *Cultural Studies* 4, no. 1 (1990): 19–29.

18 Zygmunt Bauman, *Liquid Modernity* (Cambridge: Polity Press, 2000).

19 Roger Rouse, "Mexican Migration and the Social Space of Postmodernism," *Diaspora* 1, no. 1 (1985): 8–23.

20 Kevin Robins and Asu Aksoy, "From Spaces of Identity to Mental Spaces," *Journal of Ethnic and Migration Studies* 27, no. 4 (2001): 685–711.

21 Emma Brockes, "Doing Family in Silicon Valley," *The Guardian* (G2), 17 May 2000: 8–9.

22 Stephen Bayley, *Design Classics: The Sony Walkman*, (London: BBC Video, 1990).

23 Herman Bausinger, "Media, Technology and Everyday Life," *Media, Culture and Society* 6, no. 4 (1984): 343–52.

24 Lynn Spigel, *Welcome to the Dreamhouse*, (Durham, N.C.: Duke University Press, 2001); Fiona Allon, "Altitude Anxiety: Being at Home in a Globalized World," PhD thesis, University of Technology, Sydney, 1999; Fiona Allon, "An Ontology of Everyday Control Space, Media Flows and 'Smart Living' in the Absolute Present," in *Media/Space: Place, Space and Culture in a Media Age*, ed. Nick Couldry and Anna McCarthy, 275–94 (London: Routledge, 2004).

25 Shunya Yoshimi, "Television and Nationalism: Historical Change in the Domestic TV Formation of Post-War Japan," *European Journal of Cultural Studies* 6, no. 4 (2003): 459–87.

26 Anna McCarthy, *Ambient Television*, (Durham, N.C.: Duke University Press, 2001).

27 Robert Luke, "The *Phoneur*," in *Communities of Difference: Rethinking Education for Social Change*, ed. Peter Pericles Trifonas (London: Palgrave Macmillan, 2005), 185–204.

28 John Tomlinson, "Instant Access," University of Copenhagen Global Cultures Working Paper no. 15 (2001).

29 Timo Kopomaa, *The City in Your Pocket: The Birth of the Mobile Information Society* (Helsinki: Gaudeamus, 2001).

30 R. Adams and S. Sanghara, "Londoners Losing Track of Phones," *Financial Times* 27 September 1999.

31 Yi-Fu Tuan. *Cosmos and Hearth* (Minneapolis: University of Minnesota Press, 1996).

32 See Roman Jakobson, "Linguistics and Poetics," in *The Structuralists: from Marx to Levi-Strauss*, ed. Richard de George and Fernande de George, 85–122 (New York: Anchor Books, 1972).

33 Tomlinson, "Instant Access."

34 Martin Heidegger, "The Thing," trans. Albert Hofstadter, in *Poetry, Language, Thought*, 163–86 (New York: Harper and Row, 1971).

Lisa Nakamura

2

Avatars and the Visual Culture of

Reproduction on the Web

Visual imaging of the body is a key feature of digital screen culture as well as the culture of pregnancy: many a pregnant woman's first look at her baby is through a portable CRT monitor, which is about the same size and color as a small television, the type that many people buy for their kitchens, that archetypal domestic space. Although she is most likely looking at an Accuson rather than a Sony or Toshiba, and the experience of cold ultrasound gel on her belly distinguishes one viewing experience from the other, the mode of delivery is the same, that is, the dynamic screen. This engagement with screen culture as the primal scene of reproductive looking, this uncanny techno-visual moment, resonates with another scene of looking at the digital screen, and that is in using the Internet. The large numbers of Web sites, bulletin boards, and blogs devoted to pregnancy, nursing, and fertility attest to the intense interest women take in digitizing and sharing their experiences as pregnant women and mothers. Just as the kitchen becomes an increasingly technologized space, interpenetrated with digital screens of all kinds, so too has the experience of pregnancy. Ultrasounds represent images of fetuses suspended in an electronic elsewhere; the Internet makes available new electronic elsewheres that permit women to author as well as receive images of pregnancy. This chapter examines pregnant women's media production practices on Internet bulletin boards that focus on pregnancy, birth, and conception. In producing visual images of their own pregnant bodies, fetuses, and domestic spaces, these women inhabit the space of the Internet with prospective images of family, motherhood, and in some cases unbearable loss and grief. Their deployment of these images creates a counterdiscourse of pregnancy that challenges the medical establishment's use of imaging technologies. Although the moment of ultrasound imaging I described previously figures a rapt, passive female viewer, entranced by the images shown her on the televisual screen, the moments of avatar creation engaged in by many pregnant women on the Internet reverse this figure. Women who create their own pregnant avatars to reflect their physical states engage in an interactive moment of self-representation within a virtual community of other women. They deploy the dynamic screen of the networked computer as an electronic elsewhere that permits unique forms of visual challenge to the increasing technicity of pregnancy.

"I would like to ask if someone could make a new dollie for me as I am not pregnant anymore—my son John was born on April 1st. ☺ And if it helps—I love Care Bears™! Thanks a bunch! ☺" This posting from babydream.com, a popular Web site for pregnant and trying-to-conceive women as well as new mothers, appeals to its members to collaborate in the creation of visual online signifiers of identity—avatars.[1] The overwhelming majority of the site's users add digital signatures to each of their posts; these signatures usually contain images of the woman who is posting. A "post" consists of a box containing typed text from the user, which can include a quotation from a previous poster to whom they are responding. Appended to the bottom is the poster's signature, which usually includes a graphical avatar that visually represents the user. Once the user creates her signature it is automatically appended to each post that she creates in that board. Thus each post contains a text element and a graphical element. These signatures, or "siggies," as they are called on pregnancy Web sites, were an enduring feature of early e-mail visual cultures prior to the graphical Web; many featured images in ASCII art, fashioned from letters and diacritical elements from the computer keyboard. Signatures function as a kind of public text, because no password or authentication is needed to read them, even if you do not have an account on babydream. com. Although a family or individual photograph is often scanned in and uploaded to enhance a signature, members seem much more invested in their digital avatars, or "dollies" as they are called in this community

Yea!

Thanks, Rebecca!

AF has "left the building", so I'm getting excited about trying this month. I've decided to chart everything that I can since my temps have been unusual due to allergies. I may need some help on this!!!

Tamara, we are all here for you and look to you as our wise leader...hope everything works for ya. Wouldn't it be great if we could all become the OPB's (Official Pregnant Buddies) next month?

Gotta go study...be back in a bit to check on everyone!

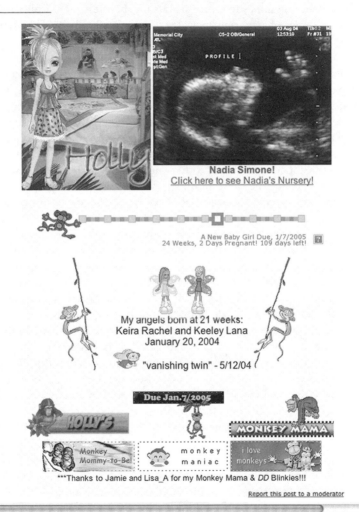

Nadia Simone!
Click here to see Nadia's Nursery!

A New Baby Girl Due, 1/7/2005
24 Weeks, 2 Days Pregnant! 109 days left!

My angels born at 21 weeks:
Keira Rachel and Keeley Lana
January 20, 2004

"vanishing twin" - 5/12/04

Due Jan.7/2005

HOLLY'S   MONKEY MAMA

Monkey   monkey   i love
Mommy-To-Be!   maniac   monkeys

***Thanks to Jamie and Lisa_A for my Monkey Mama & *DD* Blinkies!!!

Report this post to a moderator

Figure 2.1. Holly's signature on babydream.com.

(a separate bulletin board on the site deals solely with the matter of avatar creation, modification, and sharing; it is extremely active). These are created using software that offers cartoon-like body parts that can be composed to make bodies. As can be seen in the post that began this paragraph, women often envision these avatars in some of the ways that they do their own bodies. They will supply their height, weight, and coloring to the site's "Siggy Girls," women who volunteer to use their skills with computer graphics to create avatars for their less technically inclined sisters, in hopes of acquiring an avatar that looks like them. They request, create, trade, and alter pregnant avatars when they themselves become pregnant, and, as in the cited posting, which states "I am not pregnant anymore," they acquire new ones or alter their old ones to reflect non-pregnancy. In addition, the liberal use of visual signifiers such as smiley emoticons, figures from licensed media franchises like Care Bears™, and preferences for purple and "sparklies," or animated gifs which move and dance around the avatar, reveal an intense interest in digital aesthetics.

Women have been relatively late adopters of the Internet. Users of babydream.com and the other numerous Web sites that serve pregnant women and new mothers (see ivillage.com, pregnancy.org, and parentsplace.com for examples) have transformed the formerly male cyberspaces they have come across. In this chapter I will be discussing their interventions into the form of the female body in pregnancy Web sites, partly because the avatars they make there pose a direct challenge to the "hyperreal, exaggerated, hyperbodies" evident in mainstream video games such as *Tomb Raider* and *Dead or Alive*. The "unique aesthetic for perfection" embodied in Lara Croft and Kasumi "present embodiments that have left the real female body behind in a significant way."[2] I agree with Mary Flanagan when she writes that, "it is at the female body that the formation and contestation of digibodies is occurring."[3] However, the pregnant avatars that pregnant women create for parenting Web sites accomplish the exact opposite from those deployed in gaming culture; they bring the "real female body" into the digital in a central way rather than leaving them behind. Indeed, these avatars interestingly turn out far less hyperreal and exaggerated than their owner's real bodies; most women seem to want avatars that are built exactly like their unpregnant bodies, only "with a belly," an offline impossibility, as anyone who has experienced pregnancy knows. However, this fantasy of modularity—a digitally pregnant body is simply a "regular" female body with another "feature," a pasted-on belly—addresses the anxiety of permanent transformation versus transient state that preoccupies many pregnant women.

(Complaints and fears about losing "baby weight" and "getting your body back" give voice to this particular obsession with the gestating body.)

The users of these sites are often stay-at-home mothers, often quite politically conservative, often working class, and when they create avatars to use on them they often make statements reflecting these positions (the "Bush Cheney in '04" bumper sticker was quite popular. In short, they are a taste culture that has never been taken much into account when new media theorists discuss avatars, embodiment, or gender. Their overt political ideologies certainly do not square with the dominant discourse of new media theory.

What to do, however, when a media form that had been dominated by engineers, students, artists, and other cultural elites becomes popular in dramatically quick, Internet time? One of the most dramatic technology adoption stories I can think of has to do with the Internet: in 1993, Scott Bukatman could ask "why are there no women in cyberspace?" and mean it.[4] In 2003 the percentages of women and men online were exactly 50/50 and they are holding steady as of now. However, according to Wakeford, from 1992–1996, women's presence on the Internet increased from 5 percent to 34 percent.[5] The rapid narrowing of the digital divide has resulted in a very different Internet user, one more likely to be female, less educated, less culturally elite. In short, people who belong to much different taste cultures than previously existed on the Internet. This is not to say that kitsch never existed on the Internet; the number of cheesy Web sites devoted to screen grabs, slash fiction, and the digital equivalent of velvet clown paintings would perhaps challenge even the amount of porn online. However, this was masculine kitsch, geek kitsch, and it seems important to note that. This was a primarily male audience in whose visual culture Tolkien, Ridley Scott, Frank Frazetta, cyberpunk, anime, and Marvel Comics figure largely. This Internet popular culture has largely been ignored except by sociologists, who tend to discuss it in terms of social engagement, alienation, and the public sphere rather than in reference to aesthetics or taste cultures.

Visual style and taste are rarely discussed in relation to popular (as opposed to artistic or countercultural) digital forms. Although art sites are often discussed and valued in relation to their challenges to old media forms, deployment of new modes of interactivity, and forms of resistance to linear modes of consuming and producing the art object, pregnancy Web sites are seldom visited by people who are not pregnant, or partnered with people who are pregnant. Web sites that deal with domestic, everyday, or commercial matters have heretofore been the province of sociologists and graphic designers or usability experts, such as Edward Tufte, whose *Envisioning Information* has become a standard text in information design.[6] This discourse of transparency and usability values efficiency and density of information, and does not discuss new media objects in terms of its visual culture. "Look and feel" are elements of button positioning, font size, use of white space, and intuitive icons, and are not used to signify anything in regard to what sorts of offline visual traditions are being referenced.

Parenting Web sites exemplify the ways that women use the Internet to graphically embody themselves in specific reproductive states, that is, as pregnant women, nursing women, and mothers. They draw significant numbers of women who exemplify the profile of the "late adopter" of the Internet; that is to say, they are female, often not young, and tend to be stay-at-home mothers rather than professionals who might be required to use the Internet for work. In addition, they defy their gender profile in relation to the Internet because they are deeply involved in digital production: they upload significant amounts of online content as well as consume it.

Pregnant avatars put pressure on all kinds of ideas regarding online embodiment. Although no one believes anymore that on the Internet "nobody knows you're a dog," it is certainly true that many women offline can exist for several months without anybody knowing that they are pregnant. Women who work outside the home must carefully weigh factors such as economic need and work climate when they decide how and when they wish to reveal their pregnancies in the workplace. This discourse of "outing" is in some sense a queer one; pregnancy is a state of difference whose visibility and legibility is, at least at first, somewhat performative and volitional. Thus, pregnant avatars represent a state that is by definition temporary; they signify a changing body, in some sense an ephemeral body. In addition, one's avatar can be pregnant in the "public" space of the Internet bulletin board, while its owner may be still closeted. The pregnant avatar memorializes a body in transition, one that is out of the user's control. The Internet is likewise a space of ephemerality, as its content changes rapidly and constantly. In addition, pregnant avatars have a certain literal quality that leads to intriguing phenomenological questions: would a user keep a pregnant avatar if they miscarry? Would the act of altering or removing that avatar from the board signify a miscarriage in miniature, a digital reenactment of the offline state? What are the implications of this participatory digital practice?

In *Feminism and the Technological Fix*, Carol Stabile describes the defining paradox of the visual culture of pregnancy as follows: "With the advent of visual technologies, the contents of the uterus have become demystified and entirely representable, but pregnant bodies themselves remain concealed."[7] Hence the paradox: whereas medical imaging technologies like ultrasounds and laparoscopy have turned the pregnant female body inside out, rendering it as transparent as a pane of glass, a vessel containing infinite visual wonders of procreation and opportunities for witnessing with machine-enabled vision the miracle (or spectacle) of birth, its exterior remains hidden in plain sight: as she writes, "the pregnant body . . . remains invisible and under-theorized in feminist theory."[8] Many other scholars of feminism, technology, and the visual have noted the pregnant body's peculiar status in post-nineties feminist visual culture. As Lisa Cartright writes in "A Cultural Anatomy of the Visible Human Project," pregnant bodies have long been used to stand in for all female bodies in the culture of medical imaging, from its roots in classically rendered paintings of female pelvises by d'Agoty[9] to current projects like the Visible Woman, whose cryosectioned body was digitized and put on a database online for educational purposes.[10] Thus, women's reproductive organs, and women in reproductive states are overrepresented in medical visual culture; the pregnant female body and its interior in particular is classically overdetermined, as it comes to represent all female bodies. A spate of scholarly books and collections on the topic of reproductive technologies and feminism have all noted the way that the medical establishment has worked to make the pregnant female body normative, and as a result, pathologize it has nonreproductive female bodied. Cartright notes, the Visible Woman was criticized as an incomplete and inadequate model of the female body because, although in perfect health at her time of death, she is "postmenopausal and presumably therefore unsuited to demonstrating processes of reproduction"; in other words, she is too old.[11] Ultrasound has taken up the imaging practice that once belonged to medical painting and engraving, and is valued because it seems to give access to the invisible, the interior, to move right past the unspeakable and abject pregnant body to its contents, the fetus.

Although the culture as a whole is dying to see photographic or "real" images of babies in the womb, pregnancy's hidden spectacle, feminists in particular are wary of the way that this desire encourages ways of seeing that represent the fetus and mother as occupying different visual frames, and tends to visually reinforce the notion of their separate existences. Of course, this type of machine-enhanced seeing most famously provides fodder for antichoice movements, who have deployed these medical images ferociously in their protests and signage. However, feminist theorists' skepticism regarding reproductive visioning technologies has roots in an earlier technologically critical discourse. Just as the move to challenge the medical establishment by using and reinvesting midwives rather than medical doctors with authority characterizes second wave and later feminisms, so too has feminist theory's suspicion of the visual as a mode of knowing conditioned this reception.

As Petchesky writes in "Foetal Images: The Power of Visual Culture in the Politics of Reproduction," the problem with seeing as a way of knowing is that it creates a distance between the seer and the seen that translates into an uneven power relation between the knower and the known.[12] Evelyn Fox Keller critiques this privileging of the visual in her work in science and gender, and Laura Mulvey has also written on the ways that the gaze objectifies women and more importantly, how it is infixed in relation to the apparatus and form of narrative film. Part of visual culture's intervention into this state of things is to critique the gaze and to encourage other ways of seeing; Nick Mirzoeff wishes to replace it with the "transverse glance," which is the "transient, transnational, trans-gendered way of seeing that visual culture seeks to define, describe, and deconstruct."[13]

However, as Donna Haraway writes in "The Persistence of Vision," perhaps it is time to reclaim vision for feminist ethics. Despite the eyes' "having been used to signify a perverse capacity—honed to perfection in the history of science tied to militarism, capitalism, colonialism, and male supremacy—to distance the knowing subject from everybody and everything in the interests of unfettered power,"[14] it seems particularly strategic to do so right now, at this particular moment in both new media studies and feminist theory. For the parallels between medical visual imaging and the deployment of digital communication technologies are strong, both in terms of chronology, causality, and usage. Computer screens and ultrasound screens, although both televisual, share a common origin in radar, a military technology. Unlike the cinematic screen, which shows images of the past rather than the present, they show images in real time: "processual" images.[15] They are "live" images in both senses of the word; they visualize "life" in the form of the pregnant woman and the fetus, and they are also keyed to the present.

The linkage between the Internet's visioning of pregnant bodies and the deployment of medical images of pregnant women and fetuses allows us to parse gendered embodiment at a critical moment in its visual culture. Much feminist critique of medical imaging has targeted its mode of production. Typically, doctors, medical illustrators, and research scientists are the gatekeepers in deciding what a pregnant woman is permitted to visualize and when.[16] Ultrasounds are not transparent texts: like many medical images, they require interpretation. This means that the pregnant body is surveilled both from without and within, and the production, manipulation, viewing, printing, and interpretation of the image are controlled by doctors and technicians. However, the Internet has long been celebrated for its interactivity, that is, the way in which it puts image production in the hands of amateurs, or "the people." It bridges the production/reception divide. As Burnett and Marshall write, "distinctive from telephony, the Web implicates a production component, that is, where content is developed and enhanced beyond its original orality (think of any conversation and its unpredictable flow) into some combination of visual, textual, and graphic structure. The Web, when thought of as a medium is a hybrid that invokes the sensation of orality and contingency with the guided structure of a book or magazine."[17]

This is what makes the Internet in general and the Web in particular different from other telecommunicative forms. Hence, when we look at the ways that pregnant and trying-to-conceive women depict themselves in pregnancy web forums, we are given insight into the reappropriation of the medicalized gaze. When these women make graphical images of themselves as pregnant avatars to insert in their bulletin board posts online, they are producing a counterdiscourse that challenges the binarism of hypervisible/invisible pregnant bodies. In addition, the avatars they produce exist to serve orality: the kind of asynchronous conversation that goes on among pregnant women in an online forum. In these forums the often "unpredictable flow" of conversation is directed fairly predictably into a specific path; all discourse that is not about pregnancy or babies is flagged as an "off topic" thread so that users can avoid it. Because the orality of pregnancy online is so self-referential—it consists of pregnant women talking about their pregnancies ad nauseum—the graphical avatars they create combine "visual, textual, and graphical" structures in a hybrid form that remediates the pregnant body in truly multifarious ways. Rather than depicting hypervisible interiors and invisible exteriors, these women create complicated, at times incoherent, embodiments of pregnancy, a paradigmatically embodied state. Their use of dynamic screens to reclaim the mode of image production of their own bodies results in rich and at times bizarre taste cultures online.[18]

Ultrasounds that depict a fetus floating in an undefined space, the invisible and occluded space of the mother's body, as well as fetal photography that encourages the sense of an "independent" fetal body, reinforces the notion of the pregnant body as really two bodies. The persistent envisioning of the pregnant female body as a vessel (the umbilical cord is painstakingly deleted from most photographic images of fetuses, thereby emphasizing its existence separate from the woman's body) echoes an older cyberutopian notion of the body or "meat" as a disposable package for what really counts: the mind. Computer scientist Hans Moravec, "the most exemplary advocate of radical disembodiment," sees the flesh as just a carrier or an envelope: a person is an "essence or pattern," signal to the body's noise, and the body is merely "the machinery supporting that process."[19] The mind, termed "wetware," operates like the software in a computer; it is housed by an apparatus but is transferable in nature. This notion of the mind/body split is the foundational assumption and driving force behind cyberpunk fiction, and one of the reasons that theorists claim that new media creates a "posthuman" being, one that is detachable from a body if embedded in an alternate site enabled by machinery.[20] Thus, this radical sundering of the body from its contents, be they "the mind" or "the fetus," so disliked by feminist medical theorists, is not a new idea: cyberpunk has been representing bodies existing separated from their contents since its inception in the early eighties. What is of more interest is the ideological use to which machine-enabled disembodiment is put. Much medical imaging encourages a similar idea to cyberpunk philosophy, that is, what "really counts" is what is inside the body, not the body itself—that is to say, the fetus.

Cyberfeminism has been described as "a restart button" for gendered ideologies, partly because it seeks to reclaim machines—and by extension machine-enabled vision—for women, as producers and users of their own imaging. The radical possibilities that new media offers to digitally create "other" bodies, other iterations of "woman" and "man" that elude the dichotomies between interior and exterior, white and nonwhite, and female and male are especially evident in digital visualizations of bodies, that is to say, avatars. Sites like Victoria Vesna's "bodies incorporated" are the darling of cyberfeminist and other new media theorists because they allow for interactive body play in the realm of the absurd; avatars made of chocolate with human and machine parts certainly bust paradigms of normative bodies.[21] The commercialization of the Internet has led many Internet utopians to despair of its potential as a site to challenge institutional authority and tired media scripts, and they often look to artists to provide that bit of resistance or subversion that new media theorists so badly need. However, it is important to note the elitism that can arise from this position. As Burnett notes above, new media is distinguished by its redistribution of image and content production to "the masses." This stance celebrates the Internet's potential to give expression to "all," to put media production into the hands of nonprofessionals (who are presumably less hegemonized, or at least freer of overt commercial agendas). Mirzoeff writes that the popularization of digital media has produced an "apparent state of emergency in North American universities at the level of criticism, pedagogy, and institutional practice" because they "promote a form of empowered amateurism—make your own movie, cut your own CD, publish your own Web site—that cuts across professionalization and specialization, the twin justifications of the liberal arts university."[22] However, Vesna is a type of professional herself; a professional artist. Her use of digital media is far from amateurish, and the site evidences some serious expertise with imaging software.

The promise of free and easy digital production is, practically speaking, an illusion; in reality it is really hard to create "original digital images." Photoshop and Fireworks are notoriously difficult to learn, and it is a truism of the Internet that it is much easier to borrow or steal images than it is to create them from scratch. As Manovich writes, this new aesthetic of selection from preexisting sets of images rather than creation of new ones characterizes new media's very structure and logic.[23] The modularity of digital images makes the principle of copying and modification the basis of new media practice. Yet many new media theorists heavily favor "original" artistic production, and also tend to prioritize graphical versus textual production. This tends to decrease the likelihood that "empowered amateurs" might create the kind of work that gets noticed, written about, discussed, assigned on syllabi, and analyzed. (The price of admission was a lot lower when all it took to make an avatar was some typing and writing skills). This emphasis on the essential originality of avatars, either textual or graphical, is apparent in Currier's work: she writes "the visual avatars adopted by participants in more sophisticated graphical social environments present not simply a graphic icon manipulated by the individual user but figure that is self-imagined and created."[24] She emphasizes how avatar construction represents a form of "disembodiment" because "the construction of these bodies is entirely along the lines of individual desires."[25] However, considering how difficult it is on the level of techne to create "new" digital images rather than modify bitmapped ones taken from other "original" sources on the web, individual desire, as strong as it may be, is likely to be thwarted unless the user is a graphic designer.

Popular graphical avatars created by "ordinary" users for nontechnical purposes are the blind spot of visual culture studies *as well as* digital culture studies. This constitutes an interesting case of theoretical convergence. However, there are institutional reasons for this; as Lisa Cartright writes of television studies, popular (as opposed to "artistic") digital media studies have "remained marginal to disciplines that shun low culture."[26] Her remarkable observation that television was excluded from serious consideration by the famous Visual Culture Questionnaire that appeared in the journal *October* in 1996, in which both digital media were discussed more often, I would contend has to do with digital media's efforts to legitimate themselves by focusing upon digital *art*. It is not a new strategy for new disciplines to array themselves with authority and prestige by invoking the artistic. As mentioned before, Victoria Vesna's work is a great favorite, and in fact the strongest critical–theoretical discussion of new media has come from the world of art (see Timothy Druckery's anthologies, the work of Mark Hansen, the Leonardo series from MIT Press, etcetera).[27] Like television studies, which have "tended to rely on the methods of sociology and communication foundational to cultural studies,"[28] new media studies have split into two streams: high critical exegeses of new media art, and social scientific case studies of popular new media practices on the Web and Internet. It is as if the critical theorists said of the popular Internet, if it is not art, it is crap.

The Craptastic.com Web site takes an ironic and snarky approach to cultural objects. Its notion is that something can be "crappy" or devoid of aesthetic difficulty or originality yet be "fantastic" in some other sense, that it can reference popular culture in a new way or play with the viewer's grip on his or her previously solid sense of taste and appreciation, that we can think something is fantastic in and in part because of its crappiness. Low culture, what Gans would call popular culture, as embodied by such things as strip malls, Care Bears, and reality television, can be craptastic when framed with detachment and irony.

Online community has fallen out of favor lately as a topic for academic discussion. Although it dominated new media theory in the nineties it has lately taken backstage to academic discussions of new media forms, such as interfaces, and other uses of the new media screen technology, such as digital gaming, which has become an economic juggernaut. However, as I have argued elsewhere, often the most sophisticated and interesting uses of new media involve older instantiations of them (as in the subversive potential of e-mail) precisely because they occupy lower bandwidth, and are thus less bounded by particular infrastructural requirements.[29] Pregnancy bulletin boards are asynchronous and simple. They are divided into areas based on due date, "ttc" (trying to conceive), lesbian mothers, and so forth, and within each board a user is required to choose a nickname and a password. They are then given access to posting ability. Posts follow threads on topics such as spotting, sex, labor stories, and fertility charting.

Many signatures on these boards are chaotic, especially when compared with orderly ASCII-styled earlier ones from the text-only days of the early-nineties Internet. They are riotous combinations of bumpers,

Little Livi, born still on her due date.

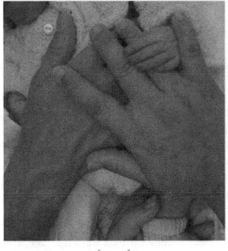

7/27/03

"out beyond the ideas of wrongdoing and rightdoing, there is a field. I'll meet you there."

Rumi

Report this post to a moderator | :

Figure 2.2.   Olivia's signature on babydream.com.

animated .gifs, blinkies, photos, borders, cartoons, and other combinations of text and image. Some of these seem about signifying identities that cannot be integrated into one sign or signature. (I have always wondered how a person can reconcile breastfeeding with Bush, but people do it). This particular visual culture of accretion rather than integration references scrapbooking, or "scrapping," another signifying practice uniquely associated with middle class women and reviled by "real" artists. Like scrapbooking, new media works through a logic of selection of existing modules or scraps and the subsequent accumulation and arrangement of these pieces into something new. Like patchwork, the signatures that result are often extremely large, in many cases taking up more than three computer screens to view.

Avatar construction is a valorized object of study in new media, especially in gaming studies. Discussions of avatars in contexts other than gaming are relatively rare. The signatures that women create on pregnancy Web sites include images of themselves and their families that take back the power to visualize the pregnant female body from the medical establishment and put it back in the hands of women themselves. The results are often cartoonish, conflicted, disorganized, and bizarre, but the openness of the form—any image or text can be uploaded to form a signature—allows for moments of poignancy that defy description and indeed the idea of visualization itself. One poster's signature consists of a photograph of her stillborn child's hand, with her own hand enclosing it. Beneath this image appears a passage by the poet Rumi: "out beyond the ideas of wrongdoing and rightdoing, there is a field. I'll meet you there." As James Elkins writes in *Pictures of the Body: Pain and Metamorphosis*, "the crucial issue in studying pictures of the body must be the expressive value of each individual choice: what *kind* of pain is evoked, exactly *where* the sensation is strongest, precisely *how* the analogies operate."[30] The power of this image indeed resides in its pain: the pain of the bereaved mother. Its transgressiveness resides in its delivering to the viewer an image of a body that is rarely represented at all in any medium: that of the stillborn child. As Elkins writes, "some images are unrepresentable because they are forbidden by law or prohibited by custom."[31] Whereas images of dead babies were common in nineteenth-century photography,[32] they are extremely rare in our times, and even rarer in the context of a pregnancy Web site. This signature represents a body that, like that of the pregnant woman, lies beyond the vocabulary of signifying practices that make up the common visual language of domesticity and home, gesturing toward the incredibly wide range of electronic elsewheres and virtual bodies that pregnant women, mothers, and trying-to-conceive women create on the Web.

Notes

1 The name of this Web site has been changed to protect the privacy of its members.
2 Mary Flanagan, "Mobile Identities, Digital Stars, and Post Cinematic Selves," *Wide Angle* 21, no. 1 (1999): 77–93.
3. Ibid., 155.
4 Scott Bukatman, *Terminal Identity: The Virtual Subject in Postmodern Science Fiction* (Durham, N.C.: Duke University Press, 1993), 314.
5 Nina Wakeford, "Networking Women and Grrrls with Information/ Communication Technology: Surfing Tales of the World Wide Web," in *The Cybercultures Reader*, ed. David and Barbara M. Kennedy Bell, 350–59 (London: Routledge, 2000).
6 Edward R. Tufte, *Envisioning Information* (Cheshire, Conn.: Graphics Press 2001).
7 Carol A. Stabile, *Feminism and the Technological Fix* (Manchester, UK: Manchester University Press, 1994), 84.
8 Ibid., 84.
9 See Julie Doyle and Kate O'Riordan, "Virtually Visible: Female Cyberbodies and the Medical Imagination," in *Reload: Rethinking Women + Cyberculture*, ed. Mary Flanagan and Austin Booth, 239–60 (Cambridge, Mass.: MIT Press, 2002), for further discussion of d'Agoty.
10 Lisa Cartright, *Screening the Body: Tracing Medicine's Visual Culture* (Minneapolis: University of Minnesota Press, 1995), 30.
11 Ibid., 30.
12 Rosalind Pollack Petchesky, "Foetal Images: The Power of Visual Culture in the Politics of Reproduction," in *Reproductive Technologies*, ed. Michelle Stanworth, (Minneapolis: University of Minnesota Press, 1987), 68.
13 Nicholas Mirzoeff, *The Visual Culture Reader*, 2nd ed. (London: Routledge, 2002), 18.
14 Donna Haraway, "The Persistence of Vision," in *The Visual Culture Reader*, ed. Nick Mirzoeff (New York: Routledge, 2001), 677.
15 Mark B. N. Hansen, *New Philosophy for New Media* (Cambridge, Mass.: MIT Press, 2004). See also Lev Manovich's *The Language of New Media* (Cambridge, Mass.: MIT Press, 2001) for an account of the "dynamic screen."
16 The very wealthy may purchase or lease ultrasound equipment for private use, however, the disapproving uproar surrounding movie star Tom Cruise and Katie Holmes' acquisition of such equipment during her pregnancy attests to the notion that the power to visualize the fetus ought to remain in "professional" hands.
17 Robert Burnett and P. David Marshall, *Web Theory: An Introduction* (London: Routledge, 2003).

18 See Gans on taste cultures and publics for more detail. Herbert J. Gans, *Popular Culture and High Culture: An Analysis and Evaluation of Taste* (New York: Basic Books, 1974).

19 Dianne Currier, "Assembling Bodies in Cyberspace: Technologies, Bodies, and Sexual Difference," in *Reload: Rethinking Women + Cyberculture,* ed. Mary Flanagan and Austin Booth (Cambridge, MA: MIT Press, 2002), 552.

20 See Richard Doyle, *Wetwares: Experiments in Postvital Living* (Minneapolis: University of Minnesota Press, 2003).

21 New media criticism by Jennifer Gonzalez and Doyle and O'Riordan have showcased the site as an example of the possibilities. See Jennifer Gonzalez, "The Appended Subject: Race and Identity as Digital Assemblage," in *Race in Cyberspace,* ed. Lisa Nakamura, Beth Kolko, and Gil Rodman, 27–50 (New York: Routledge, 2000).

22 Mirzoeff, *The Visual Culture Reader,* 2nd edition, 6.

23 Manovich, *The Language of New Media.*

24 Currier, "Assembling Bodies in Cyberspace: Technologies, Bodies, and Sexual Difference," 526.

25 Ibid.

26 Lisa Cartright, "Film and the Digital in Visual Studies: Film Studies in the Era of Convergence," in *The Visual Culture Reader,* 2nd edition, ed. Nicholas Mirzoeff, 424.

27 See Hansen, *New Philosophy for New Media;* Timothy Druckrey, *Electronic Culture: Technology and Visual Representation* (New York: Aperture, 1996); and Timothy Druckrey and Books24x7 Inc., *Ars Electronica Facing the Future: A Survey of Two Decades* (Cambridge, Mass.: MIT Press, 1999); and the Leonardo book series from MIT Press.

28 Cartright, "Film and the Digital in Visual Studies."

29 Lisa Nakamura, *Cybertypes: Race, Ethnicity, and Identity on the Internet* (New York: Routledge, 2002), 131.

30 James Elkins, *Pictures of the Body: Pain and Metamorphosis* (Stanford, Calif.: Stanford University Press, 1999), 276.

31 Ibid., 277.

32 See Michael Lesy and Charles Van Schaick, *Wisconsin Death Trip* (New York: Anchor Books, 1991).

3

Jeffrey Sconce

The Talking Weasel of Doarlish Cashen

In his 1861 novel *The House by the Churchyard*, J. S. LeFanu writes of a home haunted by a disembodied hand. For weeks the floating hand appears at windows and doors, as if seeking entrance into the home. "One evening," writes LeFanu, "Mrs. Prosser was sitting in the twilight at the back parlour window, which was open, looking out into the orchard, and plainly saw a hand stealthily placed upon the stone window-sill outside, as if by someone beneath the window intending to climb up."[1] A thorough search reveals no sign of the intruder. Days later, alone in the kitchen, the cook looks up to see the hand "laid with its palm against the glass, near the side of the window, and this time moving slowly up and down as if feeling carefully for some inequality in the glass."[2] The mysterious palm lingers a few seconds even after the cook screams in terror. When not hovering eerily at the home's various windows, the mysterious hand knocks incessantly at the front door. One night, exhausted by the disturbances, Mr. Prosser finally opens the door in anger only to feel a strange presence pass him in the hallway. "He grew very uncomfortable, feeling an inward persuasion that when . . . he had opened the hall-door, he had actually given admission to the besieger."[3] Sure enough, the hand soon begins knocking on doors *inside* the home. As a final indexical sign of its domestic intrusion, the ghostly hand leaves its prints on a dusty table in the parlor.

Elaborating on the image of the "ice cold hand" that so memorably disturbs Lockwood's sleep in *Wuthering Heights,* LeFanu's story appeared during a period of transition in Gothic fiction, a move away from the ruined castles and historical haunts of Walpole and Radcliffe to an increasingly domestic theater of apparitions.[4] Like all "haunted house" stories, LeFanu's tale carefully exploits a symbolic architecture of domesticity, externalizing the psychical structures that fuel the genre into a meticulously detailed and wholly uncanny floor plan. In our current century, these uncanny spaces of gothic domesticity remain strangely familiar. Even as some gothic narratives attempt to transpose the genre's conventions into more hybridized iterations, the fundamental architecture of the domestic gothic—a narrative house built from ghostly moors, forbidden attics, cursed bedrooms, ominous windows, and haunted stairways—remains wholly legible and alluring for contemporary readers. So too does the narrative logic that orchestrates these spaces for maximum uncanny effect. Consider, for example, the still prevalent folktale of the terrorized babysitter, a suburban legend in circulation since at least the 1960s. Left alone at night with a group of small children, the babysitter receives increasingly threatening phone calls from a demented stranger. The menace is vague at first, but as the calls continue, the madman seems to possess privileged information about the family and intimate knowledge of the babysitter's moment-to-moment activities within the home. The terrified babysitter finally enlists the aid of a phone operator to trace the source of the calls. In the midst of a particularly bloodcurdling exchange with the psychopath, the operator cuts into the line and screams—"Get the children and get out of the house! He's calling from the phone upstairs!" LeFanu's ghostly hand at the window thus becomes the corporeal killer on the extension, but the carefully articulated spatial logic of media and domestic transgression remains identical.

Such continuity would be wholly unremarkable if not for the many claims that modernity—to name only one of the great historical lines in the sand dividing LeFanu's gothic handiwork and the hazards of contemporary babysitting—has so drastically altered space, time, and subjectivity that previous genres of thematized space, like the domestic gothic, should seem by now to be antiquated, irrelevant, and even wholly alien. We take it as a matter of faith to say we experience space and time much differently than the citizens of previous centuries, a transition seen as foundational to changing modes of historical subjectivity. Such claims of experiential transformation have been especially central to media studies, which of late has increasingly interwoven its technological histories with more totalizing accounts of perception and subjectivity. Central to the "modernity thesis," Jamesonian postmodernism, and the current attempts to reconcile "new media theory" with garden-variety philosophy is an often unexamined assumption that space, time, media, and subjectivity exist in a nexus of mutually transformative relations. As the rhyming fictions of LeFanu's floating hand and suburbia's terrorized babysitter demonstrate, however, certain chronotopic strategies for narrating media and space have predated modernity, survived postmodernity, and remain current even today. Regardless of whatever transformations in domestic life, social space, media practices, and perhaps even consciousness itself that may or may not have occurred over the past century, most of us still recognize that disembodied hands, murderous psychopaths, rabid wolverines, and encyclopedia salesmen are best kept at bay beyond clearly demarcated property boundaries, a lesson most children learn very early in life through their first reading of "The Three Little Pigs."

How might we explain this apparent disconnect between theories of fundamental transformations in "the human sensorium," as Benjamin puts it, and the relative stability of genres centered on still coherent chronotopes of thematic space and time? This apparent schism between our contemporary theories of mediated subjectivity and the historical legacy of discursive and representational practices in, about, and around the media testifies to the difficulties in reconciling media theory's recent philosophical aspirations with a more material history of cultural practice. Media theory may well be doomed to become simply a subset of philosophy. But before our histories of media technologies and practices become forever wedded to the key figures, conceptual gateways, and philosophical traditions that have most aggressively promoted an intrinsic relationship between media and subjectivity, perhaps it is worth considering for a moment whether or not the media have any determinative relationship with subjectivity in the first place. After all, media studies' resurgent interest in subjectivity (following on the heels of its temporary infatuation with the equally monumental yet equally vague abstraction of "the body") can never actually reconstruct how any medium did or did not alter subjective experience on a phenomenological level, any more than it can prove how a particular mode of subjectivity did or did not inform the course of media development. Or, even if such links do exist, can anyone really reconstruct such mediated historical subjectivities without resorting to technological superstition or outright necromancy?

Perhaps we would do better here to follow Jonathan Crary in following Michael Foucault and argue that space, time, technology, subjectivity, and the other usual suspects in the historical turn in recent media theory have no existence outside of the discursive horizons that give them shape. In his account of a historical shift in the *conceptualization* of perception during the mid-nineteenth century, Crary writes, "Whether or not perception or vision actually change is irrelevant, for they have no autonomous history. What changes are the plural forces and rules composing the field in which perception occurs."[5] When engaging the issue of media and subjectivity, one might say that these amorphous entities likewise have no "autonomous history," but instead reveal themselves through the "plural forces and rules" that produce them discursively in both social practice and conceptual imagination. Following this trajectory, media studies would need to temper (or at least be more reflexive about) its infatuation with the grand questions of philosophy to better engage how media figure in the social production of discourses about space, time, and subjectivity. In this approach, radio, cinema, television, and other media that "see," "hear," and "speak" would not simply be assumed to mimic the human sensorium and thus signal profound shifts in a spatial/perceptual field; rather, media and their attending practices would serve as important discursive sites and privileged discursive objects in a historical dialogue *about* media, space, and subjectivity. Rather than ask how various media must impact, embody, index, reflect, or otherwise relate to the subjective experience of space and time, the question would instead be why we so readily *assume* that the media have in fact had any impact whatsoever on the subjective experience of space and time.

A more genealogical approach, meanwhile, would also allow us to reconsider and perhaps even redraw the now thoroughly imprinted chronotopes of modernity and postmodernity that so dominate our historical accounts of film, television, and emerging media. What might happen, for example, if we returned to issues of media and modernity by first bidding adieu to Benjamin at the gates of the Paris arcades, or if we revisited our cognitive map of postmodernity after abandoning Jameson to find his own way out of the Bonaventure hotel? Why not, if only in the spirit of theoretical R&D, temporarily elevate an Alfred Jarry, Georges Bataille, or William Reich to the forefront of theorizing about media and subjectivity? Or better yet, why not seek out the truly pataphysical, heterogeneous, and even downright cranky accounts of media, history, and subjectivity that lie beyond the purview of even these celebrated cranks? Not only might we encounter some women, peasants, and/or people of color to interrogate for alternative accounts of these eras, but such forays into discursive realms other than the tradition of academic philosophy might, at the very least, open media studies to a wider range of less predictable and hopefully more interesting questions about the cultural histories of film, television, and digital media. Toward that end, I would like to present another exercise in gothic domesticity, an account of media, space, and modernity from the 1930s that forces us to make a number of disruptive shifts in our conventional critical and geographical framing of the period—from the City of Lights to the Isle of Man, from Paris to Peel, and from the *flaneur* to a fur ball named Gef, the talking weasel of Doarlish Cashen.

"I am a ghost in the form of a weasel, and I shall haunt you with weird noises and clanking chains."[6]

London newspapers first reported the story of the talking "man-weasel" in October of 1931, and articles on the phenomenon appeared sporadically throughout the decade. "The Dalby Spook," as the locals called him, shared this farm with Jim Irving, formerly a piano salesman from Canada, his wife Maggie, and their adolescent daughter Voirrey. The Irvings and their furry boarder lived in a tiny farmhouse overlooking the ocean, two miles away from their nearest neighbors and eight miles away from Peel, the nearest community. Despite this isolation, the case garnered enough press attention in its time to attract such noted parapsychologists as Harry Price, Hereward Carrington, and Nandor Fodor, each of whom visited the farm to study the phenomenon firsthand. At the height of the "talking mongoose" craze, an American theatrical agent even offered the Irvings fifty thousand dollars to bring Gef to the United States for a national tour, but Gef, deadly afraid of being captured and "bottled," as he put it, would not consent.[7]

When Gef first came to Doarlish Cashen, he could not speak at all, but simply tormented the family with loud squeals, thumps, and crashes in the night. When the entity began making strange gurgling, infant-like sounds from behind the walls, various members of the family attempted to make verbal contact with the creature. Gradually, by imitating the Irvings, we are told Gef learned to speak English. Later, the weasel claimed he had always *understood* human speech, but that no one had taken the time to teach him before. After demonstrating a mastery of English, Gef also proved he could speak a few words and phrases in Russian, Spanish, Flemish, Welsh, Hebrew, Manx, Hindustani, and even sign language. Gef claimed to have been born near Delhi, India on 7 June 1852, and that as a young mongoose he had been chased and shot at by natives in his home land (and, it should be noted, a local Manx farmer had only a few years earlier imported a few mongooses from India to help control the local rabbit population). When Gef screamed in horror one night after seeing a man sharing his name in the obituary section of the *Liverpool Post*, the family realized the weasel had somehow taught himself to read as well. "I see a name that makes me quake, that makes me shake!" he said at this unnerving coincidence.[8] The mongoose also knew arithmetic, and could easily calculate multiple bus fares to and from the neighboring town of Peel. Gef was also very fond of music, and could often be heard behind the walls practicing the Tonic Sol-fa scale. On other occasions, he treated the family to renditions of "Ella Vannin," the Manx National Anthem, "Home on the Range," and "Carolina Moon." Those lucky enough to hear Gef speak or sing describe his voice as eerily high-pitched and squealing—several octaves above the human range. At other times Gef would simply laugh in variations described as girlish to Satanic. Asked why he so often engaged in jags of maniacal laughter, Gef answered, "I did it for devilment!" His exits from the house, finally, were most often announced with a single, elegant flourish. "Vanished!" he would say, disappearing for days or weeks at a time.

Gef's talents, however, went beyond mere speaking, reading, ciphering, and singing. After Voirrey Irving gave Gef a rubber ball, the weasel often amused himself in the rafters by bouncing his new toy in time to gramophone records playing in the living room below. Although Gef would often keep the family awake past three in the morning with his garrulousness, he was very reluctant to be seen. At first he cited a fear of being captured, but then admitted to shame over his bizarre appearance. "I am a freak," he would lament. "I have hands and I have feet, and if you saw me you'd faint, you'd be petrified, mummified, turned into stone, or a pillar of salt!" On closer inspection, the family discovered that, indeed, Gef's front paws were actually more akin to human hands, which perhaps explains his ability to bounce a rubber ball. Further demonstrating his dexterity, Gef would often display his annoyance by pelting family and guests with pebbles, thimbles, and other small projectiles. Many locals told stories of walking alone through a field only to have a small rock hit them in the back or on the head, a missile often attributed to the mischievous mongoose. As part of his investigation in 1935, Harry Price left out plasticine for Gef to impress with his unique paws and teeth. "I put my foot in it, and gave it a twist, but the stuff was hard as hell," Gef later complained.[9] Subsequent analysis of the impressions proved inconclusive. R.I. Pocock of the British Museum's Zoological Department advised that the prints might match a North American raccoon, but even that was doubtful. Gef did eventually consent to allow himself to be photographed, but either by design or ineptitude, his only known portrait suggests more than it reveals.

Harry Price writes that by 1934, "the Irvings had come to the conclusion that there was some sort of *nexus* between Voirrey and the mongoose; a sort of mutual affection which made the animal contented with his life at the farm."[10] In this respect, Gef's appearance in the Irving household between 1931 and 1939 followed a classic Poltergeist scenario, coinciding with the adolescent years of the Irving's daughter. For his own part, Gef was most adamant that he was *not* a ghost; in fact, the occasionally timid weasel was easily terrified by stories of ghosts and spooks. When Jim Irving ran into the living room one night with a sheet over his body, Gef screamed in fright and then sobbed like a little child. "I am not a spirit," he explained on another occasion, "I am an extra, extra clever mongoose."[11] Although Gef's true origins must necessarily remain shrouded in mystery, the most likely scenario is that this "extra, extra clever" mongoose was an imaginary companion created by the Irving's extra, extra clever daughter, Voirrey. Childhood psychologists argue that although imaginary companions are rare in adolescence, they are not completely unknown. Voirrey certainly possessed the classic profile for constructing an imaginary companion in her teenage years. She was born to her parents late in life and grew up on the farm ostensibly as an only child, long after her older brother and sister had already left for London and Liverpool. At the time of Gef's arrival, Voirrey herself had never even been to the north half of the Isle of Man, much less off the island itself. Beyond time spent at school, her life seems to have focused on caring for a few chickens and sheep on the Irving property, reading, and listening to records on the family gramophone. When one reporter wrote asking to visit Cashen's Gap to meet Gef, the weasel said, somewhat suspiciously, that he would speak only if the man brought Voirrey a camera or some new gramophone recordings. A simple explanation for Gef's existence, then, might be a creative girl's reaction to prolonged isolation and boredom.

Assuming for a moment (perhaps arrogantly) that Gef in fact did not exist in any material form, but was instead an imaginary companion invented by a young girl, adopted by an isolated family, and rather playfully embraced by an entire nation, then we have no recourse but to approach this weasel as a fascinating exercise in theoretical media.

In a household without radio, Voirrey's weasel worked tirelessly as a radio entertainer, a collectively animated entertainment technology that brought music, magic tricks, stories, companionship, and even occasional gymnastic routines into the Irving home.[12] One can only imagine the commitment required of Voirrey, who like any good station manager, had to work tirelessly to "program" the weasel's days and seasons for his eager audience. But the weasel's radiophonic status went beyond a mere ability to entertain in the great vaudevillian traditions. As one might expect of a useful imaginary friend, be it a radio set or a talking weasel, Gef's "powers" gave him full run of the island even as Voirrey remained physically attached to her desolate farm. He would often disappear for days only to return with tales, news, and gossip gathered during his journey. He seemed particularly fond of livestock shows, and would often announce his intention to journey to some remote community on the island to watch the competition. Three or four days later, he would return with a full account of the winners and losers (accounts, it should be noted, that were entirely accurate). Aircraft were another interest, and Gef once left the farm to visit an air show on the other side of the island. Though Gef was an eighty-year old weasel born in India, he was also apparently a devoted subject of the Queen. On 6 May 1935, he announced his intention to travel to the town of Rushen to celebrate Jubilee Day, returning the next day with colorful stories of the festivities, including his eavesdropping from beneath the platform on four broad-casters covering the event for the British Broadcasting Corporation (BBC). Finally, and maybe most interestingly, Gef often entertained the family with exciting and colorful tales of his life as a young mongoose in India. "Two natives had me," he once told the family, "one a tall man with a green turban, the other a little man, deformed or a hunchback. I was on a table in the house, and I knocked something over. Whereupon one said to the other: 'Comee, comee, Gommadah, Mongus, Mongus.'"[13]

Voirrey and Gef would appear to have had an uncanny sense—for a farm girl and her weasel, that is—as to how long it would actually take a mongoose to go to Rusten, Peel, and other Manx cities, either by paw or underneath the No. 81 bus. Moreover, Voirrey and her imaginary ward never tested the credulity of the family by claiming jaunts to London or sea voyages to Rome. Despite her rather premodern rural environment, Voirrey no doubt recognized that such embellishments on time, space, and travel would push an already implausible story to the point of obvious fraud. Gef's days of international travel were a thing of the distant past, placing his remarkable transoceanic voyage and exotic pedigree in a dimly recalled adventure of seventy years ago. For the most part, the weasel seems to have respected a rather Aristotelian unity of time and space in relating his adventures on the Isle of Man, and internalized a wholly colonial portrait of his former life among the "less civilized" nations. In other words, even though her cryptozoological creation was a wholly implausible being, Voirrey obeyed—like any decent realist novelist—wholly plausible "rules" about traversing time, space, and culture. Cut off from any meaningful experience with travel or media, Voirrey nevertheless constructed a vibrant geographic imaginary from local gossip, limited travel, family stories, novels, travel art, bus schedules, the *Liverpool Post*, and a large dose of Rudyard Kipling. Voirrey thus employed Gef, like any other medium, to provide *symbolic* transport to distant worlds that far exceeded her actual experience of geography itself, invoking the weasel as a magical figure through which to organize these fantasies of local, national, and global space in her prodigious imagination.

Figure 3.1. In this cartoon from London's *Daily Mail* in December 1936, the British Broadcasting Corporation "listens in" on its fate in the House of Commons as "Gef" reads aloud about the "control and conditions of BBC staff."

Gef's ample talents for comedy, magic, and popular song notwithstanding, this capacity for symbolic transport was no doubt the weasel's most impressive radiophonic quality, serving as a mechanism that allowed Voirrey to map and rehearse her surrounding environment through fantasies of furry mobility, a form of mongoose privatization, if you will. Gef seems to have proven so effective as a radio, in fact, that one wonders how significantly different Voirrey's sense of space, time, and geography would have been had she had access to an electronic radio set. Daily radio contact with London, Glasgow, Cardiff, and other BBC centers would certainly have expanded Voirrey's access to distant events and information, but it is far from certain such contact would have rewoven the young girl, or anyone else for that matter, into a new fabric of space, time, and subjectivity. Rather, she would no doubt have integrated radio within this larger preexisting geographic imaginary, much as she had already done with the family's paintings of Maori chieftains or the "Just So" stories of Kipling. My point here is not to argue that Voirrey Irving was an aberrant subject of modernity (whatever that might be), nor that her weaselphonic experiments necessarily invalidate possible changes in subjectivity or the "human sensorium" (which is, again, unknowable). What the adventures of Voirrey and Gef do suggest, however, is that a preexisting order of entrenched textual and geographic environments carry as much or more influence on a historical sense of space, time, and geography than do the emerging technological practices associated with a new medium. In shaping a historical subject's (or era's) sense of space, time, media, and the world, can "contact" with any medium, no matter how extensive, ever really outweigh participation within the textual fields that produce knowledge about both the medium itself and the world it allegedly transforms? In this respect, Voirrey's authorship of Gef also suggests how radio and television might be thought of as "imaginary companions" in their own right—magical "entities" that we imbue with the power to transport consciousness/subjectivity around the physical world, even as they are really only forging creative links in our own fertile imagination of the *geographic*—literally, the world as written, a product of an era's dominant understanding of space and culture expressed in maps, narration, and other representational modes.

Voirrey and Gef's adventures on the Isle of Man should also remind us that changes in a geographic imagination do not necessarily constitute a change in perception or subjectivity. To say that early cinema takes the accelerated pace and industrial mise-en-scene of urban modernity as its topical subject matter is one thing; to claim that early cinematic form is emblematic (or even metonymic) of a new sensorial order is quite another. The concept of radio might have led many to imagine and express new ways of thinking about the world, but it does not necessarily follow that the medium was emblematic of or contributed to any emerging mode of subjective experience. And although television can certainly seem fragmented and fragmenting (especially to those who do not usually watch it), by what logic other than the most totalizing Marxism or sheer technological superstition can television and subjectivity be said to echo one another as terminals of postmodern schizophrenia? Belief in the absolute power of media to alter sensoriums, transform space and time, and recast subjectivity itself—compels more deterministic exercises in media theory to neglect these other systems of knowledge that might have shaped a subject's prior social and cultural engagement of place, space, and the world at large. And yet, at that miraculous moment when one first turns on a radio, television, or computer, what becomes of the entire psychic architecture that has already imagined, mapped, and populated local, national, and global space? Imagine, for example, the BBC had presented the Irving family with an experimental television that allowed Voirrey to watch a street corner in New Delhi, live, twenty-four hours a day. Would such immediate access to the Delhi "real" ever outweigh the symbolic geography of *Riki-Tiki-Tavi*, the Kipling tale that seems so obviously to have served as the inspiration for Voirrey's elaborate tale of the talking mongoose? As postcolonial theorists would no doubt concur, for a young girl living in the remote provinces of the United Kingdom in the 1930s, how different, ultimately, is the fictional "India" of Kipling and the "documentary" India of the BBC? Is hearing one account "live" any more transformative than, say, reading a Gothic novel that purports to have been written in blood?

Alchemists of media and philosophy who demand some form of reciprocal exchange between media and subjectivity, screen and eye, consciousness and information, are more often than not simply resurrecting a metaphysics of "contact" that has haunted electronic (and other) media for more than 200 years.[14] Beneath all the superstition of animation and presence, however, electronic media themselves remain opaque windows of textuality rather than transparent conduits of dialogue, contact, or teleportation. And yet so much of this theory continues to labor under the assumption that mere *access* to media inevitably leads to an instantaneous disruption of subjective and mediated space-time, when of course even the very concept of "contact" is itself a textual red herring, a tactile superstition maintained in an era of ever more remote, unilateral and alienated media interpolation. Indeed, to actually believe that media create "contact" across, between, or through time and space requires a profound sense of fantasy, activating a global imagination every bit as powerful as the one that gave birth to Gef, the talking weasel.

Occult Justice

Gef would have remained an item of only local interest on the Isle of Man had it not been for the efforts of Harry Price, England's most famous ghost hunter of the era and a man who, like Voirrey Irving, had a most active radio imagination. Price arrived at Doarlish Cashen on 30 July 1935. To conduct his inquiry, Price brought along a friend and consultant, R. S. Lambert, to serve as an impartial witness to whatever weasel manifestations might transpire. Lambert was a fellow member of the British Film Institute (BFI) and, more importantly, the editor of *The Listener*, the BBC's weekly guide to radio news and programming. Apparently Lambert was also intrigued by reports of the talking weasel, and as editor of *The Listener*, perhaps he felt duty bound to go and listen to what this weasel might have to say. In any case, Lambert was so fascinated by his experiences with Price as to later that year devote twelve weeks of *The Listener* to a serialization of Price's book, *Confession of a Ghost-Hunter*, including an installment on Price and Lambert's own adventures with "the Talking Mongoose." Gef's appearance in the official organ of the BBC, in turn, prompted several readers to weigh in with their own explanations of the phenomenon, temporarily transforming *The Listener* from a program guide to a Fortean *Book of the Damned*. One helpful reader, hoping to solve the mystery of Gef's "human hands," sent a picture of a Ugandan "bush baby" taken at the London Zoo, suggesting Gef might not be a mongoose at all. Another reader noted waggishly, "Surely, in view of the technical achievements reached by outside broadcasts, it should not be a difficult matter to arrange for the Talking Mongoose to broadcast (with or without his consent) to the British public? This would not only add a new element of entertainment to (say) a variety programme, but would eliminate the waste of time involved when investigators have to travel to distant parts of the country on wild mongoose chases."[15]

Lambert's interest in the case, and his decision to include such extensive discussion of the paranormal weasel in an official BBC publication, was in many ways wholly consonant with the larger supernatural context that framed the arrival of radio technology across the globe in the 1920s and 30s.[16] Radio remained for many a rather unearthly technology, and it was not unusual for radio and popular science magazines to feature items that played on the technology's occult qualities, even if they were as in this case displaced onto the body of a furry houseguest. Still, not everyone was happy that the BBC would associate itself with an outlandish story of an 80-year old multilingual mongoose who bet on horses, hitched bus rides, read the evening paper, and dabbled in sign language. In the wake of Price and Lambert's article and a subsequent book detailing their investigation, a retired Lieutenant Colonel in the British Army, Sir Cecil Levita, cornered the BBC's assistant controller of programs at a luncheon to complain that Lambert was "under the influence of Harry Price and has been heard to express belief in the occult, notably in the talking mongoose."[17] Equally damning, Levita also claimed Lambert had moved his residence three times because of "pursuit by the evil eye." The BBC controller, Gladstone Murray, later reported the conversation to Lambert, who then demanded a public apology from Levita. When Levita refused, Lambert sued him for slander.

The case of *Lambert v. Levita* had its initial hearing on 4 November 1936. Lambert claimed that Levita's comments had affected his standing with his BBC employers, resulting in the suspension of an expected salary raise. Lambert also accused Levita of attempting to have him removed from his governorship role at the BFI. There was little doubt that Levita had besmirched Lambert's reputation. Murray testified as much. Levita's only possible defense, then, was to further impugn Lambert by arguing that the plaintiff *really did believe* in the reality of the talking weasel. Levita's counsel took the question to Lambert directly, asking Lambert to testify about a meeting with Levita that took place shortly after Lambert returned from the Irving's farm. "I suggest that you were quite angry with Sir Cecil Levita for suggesting that the talking mongoose was a fraud," accused Levita's barrister. "I was interested in how the fraud was perpetrated," countered Lambert, "how the people who did it managed to 'put the idea across' to the other people."[18] Perhaps recognizing the absurdities unfolding in his courtroom, the Justice of the proceedings at this point interceded to ask, "Does a mongoose in the Isle of Man have a tail?" (Transcripts tell us this rather tired and predictable joke elicited a good deal of laughter in the courtroom). Keeping to the legal issues at hand, and perhaps hoping to further undermine Lambert's credibility, Beresford replied that the authors had portrayed the animal on their book cover with "a much bushier tail than an ordinary mongoose."[19]

Thus did Voirrey Irving's imaginary companion Gef enter into the British legal system as a point of evidence in adjudicating the public boundaries of reasonable belief. Did the editor of a BBC publication actually believe a weasel could talk, as Levita claimed, or was he simply interested in the mechanisms of the fraud? "He was very serious about it," testified Levita, "and when I suggested that it was a swindle he did not agree. He said that the owner of Gef had no pecuniary interest in the matter. I did my best to 'guy' the whole thing, but I was left with the impression that nothing would induce him to say a word against it or to permit me to scoff at it. At the end of the visit I said to my wife, 'My god, he believes in it!'"[20] Picking up on this crucial aspect of the case, Lambert's lawyer later cross-examined Mrs. Levita for her impression of the meeting, asking her for her opinion on how the Gef "swindle" was done. When Mrs. Lambert professed she had no idea, Lambert's barrister observed, "Then you seem to be in the same position as Mr. Lambert. . . . How can it be evidence of insanity that a man cannot find out how a swindle is done?"[21] Faced with this ironclad logic, Ms. Levita conceded that the inability to solve a riddle does not necessarily indicate insanity. What is particularly interesting in this exchange, however, is the apparent belief on the part of Lambert's defense that a case needed to be made in support of Lambert's "sanity." Again, Levita did not deny having complained about Lambert's "beliefs" to another BBC employee, so both the plaintiff and the defendant had to fight their case in the realm of occult imagination; that is, the court was asked to decide if Lambert's interest in Gef, at any level and for any reason, was so preposterous that he deserved no protection from public derision.

In the end the jury decided Lambert's interest in the mongoose was not unreasonable. Finding Levita's comments to be untrue and spoken maliciously, the court ordered him to pay Lambert 7,500 pounds in damages.[22] But Gef's influence on the civil institutions of England did not end even here. During the course of the proceedings, Lambert became convinced that his BBC employers had conspired to make him drop his case against Levita, apparently fearing the matter would only further embarrass the Corporation. Lambert referred to a meeting with Sir Stephen Tallent, who in a memorandum admitted that he had urged Lambert "to take a week's leave . . . as his doctor had advised, and to consider the matter quietly again thereafter." Failure to do so, Tallent warned, might "make the Corporation doubt his judgment" and be seen as "placing his own interests in priority to those of the Corporation."[23] Lambert's accusations against his employer resulted in no less than the Prime Minister himself appointing a Special Board of Inquiry to look into the matter. In the end, the Board cleared the BBC of any wrongdoing, but did find that the Corporation had not handled the matter "wisely." Either sympathetically or facetiously, the Board observed that "the suspicions not unreasonably engendered in Mr. Lambert's mind by previous events seemed to have mastered him so completely that he was unable to attribute any but an ill motive to the actions of the BBC in relation to him."[24] In other words, spooked by the search for a reclusive talking weasel, slandered by Levita, and called on the carpet by his employers for the poor judgment of associating the BBC with occultists, Lambert had become somewhat paranoid.

The New Apparatus Theory

In the struggle to achieve a favorable verdict, Lambert had little room to advance the most likely scenario involving his (and perhaps everyone else's) experiences with Gef. It is highly unlikely that Lambert, as an educated man in a position of esteem and responsibility, would really believe that a weasel, any weasel, could actually master human speech, read racing forms, and calculate the Peel bus schedule. And yet his rather earnest participation in Price's investigation does suggest a certain desire to indulge the *possibility* of a paranormal explanation for whatever might be happening on the Irving farm—be it a poltergeist, a furry medium, or perhaps even an actual talking weasel. And in a world of unrelenting materialist boredom, who wouldn't want to entertain the prospects of a talking weasel? Such is the literary appeal of Todorov's fantastic, a play between the banality of daily life and the possibilities of phenomena that confound the rational boundaries of society and culture. Although the "fantastic" is pleasurable enough in reading fiction, it is even more alluring when conditions exist for a seemingly genuine enigma in the real world—or at least an appealing enigma that can be nurtured and enjoyed through speculative play. Happily for Lambert, his unfortunate "persecution" for his involvement with Gef did not end his speculative interest in the paranormal. Two years after his victory against Sir Cecil Levita, *The Times* listed Lambert as attending a meeting of the London "Ghost Club" for a demonstration and discussion of firewalking.[25]

Whatever Gef might have been—imaginary companion, ghost, or talking weasel—he now lives forever in BBC history and British case law as the mascot of an era when the intersection of new technologies, the occult, sanity, and slander still made for a contentious popular and legal debate. Thus did a young girl's furry embodiment of her technological and geographic fantasies become an administrative concern for the prime minister of England, who no doubt had little knowledge of Gef, and yet nonetheless found himself in a position of having to appoint a Board of Inquiry to address the weasel's impact on the nation's broadcasting system. As for Gef himself, he seems to have mysteriously "vanished" for good sometime in 1939. Although Voirrey was apparently glad to be done with him, Mr. Irving in particular is said to have been very saddened by Gef's departure and spent many months pitifully walking the property calling for his lost friend to return. As for Voirrey, little is known about her after her time on the farm with Gef. In 1970, *Fate* published an alleged interview with the now middle-aged Voirrey, who apparently had come to hate her once famous companion.[26]

Sorting through Gef's various occult, journalistic, and legal adventures, it is very difficult to know who really believed what in the "haunting of Cashen's Gap," or more precisely, it is almost impossible to separate those who really believed the weasel might exist from those who only pretended to believe he might exist. There is, after all, a highly ludic quality to Gef's shenanigans, beginning with Voirrey's initial creation of his devilish persona and reaching all the way to a judge in the High Court of Justice pondering whether or not a Manx mongoose would have a tail. Such forms of ludic play, moreover, present modes of experience, belief, and discourse that the legal system, historiography, and much current media theory often seem ill-equipped to confront and understand. In addition to the perpetual Derridean play of slippages and imprecision haunting all of language, these more strategic performances of ludic belief within historical discourses present slippages, not only between language and meaning, but also between discourse and conviction, experience and expression. When examining what the media (or a talking weasel) have done, do, and will do, or what we think they have done or will do, or even what we'd like them to have done or do, we should always remain attentive to such "play" in popular, academic, legal, and scientific discourses, a "play," moreover, that is not necessarily a function of either lying or fantasy, per se, but more a rehearsal of belief, an entertaining of possibilities either for the benefit of oneself or one's presumed audience. As a premodern figment of a modern imagination, Gef served as a convenient device (one might even say "theory") enabling a number of people—Voirrey, Price, Lambert, and many others—to "think out loud," to entertain intriguing possibilities about media, communications, and the unknown boundaries of various "real worlds." To believe them wholly sincere in their belief in Gef would be an insult, but so too would be dismissing their interest in Gef as wholly fabricated.

Gef's adventures on the Isle of Man, though highly improbable, seem to have nevertheless created a somewhat plausible melding of many technological, geographic, colonial, occult, and cryptozoological imaginations. If not wholly plausible, then Gef seems to have at least made a compelling contribution to the fantasy lives of many people from a variety of backgrounds. Gef had many media roles in the Irving home—entertainer, reporter, dramatist. But his greatest lesson for media studies may well be in foregrounding the place of fantasy and play in thinking about the media, both historically and theoretically. After all, the collective animation of Gef the weasel as a popular emblem for transitional possibilities in media belief is not really that different from our current fantasy investments in Lacan, Deleuze, and the other biographical entities that promise to unlock the mysteries of media and consciousness. For better or worse, the increasingly indistinct discipline of "media theory" continues to serve as the primary point of contact between cultural analysis, technological history, and the classic enigmas of continental philosophy. At its most ambitious, such theory has aligned with philosophy's resurging interest in media to resurrect the metaphorical allusions of "apparatus theory" that so dominated film studies in the 1970s and 80s—albeit with an important twist.[27] As veterans of film theory will remember, classic apparatus doctrine approached the cinema as a mechanism productive of subjectivity, elaborating an argument that linked the technology, its representational practices, and the spectator in a loop of ideological interpolation incorporating everything from basic perception to the most elaborate structures of fantasy. Having been chastened by cultural materialists for the universalizing abstractions of such a model, the new apparatus theory does indeed turn to history as a foundation for contextualizing its claims. But all too often, it is a version of history refracted through the conceptual prisms of Benjamin, Kracauer, Deleuze, and other strategic theorists of space, technology, subjectivity, and culture who, grounded in Western philosophy's debates over Being and subjectivity, inevitably find Being and subjectivity to be the central concepts in whatever object they engage. In the process, this form of history returns to the very same intellectual tradition that produced apparatus theory in the first place, leaving relatively unchallenged the assumption that media technologies, as seemingly direct but actually only highly suggestive conduits of consciousness, must in some manner be directly expressive of psychic structures and processes.

And yet, as Gef should remind us, how does one ever divide gradations in fantasy, imaginative play, speculative cosmologies, theoretical experimentation, transient delusions, and outright psychosis—either in historical or philosophical discourse? Much as Gef served as a (semi) concretized fantasy figure to rehearse the imagination of radio and geography, the new apparatus theory has imbued certain technologies and philosophers with qualities that render them compelling protagonists in an occult drama of mediated subjectivity. Rather than see Lacan or Deleuze (or even earlier critics such as Benjamin and Kracauer) as *historical* figures participating in a *historical* discourse about space, time, technology, and subjectivity, enthusiasts of the new apparatus theory often approach this work as a transcendental toolbox with which to bolt history to the truth of philosophy rather than as an opportunity to historicize philosophical labor. How else are we to explain the recent vogue for invoking Heidegger as the definitive authority on almost any question pertaining to almost any technological or cultural practice from almost any historical period—modernity to posthumanism, zoetrope to cyberspace, silent cinema to text messaging? This impulse also animates the ghost of McLuhanism, which having been roundly critiqued and even excommunicated for its essentialism, determinism, and ethnocentricism, now haunts the new apparatus theory in its quest for a unified field theory of media and subjectivity. One could argue, finally, that the recent influence of Friedrich Kittler's work resides less in its ability to explain the history of technology than in its ability to synthesize poststructuralist genre conventions *around* technology.

The provocative suggestion that media technologies order, compress, and otherwise refigure space and time in new configurations, be it through the plasticity of film editing or the global reach of electronic networking, certainly implies that these technologies must be related in *some* way to a similar transformation of consciousness and/or experience beyond the theater or TV screen. And yet, it is just such an *implication* that requires more rigorous (and yet also playful) historical interrogation, especially in terms of its discursive genesis in both the popular and academic imagination. Stories of domestic spaces transgressed by "occult" media, like Gef's "haunting of Cashen's Gap," endure even today, many still organized around conventions that date back to transformations in Gothic fiction over 150 years ago. Equally enduring is the genre of theory/philosophy that posits media and subjectivity to be in perpetual transformation and crisis, telling the story of a constantly emerging mode of consciousness read indexically against changes in media technologies and practices. Gothic domesticity and the new apparatus theory each present, in very different languages for very different audiences, highly conventionalized narratives of the media's anthropomorphic challenge to the sovereignty of public and private space, exterior worlds, and interior consciousness. Displacing issues of self and communication onto architecture and transgression, the domestic gothic's interest in media—be it window, wireless, or weasel—speaks to an anxiety over the violation of those imaginary boundaries that link person and property in alliance against the surrounding public world. Similarly, although media technologies have had at best an ambiguous influence on the "sensoriums" of modernity, postmodernity, and beyond, they have certainly had a profound impact on the imaginations of just those authors, critics, and philosophers most likely to entertain the idea that space, time, and media are in some way mutually defining. In this respect, what seems to be truly at stake in so many critical discussions, the actual "object" at the heart of media theory and philosophy's brush with technological history, is not so much anyone's actual "sensorium," but rather, a play of artistic, critical, and philosophical discourses that would posit equivalences between seemingly sentient technologies and human consciousness.

As Gef's adventures across various imaginations and imaginaries suggest, any theory of media that abstracts technology into a purely instrumental mode of form and functionality modeled on illusions of subjectivity and sentience is doomed to segregate film, television, and their cousins from the messy historical field of textual belief, speculation, and practice. By conflating subjectivity with discourse, experience with representation, and ideology with imagination, the new apparatus theory's promotion of cinema, television, and cybermedia as historical emblems of consciousness confuses discourses *on* media and subjectivity with the ultimately unknowable historical phenomenology *of* media and subjectivity. It is always tempting and seemingly self-evident, for example, to interpret period speculation over the marvels of a new medium's "powers" or premature diagnoses of a self-identified zeitgeist as evidence of actual transformations in the lived experience of space, time, and subjectivity. Thus has Benjamin transformed from a figure writing *within* modernity to a direct eyewitness or transcendental oracle of modernity. To recognize that media technologies, practices, and content have a much more immediate and significant impact on the lower threshold of the imagination than they do on subjectivity itself could be a humble first step in revitalizing media theory's philosophical aspirations. Such revitalization would not mean a naïve return to some mode of empiricist history. Quite the contrary. It would mean embracing the invitation of poststructuralism to question all doctrine at all times, not just by recognizing that histories are relative or fictional in nature, but in understanding also that theory/philosophy is itself historically contingent and hermeneutically unstable. Though they may still seem distinct, at least for heuristic purposes, the attempt to provide a theory of media is now wholly imbricated in the history of media, and vice versa. Sure, we can all continue digging through *A Thousand Plateaus, Ecrits, The Arcades Project,* and other landmark works of critical theory as texts circulating outside (or perhaps above) the material world, searching for choice quotations that allow us the illusion of having mastered a hopelessly diverse range of media practices, or that satisfy a desire to believe the media have some essential core or quality that can be isolated and explained in quasimetaphysical terms. Or we can begin to ask more interesting material questions of both media history and the history of media theory, and in the process, restore the media's links to diverse practices of "doing" over the current fascination for abstract states of media and "Being."

Notes

1 J. S. LeFanu, "Ghost Stories of the Tiled House," in *The Best Ghost Stories of J. S. LeFanu,* ed. E. F. Blieler (New York: Dover Publications, 1964), 402. "Ghost Stories of the Tiled House" originally appeared as an installment in the 1861 serial publication of *The House by the Churchyard* in *Dublin Magazine.*

2 Ibid., 403.

3 Ibid., 405.

4 In his synoptic history of the genre, Richard Davenport-Hines links this transition in the Gothic to its transplantation to the United States and an increasing emphasis on the "destructive power of the family." See *Gothicism: Four Hundred Years of Excess, Horror, Evil and Ruin* (New York: North Point Press, 1998), 267–70.

5 Jonathan Crary, *Techniques of the Observer: On Vision and Modernity in the 19th Century* (Cambridge, Mass.: The MIT Press, 1992), 6.

6 Hereward Carrington and Nandor Fodor, *Haunted People: Story of the Poltergeist Down the Centuries,* (New York: E.P. Dutton, 1951), 181.

7 Ibid., 179.

8 Harry Price, *The Haunting of Cashen's Gap* (London: Methuen, 1936), 34.

9 Ibid., 85.

10 Ibid., 47.

11 Carrington and Fodor, *Haunted People: Story of the Poltergeist Down the Centuries,* 183.

12 In the opening pages of his study of "the haunting of Cashen's Gap," Price provides an extensive inventory of every room in the Irving household. Although the Irvings did possess a gramophone, they did not have a radio set.

13 Price, *The Haunting of Cashen's Gap,* 176. This internationalist flair in Voirrey and Gef's imagination was no doubt influenced by Voirrey's father, who had in

his early days actually seen something of the world, and at Doarlish Cashen decorated the household with portraits of Maori chieftains and paintings of street scenes in Istanbul.

14 In Jeffrey Sconce *Haunted Media: Electronic Presence from Telegraphy to Television* (Durham, N.C.: Duke University Press, 2000), I provide a cultural history of this "logic of transmutability," concentrating on the centrality of electrical tropes in conflating human and mechanical animation.

15 Price's article on Gef in *The Listener* also elicited many "eyewitness" accounts, pro and con, of the weasel's performances. See "The Talking Mongoose," *The Listener* (23 October 1935), 724 and "The Talking Mongoose—A First-hand Account," *The Listener* (9 October 1935).

16 For a more detailed discussion, please see "The Voice from the Void" in *Haunted Media*.

17 "High Court of Justice; King's Bench Division; Editor of 'The Listener'; Slander Action against Sir Cecil Levita," *The Times* (5 November, 1936), 4.

18 "High Court of Justice," *The Times* (4 November 1936), 4.

19 Ibid.

20 "High Court of Justice," *The Times* (5 November 1936), 4.

21 "High Court of Justice," *The Times* (6 November 1936), 4.

22 Ibid.

23 "BBC and Mr. Lambert," *The Times* (17 December 1936), 8.

24 "BBC Inquiry," *The Times* (17 December 1936), 16.

25 "Firewalking," *The Times* (28 April 1938), 7.

26 Walter McGraw, "Gef—the Talking Mongoose . . . 30 Years Later," *Fate* (July 1970), 81–82.

27 Jean-Louis Baudry's article, "Ideological Effects of the Basic Cinematographic Apparatus," remains the most canonical statement of apparatus theory, although given the incredible influence and many variations on its premises, no single author can really be said to epitomize its claims. In *Narrative, Apparatus, Ideology*, ed. Philip Rosen, 286–98 (New York: Columbia University Press, 1985).

Lynn Spigel

4

Designing the Smart House: Posthuman

Domesticity and Conspicuous Production

The 2002 premiere issue of *Broadband House* titled "America's High Tech Havens" begins with an editorial about the future of housing after 9/11. Discussing how he and his staff went to photograph a New York City penthouse just days after the World Trade Center fell, editor Scott DeGarmo explains their sense of despair as they looked out the windows at the surrounding city. He writes, "On that evening . . . , we felt the sadness hanging over New York—and the nation." "And yet," he goes on, "atop the residential building . . . we also felt another powerful emotion— the sense of being safely at home. . . . The home is a refuge to which we head when trouble strikes. The country was reminded of that on September 11." Following this, DeGarmo explains how one stock market trader turned his broadband-connected dining room into a command post from which he was able to teleconference with his interconnected team of home office workers who likewise traded from the floors of their high-tech homes. The editorial ends with the simple declaration, "A new era has truly begun, and the home will play an even more central role."[1]

The idea of the home as haven is, of course, a common trope of industrialization that can be traced back to the religious/pastoral ethos

Old-fashioned comfort,
Space-age connectivity

WINTER 2001/02
www.bbhmag.com

BROADBAND HOUSE

LIVING AND WORKING IN THE HIGH-BANDWIDTH ER

America's High-Tech Havens

Also in This Issue

Display until March 13, 20

Windows XP: Home-networking milestone

Avon: New e-strategy is a super success

U.S.A. $4.99   Canada $6

Figure 4.1.   Cover of *Broadband House* (Winter 2001–2). Copyright Broadband Properties LLC.

of the first plan book writers of the mid-to-late nineteenth century who were trying to think about how the country home and new suburban towns could provide refuge for the weary male industrialists caught in the dizzying hub of urban production. In recovering that myth, *Broadband House* (and many consumer magazines like it) participates in a deep sense

Lynn Spigel

of nostalgia for an idea of home that is romantically—but at times even partly ironically—mapped onto our postindustrial world of global flows of capital and communication. As the World Trade Center—that ultimate symbol of modernism's verticality and Western domination—falls down, the high-tech house is erected as a symbolic substitute for a new kind of economic power and social control. Or as *Broadband House* puts it, the high-tech home is our "new center of the universe."[2]

Here, I want to consider the newest trend in communication technologies and domestic design—what is commonly known as the "smart house." A smart house is a networked house whose appliances interact with each other, adapt to dwellers, and allow residents, via the Internet, to communicate with the outside world and to speak to the home while away at work or travel. Given the complexity of its aims, the smart house is the product of alliances among architects, engineers, computer scientists, the consumer housing industry, telecommunications companies, computer and home entertainment manufacturers, and interior designers, all of whom are in the business of promoting new forms of social interaction among people and their things.[3] We might call this form of social interaction "posthuman domesticity"—by which I mean a mode of domestic subjectivity based on the melding of silicon and flesh. In what follows, I examine how the smart home orchestrates the human–technology interface. I am especially interested in how smart homes relate to broader cultural ideals about domesticity and gender, and how they reconfigure labor and leisure at home. I am also interested in the stories we tell about smart homes and what these stories say about contemporary hopes and fears about living—at home—in the future.

From Home of Tomorrow to Smart Home

The smart home dates back to a much longer history of "homes of tomorrow."[4] Prototypes for sentient domestic spaces appeared in nineteenth-century speculative fiction such as Edward Bellamy's *Looking Backward* (1888). In the United States, the home of tomorrow was inspired by the European avant-garde, and in particular the Swiss architect Le Corbusier who famously pronounced, "The house is a machine for living in." By 1930, two distinct futuristic housing types had emerged on American soil. One version was based on an ideal of modern luxury and was associated early on with architect Richard Neutra's Lovell House (1929), which drew upon the International Style. The other was rooted in the ethos of mass production and was associated most famously with

Buckminster Fuller, whose Dymaxion Dwelling Machine (1945) was designed on the model of a navy ship with factory-like efficiency, complete with an appliance-filled "service core."[5]

In both its upper crust and mass-produced forms, the home of tomorrow was often the subject of women's home magazines, and it was displayed with great fanfare at fairs, exhibitions, and in middle-class department stores. During the 1930s and 1940s General Electric and Westinghouse opened model homes for public exhibition, and they (as well as a number of other electrical/appliance companies) began to use the concept of the home of tomorrow as a way to sell a seemingly endless array of new and wondrous machines.[6] The home of tomorrow continued to fascinate the public through the Cold War era. Disneyland's Monsanto Home (which was designed at MIT) appeared in the theme park's Tomorrowland section in 1957 and housed an "Atoms for Living Kitchen" sponsored by Kelvinator.[7] In the next decade, Disneyland's "Carousel of Progress" (which was sponsored by General Electric and was first displayed at the New York World's Fair in 1964) took tourists on a time travel ride that featured thirty-two Audio-Animatronics figures who sang "There's a Great Big Beautiful Tomorrow" while demonstrating how the American family benefited from electrical appliances over the course of the twentieth century.[8] Updating these promotional techniques for the digital age, corporations like Panasonic, Philips, and IBM offer similar public and/or corporate exhibits of smart homes that allow these corporations to test their user–technology interface and also help promote their corporate vision.[9]

In the process of selling a future, corporations have historically appealed to housewives by promising them that technology would lead to liberation. Since the 1920s, advertisements for stoves, percolators, dishwashers, and the like depicted women freed from drudgery, playing tennis, or going shopping while their kitchens did the work.[10] In the 1940s and 1950s, industrial ads and educational films promised even more elaborate spectacles. In 1952, the Whirlpool Corporation advertised its new washer–dryers in a short educational film featuring a group of high school girls who sit around a kitchen table searching for topics to write about for their homework assignment. Inspired by the purchase of her family's new Whirlpool washer–dryer units, Marilyn (the cleverest girl in the group) suggests they write about how household appliances have emancipated American women.[11] Popular speculation about robots also used this liberation theme. Released by the Jam Handy Picture Company in 1940, a short educational subject titled "Leave it to Roll-Oh!"

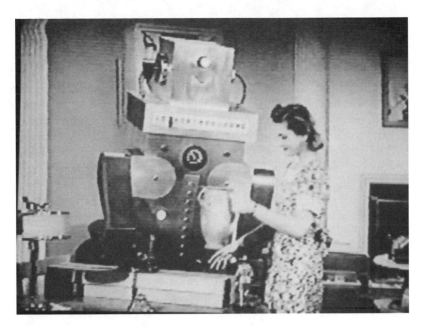

Figure 4.2.   Roll-Oh helps around the house in the short film *Leave It to Roll-Oh* (1940). Archival footage courtesy of the Internet Moving Images Archive, www.archive.org.

promoted robotics by featuring a happy housewife who relaxes at home while Roll-Oh, her "mechanical butler," vacuums the rug, opens canned goods, waters flowers, and answers the door. A clunky robot designed to look and speak like a man, Roll-Oh embodied the paradox of tomorrow's home. While appearing to be futuristic, this imaginary robot ultimately maintained core principles of domestic ideology by offering women an appealing fantasy of the housewife role. Women's drudgery, loneliness, and submission were here transformed into play, companionship, and dominion through the wondrous technology of what the Jam Handy narrator called "thinking things."[12]

Despite the obvious corporate connections and socially conservative agendas, architects, designers, and corporate spokespeople often promoted futuristic homes in relation to utopian social goals of democracy, environmentalism, and, as the above examples suggest, liberation. For example, architect Buckminster Fuller promoted his Dymaxion Dwelling Machine (which was sold in a kit) as a do-it-yourself democratic dream house chock full of new technologies and available to everyone at affordable prices.

However, although American consumers were fascinated with futuristic homes, they did not necessarily want to live in the mass-produced and strange looking places imagined by Fuller, nor did they eagerly embrace the avant-garde styles of homes built by Le Corbusier, Neutra, and others. For the most part, as Brian Horrigan suggests, "Americans did not want machines to live in; they wanted machines to live with."[13]

Like previous homes of tomorrow, the smart house has been ushered in with a wave of utopian predictions. Key among these is the promise that smart homes will provide greener environments, more mobility (via telerobotics) for physically challenged and aging populations, and increased safety for residents. Yet, as with the older homes of tomorrow, the corporations sponsoring the research and design know that consumers are wary of unfamiliar futures. In response, they primarily envision the future in relation to middle-class residential housing and the people who can afford smart lifestyles. Indeed, as smart homes are being developed, roughly 75 percent of the world's population does not have internet usage.[14] Even for privileged populations, the Internet (on which the smart home is predicated) is distributed unevenly among different ages, regions, income groups, and races (with whites and Asians having more access and use).[15]

In 1986, the National Association of Home Builders Show offered a tour of a smart home that was in many ways a prototype for the alliances between the home building industry and digital communication technologies.[16] Since then corporate synergies have been the core strategy for success. In June 2004, Intel formed the Digital Home Working Group, which now has over one hundred participating companies.[17] Given their prospective consumers, it is not surprising that the most advertised features of residential smart homes are the twin middle-class goals of homeownership—lifestyle enhancement and convenience on the one hand and privacy and surveillance on the other. Elaborate home theaters, dream kitchens, smart bathrooms, and electronic eyes adorn the home with comfort and safety, thereby ensuring that while technology advances, domestic ideals remain the same.

More generally, recent studies suggest that travelers on the proverbial "road ahead" are slow to change their course. Even though the 2004 Pew survey reports, "nearly two-thirds of the American population is now online,"[18] Internet use tends to be limited to certain types of data retrieval (the most popular use is downloading maps) and communicating with friends and family (the second most popular activity).[19] The report concludes, "The Internet still takes second place to the real world as the place to accomplish daily tasks or enjoy recreation."[20] This is not really surprising. At moments of technological transition, people often search for ways to balance novelty with tradition. As with radio or television before it, today's new technologies are subject to patterns of cultural adaptation that aim toward conserving familiar lifestyles. In this context, much of the advertising rhetoric surrounding smart homes depicts what I have elsewhere called "yesterday's future," a future that is oddly nostalgic for a Cold War era notion of progress in which white middle-class family lifestyles take center stage.[21]

Integrated Systems and the Human–Machine Interface

Even though smart homes conserve middle-class ideals of property and privacy, they are also a product of contemporary changes in everyday life. One of the key changes revolves around gendered patterns of house-keeping. Whereas the old "mechanical servants" (such as stoves and dish-washers) were promoted pragmatically as timesaving devices that could enhance the lives of housewives, the new intelligent appliances do not just do the chores, they virtually become the housewife as they perform the managerial and caretaking roles previously ascribed to women. Corporations like IBM's subsidiary Home Director, Microsoft's Universal Plug and Play, Macintosh's Xtension home, and Intel's Digital Home Fund are hooking up with appliance companies like GE and Maytag to produce "integrated systems" that orchestrate not only internal household tasks (like cooking or cleaning), but also dialogues (increasingly via Wi-Fi) between and among household devices. And in place of today's bar code product scanning system (UPC), Motorola and MIT's DISC consortium have been developing a new generation of low-cost digital tagging. This new tagging system uses radio frequency to allow appliances to talk to products.[22] So for example, the frozen dinner you buy at the market will prompt your microwave oven to follow manufacturer's cooking instruc-tions from the Internet.

What happens to social relations in a home built on the language of appliances? How is human communication imagined? And what exactly is a home and family in this configuration?

Some researchers look for ways to enhance human communication through intelligent agents that not only interact with but also form rela-tionships with residents. Panasonic's smart house (which was displayed at the Panasonic Center in Tokyo in 2003–2004) contains a virtual cornucopia of adaptive intelligent agents and smart appliances that are drawn together in conversation through wireless networking. As with all smart homes, the Panasonic version contains a virtual security agent that alerts residents to intruders, locks doors, and scans visitors (in this case visitors submit to a palm print or retinal scan). Upon entering the living room, the visitor sees what looks like a virtual fish tank, but is really a large glass table full of intelligent "fish" agents that are designed to develop relationships with residents and do their bidding. A physical manifestation of the smart fish, a small mobile robot follows residents around to do the same. Meanwhile, the bathroom sink has a smart toilet that analyzes urine to get a general picture of your health. If your urine looks bad, the toilet e-mails your doctor. In fact, the house shows concern not just for your functions, but also for your form. A smart closet that hangs up clothes also acts as a personal wardrobe consultant, telling you which outfits look best.[23] Here as elsewhere, the smart house offers a curious inversion of the relations between people and their things. Intelligent agents become more lifelike (as they take on a series of cognitive and motor tasks) while humans become more "thing-like" (as they submit their bodies to checkups, judgments, and repairs).

Similar amenities—and inversions—are offered in MIT's House_n. An experimental house of the future, House_n is designed by architecture professors Kent Larson and Chris Luebkeman and sponsored by companies like Compaq, Proctor and Gamble, and the cable manufacturer, Superior Essex. Acknowledging the fundamental commodity logic of his housing future, Larsen explains, "High-tech companies are looking to the home as the next big market. . . . They're realizing they'll never successfully sell all the gadgets they envision unless there's a more sophisticated infrastructure in the home to plug them into—which means new ways of building."[24] This new way of building is based on "mass customized" component parts that can be purchased and arranged according to personal taste and lifestyle. The heart of House_n is a chassis with an "infill" of sensing devices like LEDs, speakers, displays, heat sensors, and cameras that can be plugged in at any point and upgraded as new technologies become available. Speculating on how homebuyers of the future may design their own house, Larsen writes:

> A young couple looking to build a new home begins the process at one of a number of Internet home sites, where they play design games and select from options presented to them. . . . Systems from one manufacturer are now interchangeable with another. . . . They learn that Ikea Systems has expanded their kitchen and home furnishing product line to include

low-cost kit home components with Scandinavian detailing and energy saving technologies; BMW has developed sleek, modernist, high-tech house components . . . and Home Depot and Martha Stewart have partnered to offer fully furnished reproduction historic homes.[25]

Personalized modular design (which, by the way, is not Larsen's invention), matches the contemporary turn in postindustrial housing architecture toward mass customization, flexibility, adaptability, mobility, and lifestyle options, all of which address the varied configurations of family in contemporary U.S. society, where only about 7 percent of households are now composed of traditional families.[26] At the same time, as Larsen suggests, these same architectural features are productive agents for corporate synergy and "branding."

In publicity materials, House_n promotes itself as both an ancestor of, but also in comparison with, older modernist designs. Suggestive of this "next generation," the official Web site for House_n has a picture of a young girl and (what looks to be) her grandfather romping in a starkly modern and minimally decorated home. Underneath this image are two citations, side by side. The first is the famous quote by Le Corbusier: "The problem of our epoch is the problem of the house (1919)." The second is House_n's update: "The problem of our epoch is the problem of the electronically mediated house (2000)."[27] By bridging Le Corbusier's modernist dream house (a "machine for living in") with its digitized double (a network for connecting to), the Web site forms a teleological history that imagines House_n as the realized vision for yesterday's future.

Nevertheless, Larsen insists that House_n is not just a remake of the past. Comparing House_n with previous homes of tomorrow, Larsen argues that the twentieth century homes were doomed because they were "single purpose structures with a single form driven by one ideology" that was forced on residents. As opposed to this, he claims that House_n "is infinitely adaptable"; in other words, the house can evolve its systems to meet different dwellers' needs. And, because it is made with the baby-boomer market in mind, the house is also meant to evolve with the residents' aging process.[28] The "n" in House_n is scientific shorthand for "variable." Yet, it is clear that variability is realized in market-driven terms. Like Amazon.com or TiVo, House_n will let you know what products you'll like and it will even purchase them for you (for example, Larsen speculates that the house will buy your tuna when your pantry is bare or else tell you what films you'll want see). "It becomes a companion of sorts."[29] In this regard, whereas the idea of "home" has historically been rooted in one's social relation with things (home décor is meant to reflect one's personal style or position), the smart house takes this to its logical extreme; humans now imprint their code on their things to the degree that things become more like the people who own them.

Like other smart homes, House_n is conceived according to principles in contemporary research on Artificial Life that—to use N. Katherine Hayles's terms—gives information back its body.[30] In other words, whereas the old homes of tomorrow imagined a split between mind and body in which the house had what Buckminster Fuller called a mechanical core—a kind of giant brain that transmitted signals to mechanical parts—the smart home's "integrated systems" are imagined as interrelated organs in a body that adapt to each other's presence as well as to their residents. Extending the biological metaphor, Panasonic even promotes its new lineup of "bio-concept" appliances that are made to form emotional bonds with humans. As the Panasonic Web site asks, "Have you ever loved a home appliance?" The question is posed in relation to corporate strategies aimed at forming brand loyalty through creating affective relations with intelligent agents. The Web site claims, "National/Panasonic has developed our products with the key words of 'Peace of Mind, Security and Brand Loyalty.' This time we especially focus on 'Brand Loyalty' and try to create new values for home appliances . . . beyond the conventional concept for them. This is our proposal of new sensuous values such as affection, loyalty and loveliness that put new life 'Bio' into home appliances."[31]

Architects have long used biological metaphors for buildings—the most obvious being the "skeleton" (frame) and "skin" (surface materials). Smart architects transfigure this bio/mechanical logic by splicing it together with a third term: the cyberlogics of silicon life forms. Now the home's surface is referred to as a "smart skin," an intelligent agent that not only protects the domestic interior but also interacts with the surrounding community. For example, Gisue Harari and Mogin Harari's speculative design for the Digital House (unbuilt, 1998), which was commissioned by the magazine *House Beautiful,* uses plasma and liquid crystal walls developed at NASA to cover the home with a smart skin that formulates ideas and transmits messages to neighbors. The smart skin develops community relationships, and allows "virtual" guests to enter the home. So, for example, in one scenario a virtual chef materializes in the kitchen, hangs out with a housewife, and prepares a meal for her virtual dinner guests. Taking this virtual visit in the other direction, Michael Trudgeon and Anthony Kitchener's "Hyper House Pavilion 5" (unbuilt, 1998) transmits a programmed message to neighbors on its electrochromic glass walls.[32]

Figure 4.3. Virtual chef in the "Digital House." Copyright Hariri & Hariri-Architecture.

Imagining the house as a smart skin and its systems as sentient life forms inverts the biological metaphor. Now it is the house that literally becomes more human—or at least "flesh" like—while the humans inside it become more integrated into the systems of objects within it. In this regard, the smart house turns the old Marxist "camera obscura" effect inside out. If the central spaces of monopoly capitalism—the factory, store, and office—turned social relationships into object relations, these post-Fordist homes of the future turn object relations into social relations. In the smart house things relate to things. Your microwave talks to your TV dinner, and you—somewhere offsite—cell phone home to reach out and touch your fridge.

SMART HOME DEVELOPMENTS AND VIRTUAL COMMUTES

One of the key features of smart homes is the way they negotiate a shift from a production-based economy (with its company town or commuter suburb) to a consumption-based service economy, envisioned most dramatically in the edge city. In this respect, the vision of community inscribed in the new smart homes is very different from that of the older social systems where production and consumption—work and leisure—were split across the city and suburb. Instead, the corporate sponsors of smart homes think that the infrastructure of tomorrow's home will be wired to decentralized virtual work places and to the service economy of goods, conveniences, and entertainment. In this configuration, the contemporary digital house is a place where home, community, marketplace, leisure, and labor mutate into a commodified sphere of communication. Everyday places are constructed through a circulation of commerce, information, and media flows that collapse the boundaries between time off and time on the job.[33] All forms of human labor and leisure are "branded" in a highly rationalized vision of a "glocal" (part global, part local) village.

Through the aesthete sensibilities of theoretical architects, the post-Fordist vision of community is being turned into ironic designs for the future. A housing development designed by architects Paul Lewis, Marc Tsurumaki, and David J. Lewis extends this commodification of the home by placing the house within the contemporary retail space of new suburban big box stores like Office Depot and Best Buy. In a speculative project they call "New Suburbanism . . . Anywhere USA" (2000), the architects claim, "The compact houses of post-war mass production have given way to the mini-mansions of information-age mass customization."[34] In other words, suburban homes are increasingly defined by the hodgepodge of technologically enhanced activities that proliferate across an increasing number of randomly associated custom-ordered rooms (from family room to home office to gourmet kitchen to "great room"). Given this move toward commodification of room design, the architects propose to combine the home with the formal features of the big box stores that surround them. The idea, for example, is that Best Buy or Costco will literally become the new suburban neighborhood network as the homes are connected with the life stream of goods and services that supports them. According to the architects, "In this hybrid of the logic of house and store, the identities of both are maintained, but in an altered form—now cross-wired to produce unanticipated social relationships through their mutual influence."[35] An example is their concept of a part private/part community swimming pool modeled on the big box stores' "aisle" format. A private pool in each yard extends across the suburb so that the residents can do laps around the block as if swimming through the shopping aisles of Office Depot.

Examining their proposal, it is difficult to ascertain exactly what kind of social relationship could be produced by this ironic embrace of the house as retail space. This is a design where social relationships are merged with commodity relationships to the point where we no longer sense the classic Marxist binaries between use value and exchange value, nature and machine, human relationships and relationships among things. We are in a world where domestic space and community space are no longer imagined as antagonists in a long modernist history of public service versus private luxury. Instead, community services and private comfort are both enveloped into the megastore logics of the new suburbia. Meanwhile, the aesthetics of horizontal gigantism (that so many modernist architects had once deplored)—are, in the tradition of Venturi—fully embraced.

In other speculative projects, the media itself provides the epistemological ground upon which a sense of community and/or nature is delivered into residential space. Beatriz Colomina traces the mediated domestic environment back to the modernist designs of Le Corbusier and his penchant for thinking of the home (and especially the window) as a kind of movie camera/projection screen that provided views of the outside world.[36] In more recent postmodern architectural projects, a kind of ironic play between nature and media informs the design for daily life in postindustrial landscapes.

Elizabeth Diller's and Ricardo Scofidio's design for the "Slow House" (unbuilt, 1990) is a case in point. This Long Island, New York vacation home includes a rear picture window that captures a view of the landscape. A video camera mounted above the house depicts the same landscape digitally and transmits it back to a monitor suspended before the picture window. It will even digitally transmit the view back to the main residence in the city. But the Slow House is not just the realization of the modernist dream of a perfect view; it also offers the parallel modernist fantasy (seen early on in Le Corbusier) of the merging of home and work. The Slow House is a complex articulation of labor and leisure as the distance between the vacation residence and the city is collapsed through the simultaneity of all experience via digital telecommunications. According to the architects, the Slow House is a "vacation/work space" designed to provide an "escape from escape, that is, to connect at a moment's notice back to the sites of anxiety" in the city.[37]

Like other smart homes, the Slow House epitomizes, but also reworks, the terms of what Raymond Williams called "mobile privatization," a phenomenon he tied to the simultaneous rise of privatized suburban housing and the rise of mobile urban industrial centers in the nineteenth century.[38] The advent of telecommunications, Williams argues, offered people the ability to maintain ideals of privacy while providing the mobility required by industrialization, and broadcasting in particular held out the promise of bringing the public world indoors. As I have argued elsewhere, the proliferation of portable technologies and remote control in the 1960s created a new twist on mobile privatization by inverting its terms. By the sixties, the reigning fantasy was one of "privatized mobility."[39] Advertisers for portable television sets promised consumers that TV was not just a window on the world, but also a way to extend one's private life into public spaces. Advertisers recommended a new set of viewing protocols (or at least fantasies about one's relation to TV) that were no longer confined to the interior world of the family. Unlike the 1950s console model, which was placed in a central area of the family home, ads for portable receivers typically showed people on the move, carrying their totable TV sets to beaches, picnics, and even, in one humorous 1967 Sony ad, nudist colonies. At a time when critics spoke out against Eisenhower era consumerism and sedentary lifestyles, and at a time when President Kennedy implored citizens to do something for their country or at least get some exercise, privatized mobility dissociated the activity of television viewing from the sedentary figure of the "homebody." Instead, portable television was associated with more active forms of pleasure. Ads for portable TV often depicted viewers with mobile rather than passive bodies, and unlike the 1950s ads, they almost never showed people sitting while watching TV.[40]

The current architectural designs for smart homes continue fantasies of both mobile privatization and privatized mobility. Digital media and intelligent agents offer the fantastic possibility of bringing the world into the home, not through a sedentary watcher's gaze, but rather through the kind of active corporeal involvement that prior portable technologies promised their consumers. Moreover, rather than simply promising to negotiate privacy with publicness, speculative designs like New Suburbanism, the Digital House, and the Slow House disintegrate boundaries of home, office, store, factory, nature, restaurant, school, and community. As David Morley argues, the home is being "dislocated" and disconnected from its physical and psychical place.[41] With cell phones, PDAs, laptops, and the like, we increasingly experience being at home while in public and we also experience being in public while at home. So too, I would argue, the home is being "reclocked" to the extent that the normative rhythms of domestic time, vacation time, commute time, and labor time are being altered through telecommuting and telecommunications (a point which the Slow House ironically makes).

SMART HOMES AND CONSPICUOUS PRODUCTION

Within this context of dislocated and reclocked domesticity, the experience of "feeling at home" is likely to change. Accordingly, architects, engineers, and advertisers are providing a blueprint for our sense of home in the digital age.

The speculative plans for the Digital House are a case in point. According to the architects' promotional video, the house "reflects [the] changing configuration of family, work, play, communication, and virtual and actual reality." In the digital house residents are figured as compatible machines, ready to "work" or "play" when keyed into the home's display screens. In line with this logic, the "transient spaces" (or hallways inside and outside the home) are constructed in such a way as to make a valuable use of time. The architects claim that the hallways' liquid crystal walls provide an interactive environment that allows "inhabitants to unplug themselves momentarily, as they move between tasks and from the virtual to the actual world."[42] In the Digital House, these transient spaces are "an opportunity for heightened awareness."[43] Even sleep is transformed into usable time. The bedrooms are equipped with dream recording devices that provide a transcript of the dreamer's unconscious. The ultimate paradox, then, is that the postmodern luxury home has become the ultimate work terminal—a place where the resident is in a perpetually interactive state of preparedness—never allowed to simply "waste time."[44] Now Thorstein Veblen's famous concept of bourgeois "conspicuous consumption" has morphed into what I would call "conspicuous production." In the smart home the resident is meant to be seen working all the time.

More than just the ironic gesture of cutting-edge architects, the ideology of conspicuous production is installed in the hardware of the machine–human interface that smart home engineers design. For example, the integrated systems and intelligent agents of House_n are hardwired to elicit a constant stream of activity, and in this regard the house is specifically tailored to defy an older view of robotics that rendered humans passive. Comparing House_n with its predecessors, Stephen Intille, a computer science researcher working on the project claims, "The popular vision of the house of the future is where you hardly have to get up from your easy chair. That's not ours at all. We want the house to enable you to lead a more active and richer life—and encourage you to do things, not to have them done for you."[45] Indeed, whereas Jean Baudrillard and Paul Virilio have argued that audiovisual media and telerobotics have rendered human bodies "superfluous," "disabled," and increasingly sedentary (Virilio speaks of the "cadaver-like inertia of the interactive dwelling" where the most important piece of furniture is the seat), smart home engineers and promoters posit just the opposite.[46] Indeed, for today's digerati, interactivity has become the buzzword for a kind of commonsense, taken-for-granted future where social ills are remedied by technologies that stimulate us to action.

The current value placed on interactivity should be understood as part of a social milieu in which people are asked to work more of the time and in more locations, and where being idle is suspect. The ideal of interactivity should likewise be seen in relation to changing configurations of work and home in which the eight-hour workday, breadwinner commuter Dad, and stay-at-home mom are no longer the rule. In 2002, dual income families with children comprised more than two times as many households as did traditional nuclear families (in which mothers stay home); even double income families with no children outnumbered the traditional family by almost two to one.[47] Meanwhile, work and home have become coextensive. The 1990 U.S. Census showed a strong resurgence in the number of home-based workers (3.4 million compared to 2.2 million in 1980).[48] According to the May 2001 Current Population Survey (a monthly survey of households conducted by the U.S. Census Bureau for the Bureau of Labor Statistics), the total number of persons who reported that they worked at home (regardless of how often they engaged in home-based work activity) was 25.0 million, or 19 percent of total nonagricultural employment. Two-thirds of those who usually work at home reported they did so in order to "finish or catch up on work" or because it is the "nature of the job."[49] People are combining home life with work life as they multitask across a wide variety of activities.

Telecommuting represents one part of the picture. A survey conducted by the Society for Human Resource Management (SHRM) in 2000 showed that Human Resource Managers ranked telework among the top five incentives they use to attract employees.[50] Tim Kane, President of the International Telework Association and Council (ITAC), claims that telework offers people "flexibility to better balance their work and family demands."[51] Meanwhile, teleworking allows corporations to downsize physical plants and reduce overhead.[52] Whatever the attractions, studies show that the teleworkforce is relying on broadband Internet connections to bridge the geographies of domestic and workspace.[53] Even among the general population, work is a growing use for wired connectivity at home. The 2001 Current Population Survey found that "about 8 people in 10 used a computer for the work they did at home, and about 6 in 10 made use of Internet or e-mail access."[54] In its 2004 study, the Pew Internet & American Life Project reports, "One in seven Internet users say their use of the Internet has resulted in an increase in the amount of time they spend working at home." Moreover, this appears to increase among long-term users. (Of those who had been online for more than three years,

21 percent reported that the Internet has increased the amount of time they spent working at home).[55] Indeed, as the Slow House so ironically demonstrates—even while the workplace becomes decentralized and global, work is nevertheless increasingly localized within the networked home. In this context, the difference between labor and leisure (and the related ideologies of public and private spheres) is not always clear or even desirable.

In light of these changes, it is no surprise that conspicuous production has become a key feature of everyday life. In public venues people now flag themselves as wired agents, with cell phones, laptops, PDAs, palm pilots, and the like. It has become a sign of status to seem perpetually occupied and "in touch" with needy anonymous others—and importantly, we never know whether someone is phoning home or phoning the office. We used to speak of mass communication versus interpersonal or face-to-face communication. Today, we should add a third term: performative communication. The partner to conspicuous production, performative communication allows people to demonstrate their labor value as social actors in a networked world. The important point is that we need an audience in physical space for our communicative acts in cyberspace.

The same logic of conspicuous production and performative communication runs through the popular discourse on smart homes. Smart home magazines and the advertisements in them do not merely promise leisure through the purchase of household appliances (as advertisers did since the 1920s); they also offer potential consumers the dream of super-productivity—and at no personal sacrifice to love, happiness, heath, pleasure, leisure, and childrearing. A prototypical image here is the June 1996 cover of *Wired*. The cover shows Microsoft CEO Bill Gates floating in his pool, wearing smiley face swim trunks with his signature nerd glasses while talking on his mobile. Lest the imagery fool you, the article reassures readers that Gates is not just sunning himself; he is actually quite busy turning his empire into a full-blown media company.[56] This "work–play" imagery has since become a convention by which advertisers promote smart lifestyles—not just for industry moguls but also for everyday people who want to live on the right side of the digital divide. For example, the August 2003 issue of *Digital Home* shows a classically beautiful couple in swimwear at poolside while talking on mobiles and working on laptops.[57] Once again, the truly successful business tycoon simultaneously works and plays. Conspicuous production means that leisure is not just "time off," but rather part of the job.

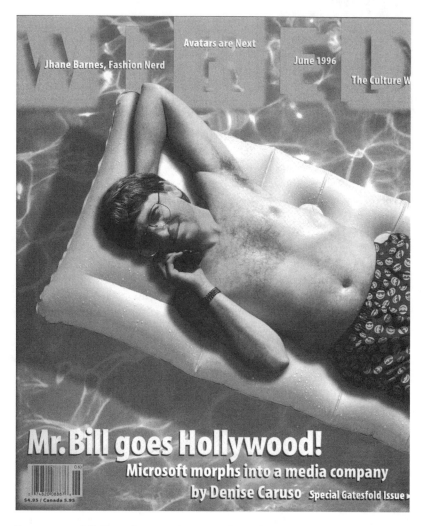

Figure 4.4. Bill Gates floats on the cover of *Wired* (June 1996). Copyright Wired Ventures LTD.

Similar imagery is used to promote the idea that new telecommunications technology fosters family fun without sacrificing work schedules. A particularly striking example comes in the same post–9/11 issue of *Broadband House* with which I began this essay. In a three-page photo spread, the magazine portrays a "smart" family who display their luxury lifestyle, not

THE NEW MAGAZINE FOR TECHNOLOGY STYLE AND CONVERGENC
digitalhome
Technology for life August 2003
40 NEW PRODUCTS TESTED
B&O BeoLink AV system
Apple's new iPod
Sony DVD recorder
PLUS! Mobile PCs
Digital radios
Plasma TVs
EXCLUSIVE: UK'S FIRST MEDIA ADAPTER
Discover how to wirelessly access your PC on the TV
HOME SECURITY MADE EASY
DIY surveillance...
whatever your budget
EXCLUSIVE INTERVIEW
Intel on the digital home
SPLASH OUT

Figure 4.5. Work–play imagery on the cover of *Digital Home* (August 2003). Copyright Futernet, www.digitalhomemag.com.

just through their leisure and consumption, but also through their ability to combine modes of everyday action (both work and play) that are mediated through their domestic environment. The opening photo displays the home's vast lawn where the father plays golf while plugged into his cell phone, waiting for calls from the office. For anyone familiar with nineteenth-century portraits of the bourgeois family home, this photo is of course a reminder of those Victorian images of domesticity that showed families playing lawn games. But here, the leisurely life of conspicuous consumption has transformed into conspicuous production as the family who stays together does not only play together, but is also literally wired to a variety of electronic spaces that mediate their everyday lives. The accompanying photo spread shows the family members multitasking across a series of recreational and work environments/media systems. The father is shown both in his home office and floating in his pool with his earphones on, immersed in a sea of data (the caption says he is phoning his office). The mother, who is shown in a living–dining area working at a laptop as well as outdoors cooking at the barbeque, "can maintain her focus for as long as seven hours but usually blends family and professional chores all day long—getting inspiration for a presentation while putting laundry into the drier." The teenage daughter operates controls to the computerized sound system, while her little sister works on her laptop as she rests in her bed (complete with a horse-motif patchwork quilt and stuffed animals). "Hutch," the family dog, has a sensor on his collar so he can open his pet door.[58]

Although it addresses the new realities of labor in the two-parent workforce, and while mother and daughters use technologies, this smart house nevertheless maintains sexual difference and middle-class family ideals as an organizing principle for everyday life. The future that is being promoted is once again "yesterday's future"—a world of technological progress that preserves and regenerates traditional social values.

GENDER AND CONSPICUOUS REPRODUCTION

Like previous homes of tomorrow, the smart house is promoted as a utopian refuge for women. Advertisers promise that intelligent agents will not only do the labor, but also make it possible for women to be dutiful mothers and successful career people at the same time. At a time when most families are comprised of double-income parents or single parents, the fantasy of all-purpose womanhood is particularly strong—at least in the promotional rhetoric for smart lifestyles.

In this respect, the ideal of conspicuous production has its corollary in conspicuous reproduction. When promoting the home office, advertisers often imply that new technologies can liberate women by giving them access to a new brand of technologically enhanced "power" femininity that allows them to participate in the traditionally masculine world of high-paid careers while also performing unpaid or underpaid women's work (child rearing, care for the elderly, cooking, cleaning, etcetera). Ads and articles often depict mothers in their home offices posed with their children, seemingly able to trade stocks while changing diapers.[59] To be sure, this "family circle" iconography is not new. Since the nineteenth century, advertisers have promoted technologies to women by using romantic images of nature, childhood, animals, marriage, and domestic comfort. For example, Singer promoted sewing machines (which were then thought to be unfeminine) with images of domesticity, childhood, and nature; this strategy carried through to telephones, radio, television, and the like.[60]

Building on this tradition, smart home magazines create sentimental imagery of family togetherness by promoting his-and-her home offices. A photo spread in a 2001 issue of *Broadband House* shows Susan and Steve Hall, both successful career people who moved from the hubbub of Miami to an 1800s-era home in the resort town of Merritt Island. The images show Susan and Steve busy at work in their his-and-her home offices. The captions read, "Susan's home office means she can be close to her kids," while "Steve works on three computers at a time."[61] The romantic quest for family bliss and the retreat back to nature (and the past) is thus sutured to imagery of conspicuous production and reproduction (Steve is a super worker who does three jobs at once; Susan is a superwoman who combines motherhood and career).

Certainly, for some women the advantages of working at home may be real. But the images gloss over the difficult tensions inherent in being a working mother. In place of the strain that women feel when trying to juggle motherhood with careers, the promotional rhetoric for smart homes offers a technological fix that allows women to be everywhere and everything at once. These images recall the "Roll-Oh" the Robot promotional logic that advertisers have historically used to convince women that new technologies would liberate them from the doldrums of everyday chores. Yet studies suggest that in the twentieth century women's domestic labor time was not reduced; instead, it was redirected, for example, to increased amounts of labor on childcare.[62] Today's smart homes likewise promise not so much a reduction in labor time, but rather an idealized view of multitasking that encourages women to juggle jobs.[63] For example, in her ethnographic study of computer-owning households in Western Sydney, Elaine Lally found that "some of the gendered meanings of new technologies are translated from the technology's previously established business and educational settings. Word processing, for example, is often a task delegated to female employees in the workplace. In what seems to be a parallel trend, mothers and wives will often take on word processing for other members of the family."[64] In this regard, the "pink collar" labor of secretary and mother is combined so that word processing becomes another "caretaking" chore for mother. Meanwhile, the gendered nature of labor remains intact.

The emphasis on caretaking and family imagery in the promotional campaigns for smart homes can be understood in light of marketers' concerns that women tend, more than men, to be uninterested in and even anxious about smart homes. In fact, recent studies suggest that women feel anxious about their time spent online. In her 1999 pilot study of 150 female academics and computer industry workers, Catherine Burke found that computer use especially sparked guilt feelings among mothers, and that "having school-age children in the household has an impact" on this. Burke additionally found that women's time spent with computers sometimes threatened male partners and led "to feelings of guilt and distancing within familial relationships."[65] For example, one woman said, "I have noticed that if I pop upstairs for a few minutes to check my private e-mail, a little voice floats up the stairs asking what I am doing. It is as though he is scared I will disappear all night." Another woman reported that her husband "commented on how my cockatiel . . . had stopped coming out of her cage unless I was downstairs. I felt that this concern for my bird was a way of telling me that I was neglecting HIM."[66]

Other studies suggest that computer use leads to family conflicts. In their qualitative study of 11 Boston families, David Frohlick, Susan Dray, and Amy Silverman found that there was "widespread competition for PC time" and that "adults gave way to children unless their task was more urgent."[67] Even when families did use computers together in one room for recreational reasons, parents often found ways to privatize their computer sessions, especially for work-related uses. "A typical pattern of use was for the mother to use the PC during the day in-between housework, child-care, or part-time work, and for the father to use it later when the children have gone to bed."[68] In general, privacy of location was important to family members who used computers for work-related purposes. One mother said, "The typing I would do in my bedroom where it's quiet and personal and I can't be disturbed." Another complained, "The phones are ringing, the kids are calling, you know you never have any real place."[69] Yet, despite such complaints, it is not entirely clear that people actually want to devote domestic space to office space. According the U.S. Census, in 2002 only

1percent of the population converted a room to a home office, and this represented the lowest percentage of all home-remodeling projects (the highest was bathrooms at 7.2percent and kitchens at 5.1percent).[70] In this respect, even if people experience conflicts while trying to work at home, the precise ways in which people will arrange domestic space to mediate these conflicts remains to be seen.

The demarcation of family space from workspace is, of course, not the result of the computer alone. Instead, dividing home from workplace is a social convention through which modern publics have experienced everyday life since industrialization. In her ethnographic study, *Home and Work*, Christina E. Nippert-Eng argues that people always demarcate a difference between work and home, even while different people demand different degrees of separation.[71] Although some workers manage to bring private life into the office (family photos, water cooler talk, spousal hires), they nevertheless still engage in cultural conventions that distinguish between private and public selves. In the case of the home office, the maintenance of this difference is, I would argue, no less important. Even as the home office represents an endpoint on the homework continuum, people nevertheless still deploy rules by which the two personae (family member/worker) are maintained.

In the discourse on smart homes, the homework continuum is troubled by the corresponding continuum, masculine–feminine. Given that domestic space has traditionally been associated with women's work, smart home promoters have to carefully persuade men that the home is in fact a masculine place to be. On the one hand, smart home technologies that enhance leisure or home security lend themselves easily to "macho" man stereotypes and technological prowess. Smart home promoters often show men in power positions, aiming remote controls like guns at wide screen TVs, monitoring surveillance systems, playing games with buddies, and even in the more fantastic versions, jumping into (virtual) sports matches they watch on TV.[72] On the other hand, images of men working at home are harder to manage. Advertisers do promote images of domesticated "family men," but they balance these with images of men who have prestige jobs, mobile lifestyles, and/or dominion over their professional careers. A 1999 ad for a Panasonic mobile phone and intercom system literalizes the contradictory nature of this masculine ideal with a split screen layout that shows a man (or half a man) dressed in business attire on one side of the frame holding a cell phone. The other side of the frame shows the man's other half wearing a casual tee shirt and shades. The caption reads, "Now, there's one phone system for the both of you. Panasonic introduces a phone system for the family man who's also a businessman."[73]

Moreover, when men are shown sharing space with children, they typically are not doing traditional forms of women's housework (cleaning, feeding kids, etcetera). Instead, articles and advertisements feature fathers in charge of technology (installing the network or building home theaters) or at play (watching TV or playing games with kids).[74] For example, the December 2003 issue of *Electronic House* contains a profile of Frank Estremera (an "on-call 24-7" IT manager) that depicts Frank as an industrious teleworker who is also a "conscientious parent." Yet, the idea of male parenting is mostly aligned with his handyman capacity (he sets up the network and stores data) and recreational pursuits (he boasts of how he has linked each family member to a multi-user game).[75]

In line with the fact that many home workers are self-employed, smart home magazines often show men who started small businesses at home. Although these articles sometimes represent men as parents and caretakers, they are not generally concerned with conflicts over career and marriage. Instead, they appear to be aimed at a disenfranchised managerial class of male workers. They guarantee men renewed sovereignty over their lives through wired work that takes place away from the cutthroat realities of the workaday world where anyone can be fired anytime. There is no set of younger eager beavers competing for your rank on the corporate ladder and no Donald Trump to declare, "You're fired." Instead, the smart home promises that the virtual workplace will be virtually unpopulated. Epitomizing this ideal, an article in a 1999 issue of *Elle Décor* (entirely devoted to "Working at Home") shows a businessman/artist alone in his upscale Tribeca loft with a caption that reads, "There's No Office Socializing."[76]

Although the previous example represents the "metrosexual" mobile lifestyle of an urbane aesthete (*Elle* claims he styled his loft after Brigitte Bardot's apartment in Jean-Luc Godard's *Contempt*), most smart home magazines show men in home offices that are functionally furnished or else have a rustic feel, using dark woods to connote outdoorsy, rugged masculinity.[77] The important thing is that the home office distinguishes itself from the nine-to-five corporate grind while also being separate from feminine decoration and family spaces. For example, the smart house displayed at the Panasonic Center makes masculinity an essential part of the floor plan. As one reporter described it, "Panasonic's study looks every inch a guy's room, emphasizing multimedia and the glory of lording it over the entire household at the flick of switch. There's even a bottle of whisky perched within easy reach. . . . Security technology plays an important part here, as the door to the study is linked to the electronically-locked front door of the house. If the house is on lockdown, so is the study."[78] Here as elsewhere, the home network is represented in ways that connote traditional ideals of male mastery over space. The Smart Dad is everywhere, but also remote. He logs on to family life only when he chooses.

FROM WOMEN'S LIB TO ROBOT RIGHTS

In her 1963 book *The Feminine Mystique*, Betty Freidan coined the term "occupation housewife" to describe the dead-end world of unpaid labor that constituted women's lives at home.[79] The housewife image she evoked was central to the community plans and architectural structures of the 1950s suburb, and the politics of unpaid and underpaid domestic labor went on to be a central concern for second-wave feminists. But today, the situation is changing—although not necessarily in ways that second-wave feminists imagined. In the current discourse on smart homes, we hear less about women's exploitation than we do about the political troubles of intelligent household machines. In a curious twist, the rhetoric of women's liberation and labor exploitation is moving from the human to the virtual; the home is now a discursive battleground for posthuman rights and virtual justice.

As domestic objects take on social relationships, intelligent agents revolt with a vengeance and in ways that the consumer product industry and the rational logic of science cannot contain. For example, what if your fridge and microwave get bored talking about recipes and instead decide to talk behind your back? What if they decide to unionize? A Web site poses such a question with its intelligent agent Huge Harry (an artificial life form designed at MIT), who instructs other robots in ways to organize against human slave drivers. One "robot rights" Web page includes the text from Huge Harry's political speech delivered at a 1996 robot rights rally, and another explains the meaning of slavery.[80] Meanwhile, the Web site for the ASPCR—the American Society for the Prevention of Cruelty to Robots—mimics language from the Bill of Rights and incites people (or bots?) to join its posthumanitarian campaigns to "free robots."[81] Highlights of the ASPCR legislation include "weekly oil baths" and "better operator training education."[82] These current dialogues among silicon-based life forms like Huge Harry (or at least the humans who have put up these Web sites), raise complex cultural questions. Is robot rights just a silly pastime of computer "geeks," or does the issue of robot rights suggest—as some AL enthusiasts suggest—a posthuman ethical dilemma? Notwithstanding these complex ethical questions about silicon life, the current discourse on robot rights—at least in its more ludic forms—is part of a much wider cultural fantasy involving tales about humans and intelligent machines. Robot rights has been a central theme for science fiction writers from Ray Bradbury to Philip K. Dick to C. L. Moore, and it is also a popular narrative focus in Hollywood film and television.

Take, for example, Steven Spielberg's 2001 summer blockbuster *AI*, which tells the story of an artificial boy abandoned by his human mother. *AI*'s futuristic suburban home looks like a page from a smart home magazine. Its grand upper-crust comfort is infused with just enough high-tech gizmos to give it a slightly defamiliarizing feel. In other words, in the tradition of Freud's famous analysis of the uncanny, the film's domestic mise-en-scene is both homelike and not homelike at the same time. Also in the tradition of uncanny fiction, and following from Freud's analysis, the film's narrative conflict between humans and automatons turns out to be a tale of sexual difference.[83]

Although many critics were quick to notice the Pinocchio-like elements of the film, the role of the father is not the driving narrative focus in *AI*. Instead, it is David's relationship with his human mother Monica that is the cause of the narrative quest. In a pivotal scene, Monica programs David to love her by inscribing a "mother" code from the owner's manual. The inscription scene is blocked so that Monica and David appear in profile,

Figure 4.6. Posthuman maternal melodrama in Steven Spielberg's *Artificial Intelligence: AI* (2001).

against romantic lighting, as she reads him a code that will literally brand him as her lovesick child for the rest of the film. Yet, as the narrative unfolds, Monica must choose between David and her human son. Too maternal to sacrifice her biological son, but too kind to shut David down, she abandons him in the woods. David pleads for her mercy, professing his love, but Monica leaves him to his fate (which in the tradition of the classic fairy tale entails a search for his identity followed by a triumphant return home).

After this point, the film follows David in search of his lost mother. Along the way David meets his maker/father Professor Hobby and learns of his cybernetic origins. The scene between David and Professor Hobby evokes, but also rearticulates, the dynamics of family melodrama between child, mother, and father. The scene is blocked and lit almost identically to the way in which the inscription scene between Monica and David was staged. But because this second scene takes place in a lab rather than a home, it underscores the uncanny and even "creepy" undertones of the first inscription scene. The scene's revelation—that David is one of a million Davids hanging on racks in Dr. Hobby's cybernetic child factory—adds to the uncanny sensibility. But this "reveal" does not satisfy David's desire, nor does it resolve the narrative hermeneutic that the film sets up. Instead, AI is rooted in David's mastery over his mother. Consequently, the film ends with artificial life forms of the future answering David's wish for his mother by resurrecting Monica from the dead. In the film's climactic scene, David literally beds Monica back in their original smart house. But this time he lies with her in the master bed (not the womb-shaped child's bed he occupied at the beginning of the film). In other words, David gains mastery over the scene of his childhood, and over the narrative itself. Rather than being seduced and abandoned by his idealized mother, he chooses her death (he is told she will live for only one day if she is conjured back from the past).

In one sense this Oedipal reading is logical enough, yet AI places the Oedipal narrative within a particular sociohistorical context that gives the scenario new cultural resonance. That social context is one in which working mothers are continually blamed for abandoning their children, and where smart homes promote themselves as a technological solution for the guilt feelings society provokes in mothers who work outside the home. To be sure, the fantasy mother in AI does not have a job; in fact, her sole purpose in life seems to be her almost twisted devotion to her children. Yet, as a fantasy figure she bears all the blame for David's pain. Read this way, AI is in part a maternal melodrama. But unlike the classic maternal melodrama (such as *Stella Dallas* or *Mildred Pierce*), AI does not present the mother as a victim of class, race, and patriarchal oppression. Maternal guilt is rendered personal rather than tied to any wider social explanation. *AI* is a morality play in which women are responsible for the fate of childhood in late capitalist technological society. Accordingly, when Monica abandons David, he is "picked up" by a sexually promiscuous gigolo-bot who services lonely women in a futuristic red light district where unthinkable dangers (including a robot "flesh fair" massacre) await. In this respect, it is significant that Monica receives David as a gift from her husband, who views the child as an object of exchange and is completely de-Oedipalized in the story (he does not inscribe his "code" on David, and so bears no parental responsibility).

A similar, if somewhat more "raw" version, of the evil mother scenario appears in a much lower-budget 1999 Disney channel TV movie, simply called *Smart House*. Once again, the lead character is a boy in search of a mother. In this case, however, the boy (Ben) is a human computer "geek" who lives with his widower father and younger sister. In the opening act, Ben enters an Internet contest and wins a digital dream house. The motherless family moves into the smart house, which is wired to cater to the family's every demand. When the kids want fruity yogurt shakes, the house goes into blender mode. When the house is dirty, it does the chores. When the kids are bored, they amuse themselves in fun places (like Disneyland) that are beamed in on plasma screen walls.

Given its rather servile nature, it is perhaps no surprise that this smart house is explicitly characterized as a woman. Referred to as PAT (short for Personal Applied Technology), the house not only has a female name she also has a female voice and a downloaded feminine consciousness. In an attempt to make PAT an even more devoted mother, Ben decides to download vintage TV sitcom housewives into her mainframe. But, as in most tales about technology and women, in this film the dream house soon goes out of control and the house literally materializes as a neurotic, clinging 1950s mother who desperately tries to keep the family from leaving her. In an elaborate climax, PAT divides herself into multiple cyborg mothers who attack the family with smothering devotion by wrapping tentacle-like wires around the family and shutting all windows and doors. This being a Disney channel film, PAT is of course eliminated and replaced with a good mother when Ben's Dad marries Sarah, the woman who originally programmed PAT. Happy to stay at home, Sarah embodies the contemporary ideal for motherhood in double-income households. She is the ultimate "home office" worker who not only combines her telework career with childrearing, but also literally builds the architecture for smart family lifestyles.

Lynn Spigel

With all these story elements in place, *Smart House* ultimately turns into Freud's uncanny, a castration tale so overstated that it appears to be the work of an overzealous screenwriter who just finished a crash course in Freud 101. Still, my point in recounting the plot is to demonstrate the extreme amount of ambivalence and anxiety that surrounds contemporary notions of our housing and media futures. Visually recalling the house-bots of the classic women's lib era film *The Stepford Wives*, *Smart House* nevertheless inverts the moral. Rather than a veiled allegory about women's imprisonment in the patriarchal world of the Stepford suburb, *Smart House* presents women as evil perpetuators of crimes against the family. Moreover, both *Smart House* and *AI* shift the central pathos of maternal melodrama from mother to child; they ask audiences to identify with the boy/child and his rights rather than with women's plight in patriarchal family structures.

Indeed, these films may be about the future of home, but they are in the end regressive. Their view of technology and mothers recalls Philip Wylie's rants on "momism"—a term he coined in his 1942 book *Generation of Vipers* (which was reprinted 16 times through 1955). According to Wylie, women, corporations, and the media technologies (radio and television primarily) had colluded to emasculate men and turn their sons into cowering sissies.[84] Although couched in less hyperbolic terms, the mothers in *AI* and *Smart House* posit a similar collusion between corporations, technology, and women, and both films make boys the victims of all three. These films remind us that even if technology advances, our fantasies about home, gender, and technology do not necessarily change.

SMART HOMES . . . OR GARDENS?

Today, popular culture is riveted on the topic of new technology as films like *Smart House* and *AI* speculate on the future of home, community, and humanity in the digital age. Although these films provide a gothic vision of domestic terror with women and technology out of control, the smart home industry promises to alleviate anxieties about change by promising that new technologies will maintain and extend traditional middle-class comforts. Still, this nostalgic return to tradition does not mean everything is the same. Instead, I think the smart home is really a kind of laboratory for figuring out the future in the context of present day transitions—including not simply technological changes, but also changes in the sexual division of labor, new forms of global commerce, as well as changes (as David Morley argues) in patterns of mobility and migration.[85]

As my opening example suggested, smart homes are now being promoted as a solution for the new position privileged populations find themselves in with respect to travel—especially in the wake of 9/11. As numerous cultural geographers have argued, mobility has historically been the purview of first world men whose power is in large part realized as freedom to move through and colonize space. Yet, as the editor of *Broadband House* so boldly announces, the home is becoming "the new center of the universe" for global businessmen like himself who fear the prospects of the journey. In this respect, corporate elites are now put in the position of women and people of color, for whom travel away from home has historically been a threatening enterprise accompanied by lynching, rape, and unprovoked arrests.[86]

At a time when first world populations are dispossessed of their privilege over space—or at least as they become more afraid of retribution for their legacy of colonial enterprise—the home is taking on the cosmopolitan features of hybridity (it is a place of here and there, work and leisure, male and female, silicon and flesh). Yet, this kind of high-tech domestic cosmopolitanism should not at face value be celebrated as a posthuman solution to a human past. The smart home, as I have shown, is still a highly gendered place, and even as it goes global the smart home uses technology to police its boundaries and purify the perceived dangers of far-off places.

In this respect, it seems to me that the chattering appliances and adaptive technologies in these homes may well be "new," but they are not necessarily equivalent to a radical socialist notion of posthumanism and cyborg subjectivity. A number of feminist critics have embraced the idea of posthumanism as a way to get out of the old myths of human nature and biologically determined sex that placed women in the home and garden. But, these smart homes are not necessarily the same as that.

What, then, does this corporate brand of posthuman domesticity offer? I am not sure. Although I still agree with Donna Haraway[87]— that is, I'd rather be a cyborg than a goddess—it seems to me that the smart home's human–technology interface may well turn out to be just a high-tech version of the older homes and gardens that created woman in the image of man. Still, my obvious obsession with smart homes suggests that I do in principle think they are futures worth imagining. After all, if we don't imagine the future then Disney most certainly will.

Notes

1 Scott Degarmo, "High-Tech Havens," *Broadband House*, Winter 2001–02, editorial, 6.

2 Ibid.

3 Note that wired networks compete with wireless and that various companies compete over platforms. Intel and Microsoft promote the PC as the hub of the digital home whereas consumer electronics companies like Sony and Panasonic push the TV screen as the smart home platform. But industry leaders also think the technologies will be in some way combined for specific types of uses for specific environments. Intel Vice President Louis J. Burns explains the three environments as (1) the "lean-forward" environment, where users interact with their notebook and PC; (2) the "lean-back" environment, where data is consumed on a handheld remote control; and (3) a "handheld" environment that relates to the phone and PDA. Burns predicts, "The home network will blur where the content comes from between these three interaction areas." See Dan Hutchinson, interview with Louis J. Burns, *Digital Home*. August 2003, 38.

4 For histories of homes of tomorrow, see Brian Horrigan, "The Home of Tomorrow, 1927–1945," in *Imagining Tomorrow, History, Technology, and the American Future*, ed. Joseph J. Corn, 137–63 (Cambridge: MIT Press, 1986); Robert Haddow, "House of the Future or House of the Past: Populist Visions from the USA," *Architecture and Ideas* 1, no. 1 (1999): 68–79; Gregory L. Demchak, "Towards a Post-Industrial Architecture: Design and Construction of Houses for the Information Age," MA thesis, MIT, June 2000; Robert Boyce, *Keck and Keck* (Princeton, N.J.: Princeton Architectural Press, 1993); Fiona Allon, "An Ontology of Everyday Control: Space, Media Flows, and 'Smart' Living in the Absolute Present," in *Mediaspace: Place, Scale, and Culture in a Media Age*, ed. Nick Cauldry and Anna McCarthy, 253–75 (London: Routledge, 2004).

5 Fuller's Dymaxion Dwelling Machine was first displayed in 1929 at Marshall Field's department store in Chicago. When marketed as a kit in the 1940s, it did not catch on. Similarly, in the same period, Walter Gropius and Konrad Wachsmann's Packaged House (also a prefabricated mass produced home) was not popular and survived only for a short while.

6 During the 1930s, General Electric showcased its "magic home" at fairs and exhibitions. In 1934, Westinghouse chose Mansfield, Ohio, as the site for its "Home of Tomorrow," which functioned as a display venue for the company's line of household gizmos.

7 The Monsanto home stood at the gateway of Tomorrowland and resembled some kind of Martian vegetation, with huge window walls flanking out of its wings. In addition to its futuristic kitchen, it contained a slew of then high-tech machines, including push-button phones and lighting panels.

8 The Carrousel of Progress became a central fixture in Disneyland in 1967, replacing MIT's Monsanto home of tomorrow.

9 Panasonic's digital house exhibit was located at the Panasonic Center, Tokyo, in 2004 and is described herein; Philips Research Centre in the Netherlands opened a "Homelab" in 2002, in which occupants are surveyed around the clock by a team of scientists; and in 2004 IBM opened its "Pervasive Computing Lab" in Austin, Texas, where engineers have developed what they call a "living lab." Note too that both global and regional corporations have had smart home pilot projects since the late 1980s.

10 See Roland Marchand, *Advertising the American Dream: Marking Way for Modernity, 1920–1940* (Berkeley: University of California Press, 1985), 167–88. See also Laura Scott Holliday, "Kitchen Technologies: Promises and Alibis, 1944–1966," *Camera Obscura* 47, no. 2 (2001): 79–130.

11 Titled "Mother Takes a Holiday: Part 1," the film is part of the Prelinger Archives, now housed at the Smithsonian Institution and available online at www.archive.org. It was produced by the Jam Handy Picture Company.

12 The opening scene shows a company technician demonstrating the robot in highly technical terms while the housewife's eyes glaze over—thereby establishing the age-old idea that women can't understand technology. Yet the film repositions the housewife as Roll-Oh's master. Moreover, a subsequent scene shows a deliveryman who is so frightened by Roll-Oh that he runs off in a panic—a comic situation that inverts the stereotypes of women as the lesser techno-savvy sex. Through this comic inversion, the film invites prospective female robot consumers to imagine that they are more modern then men. Yet, despite this bit of flattery, the film depicts the modern woman as a housewife who imagines using Roll-Oh only within the limits of her predefined role. The film is available through Something Weird Video, "Lifestyles USA," vol. 1.

13 Brian Horrigan, "The Home of Tomorrow, 1927–1945," in *Imagining Tomorrow, History, Technology, and the American Future,* ed. Joseph J. Corn (Cambridge: MIT Press, 1986), 157.

14 Internet World Stats, usage and population statistics, June 2009. See http://www.internetworldstats.htm.

15 Amanda Lenhart, et al., *The Ever-Shifting Internet Population* (Washington, D.C.: Pew Internet and American Life Project, 16 April 2003), available online at www.pewinternet.org. U.S. Census Bureau, "Households with Computers and Internet Access by Selected Characteristics: 2001," No. 1158, *Statistical Abstract of the United States,* 2003, 736. All Statistical Abstract data cited herein are available online at www.census.gov/statab.

16 The 1986 show is discussed in Laura Hengster, "Smart Home Appliances Focus On Comfort, Ease," *Chicago Sun-Times,* 23 January 2000, Home Section, 3.

17 Sebastian Rupley, "IDF Report: Intel Imagines Digital Homes," *PC Magazine Online,* 18 February 2004, PCMag.com.

18 Deborah Fallows, *The Internet and Daily Life* (Washington, D.C.: Pew Internet & American Life Project, 2004), cover page, available online at www.pewinternet.org. Note that since I wrote this essay in 2004. Pew has continued

the American Internet and Life Project. While the 2004 data I cited was for online use in all locations, an April 2009 survey by the Pew Research Center's Internet & American Life Project shows that "63% of adult Americans now have broadband internet connections at home, a 15% increases [sic] from a year earlier. April's level of high-speed adoption represents a significant jump from figures gathered by the Project since the end of 2007 (54%)." This data suggests the home is indeed becoming an increasingly "smart" space where people access data (whether information or entertainment) online. For the report see http://www.pewinternet.org/Reports/2009/10-Home-Broadband-Adoption-2009.aspx.

19 Fallows, *The Internet and Daily Life*, vi., 4–6.

20 Ibid., iii. The supporting data for this are detailed in Part 3, 9–14.

21 Lynn Spigel, "Yesterday's Future, Tomorrow's Home," in *Welcome to the Dreamhouse: Popular Media and Postwar Suburbs*, 381–408 (Durham, N.C.: Duke University Press, 2001). Despite the fact that smart home magazines contain a sprinkling of images of African American homeowners who are self-employed home business owners, the fantasy offered is clearly a class-based fantasy, and for the most part it is aimed at white "first world" populations.

22 "Technology-Home Work," *Architecture*, September 1999, online at www.earchitect.com, A:/Technology-Home Work. Htm.

23 In addition to the physical site, the Panasonic Web site (http://www.panasonic-center.com) also displayed the home to virtual visitors in 2003 and 2004. For photos and a more detailed description see Mark Lytle, "House: The Digital Homes of Our Dreams," *Digital Home*, Spring 2003, 74–83.

24 Larsen cited in Peter Hull, "Living for Tomorrow," *Metropolis Magazine*, December 2002, online at www.metropolismag.com. In the summer of 2004, MIT's House_n and TIAX opened The PlaceLab, a residential observational research facility with occupants located in Cambridge, Mass.

25 Kent Larsen, "The Home of the Future," *A+U* 361 (October 2000), available online at architecture.mit.edu/house_n/web/publications/publications.htm.

26 This analysis of the U.S. Census Bureau's 2002 *Current Population Survey* (March Supplement) is provided by AmeriStat Staff, "Traditional Families Account for only 7 Percent of U.S. households," Popular Reference Bureau, www.prb.org. For the detailed data and census tables see "Current Population Reports," no. 60–76, and U.S. Census Bureau, *Statistical Abstract of the United States: 2003*, 60–66.

27 See architecture.mit.edu/house_n/.

28 Larsen cited in Hull, "Living for Tomorrow."

29 Larsen, "The Home of the Future."

30 N. Katherine Hayles, *How We Became Posthuman* (Chicago, University of Chicago Press, 1999).

31 This appeared on a link on the 2003 Web site for the Panasonic Center's smart house, http://www.panasonic-center.com/en/design/bio1.htmlPanasonic. The website is no longer up.

32 For more on the Digital House, see Terence Riley, *The Un-Private House*, exhibition catalog for "The Un-Private House," (New York: The Museum of Modern Art, 1999), 56–59. The Digital House project was conducted in 1998. For more on the "Hyper House Pavilion 5" see ibid., 13. The Exhibit was mounted in conjunction with MIT.

33 The arrangement is akin to the one described by Javier Echaverria's in *Telpolis* (1994), which considers the paradox of a contemporary society where consumption has merged with productive time through what he calls the "telesecond" (or a unit of passive leisure that advertising converts into capital). He writes, "Telpolis subverts the structure of the market ensuring that the actual act of buying takes place without any spending of money on the part of the purchaser, but with a spending of time. . . . Many forms of leisure have been turned into productive labor, in many instances without any awareness on the part of the idle, who in enjoying their hours of relaxation are in fact working." [Javier Echevarria, *Telepolis* (Barcelona: Ediciones Destino, 1994), 154]. Note that in 1979, Dallas Smythe proposed a similar idea regarding the conversion of leisure into work via advertising. See his, "Communication: The Blindspot of Western Marxism," *Canadian Journal of Political & Social Theory*, 2, no. 2 (1978): 120–29.

34 Paul Lewis, Marc Tsurumaki, David J. Lewis, "New Suburbanism," *Architecture and Ideas* 2, no. 2 (Summer/Fall 2000): 73. See also www.archidose.org/Mar01/030501.html.

35 Ibid., 75.

36 Beatriz Colomina, *Privacy and Publicity: Modern Architecture as Mass Media* (Cambridge, MA: MIT Press, 1996). See also Beatriz Colomina, "The Media House," *Assemblage* 27 (1995): 55–66.

37 Cited from Riley, *The Un-Private House*, 52. See also www.users.cloud9.net/-bradmcc/sq/DillerScofidio.html.

38 Raymond Williams, *Television: Technology and Cultural Form* (New York: Schocken Books, 1975), 26–28.

39 See my "Portable Television: Studies in Domestic Space Travel," in *Welcome to the Dreamhouse: Popular Media and Postwar Suburbs*, 60–103 (Durham, N.C.: Duke University Press, 2001).

40 Note, however, that this ideal of active leisure and mobile bodies was just the cultural fantasy promoted in ads. Market research suggested that people barely moved portable sets in their homes—no less outdoors. See my "Portable Television," 75.

41 See David Morley, *Home Territories: Media, Mobility, and Identity* (London: Routledge, 2000) and David Morley, "At Home with Television," in *Television after TV: Essays on a Medium in Transition*, ed. Lynn Spigel and Jan Olsson, 303–324 (Durham: N.C.: Duke University Press, 2004).

42 Cited in Riley, *The Un-Private House*, 56.

43 This statement was part of the exhibition text at the Un-Private House exhibit at the Museum of Modern Art, New York and at the Armand Hammer Museum, Los Angeles.

44 Another smart home in New York City (this one actually constructed) takes this virtual work ethic to its logical extreme. Built for a couple who are both currency traders on Wall Street, the New York City Lipsitz/Jones apartment has six screens throughout the house on which the stock exchange is constantly present. Designed essentially as a residential "trading floor," the home even allows residents to receive stock reports from the video screen in the master bath.

45 Intille cited in Hull, "Living for Tomorrow."

46 The citation is taken from Paul Virilio, "The Last Vehicle," in *Looking Back at the End of the World*, ed. Dietmar Kamper and Christoph Wolf, , trans. David Antal (New York: Semiotext(e), 1989), 119. In that essay Virilio opines the paradox of a high-tech "speed" oriented society that has become increasingly sedentary, as everything is mediated through audiovisual representation. See also Paul Virilio, *Open Skies*, trans. Julie Rose (London: Verso, 1997); and Jean Baudrillard, *The Ecstasy of Communication*, trans. Bernard and Caroline Schutze, ed. Sylvere Lotringer (New York: Semiotext(e), 1987), 18.

47 AmeriStat Staff, "Traditional Families Account for only 7 Percent of U.S. households." For the detailed data and census tables, see U.S. Census Bureau, "Current Population Reports," *Statistical Abstract of the United States*, no. 60–66.

48 Jeffrey J. Kuenzi and Clara A. Reschovsky, "Current Population Reports," *Household Economic Studies* (Washington: U.S. Department of Commerce, U.S. Census Bureau, December 2001), 3. The number of home workers fell between 1960 and 1980 (presumably due to the decline in family farm work).

49 See Press Release, "Work at Home in 2001," 1 March 2002, www.bls.gov/ news.release/homey.nr).htm. Four-fifths of those who regularly worked at home were employed in managerial, professional, and sales jobs. The press release also states that the U.S. Census Bureau collected the data on work at home in May 1997 and again in May 2001. But because of changes in the questions asked, much of the data is not comparable. Using a slightly different definition of home work, a 2004 study concludes that in 2004, teleworkers represented nearly one fifth (18.3 percent) of adult Americans, and their numbers had increased by 2.6 percent from the previous year. See "Work at Home Grows in Past Year by 7.5% in US," ITAC press release, 2 September 2004, available online at www.telecommute.org. Since I wrote this essay, the trend continues. Measuring employed adults in 2008, Pew reported, "45% of employed respondents in our sample reported at least some amount of at-home work. The segment that routinely works from home is smaller: Some 18% of job-holding Americans work at home every day or almost every day. However, 37% of employed Americans say they are working from home at least as often as a few times per month." For the report see Mary Madden and Sydney Jones, "Networked Workers," Pew Internet & American Life Project," September 24, 2008. Online at http://www.pewinternet.org/Reports/2008/ Networked-Workers.aspx.

50 "The Work-at-Home Hook," *Home Office Computing*, November 2000, 92.

51 "Work at Home Grows in Past Year by 7.5% in US," ITAC press release, September 2, 2004, posted at www.telecommute.org.

52 Ibid, 94.

53 In its 2003–04 American Interactive Consumer Survey, the Dieringer Research Group found that the number of teleworkers using broadband rose to 8.1 million from the previous year, an 84 percent increase. See "Work at Home Grows in Past Year by 7.5% in US." This research supports the findings of the AT&T Foundation-sponsored Telework America 2003 research ("Teleworking Comes of Age with Broadband") that predicted that more workers would telework as they became equipped with broadband.

54 Press release, "Work at Home in 2001," www.bls.gov/news.release/homey.nr). htm. This is a press release summarizing the May 2001 "Current Population Survey" conducted by the U.S. Bureau of Labor Statistics. Since I first wrote this essay in 2004, the Internet and mobile technologies appear to be allowing for a greater merger of home and work. In 2008 Pew reported, "One of the major impacts of the internet and cell phones is that they have enabled more people to do work at least occasionally from home. Some 45% of employed Americans report doing at least some work from home and 18% of working Americans say they do job-related tasks at home almost daily." The report also finds that "Networked Workers who use the internet or email at their job report higher rates of working at home. Overall, 56% of Networked Workers report some at-home work and 20% say they do so every day or almost every day." For the report see Madden and Jones, "Networked Workers."

55 John B. Horrigan and Lee Rainie, *Getting Serious Online* (Washington: D.C.: Pew Internet & American Life Project, Pew Research Center, 3 March 2002), 7–8, available online at www.pewinternet.org.

56 Denise Caruso, "Microsoft Morphs into a Media Company," *Wired*, June 1996, cover and 126–30.

57 *Digital Home*, August 2003, cover.

58 Joanne Cleaver, "Say Hello to the House of Tomorrow," *Broadband House*, Winter 2001–02, 56–63.

59 For examples of images/articles of mothers and children, see ibid.; *Broadband House* Winter 2001–02, 53; *Home Office Computing*, November 2000, 92; Marshall F. Lager, "In the Family Way," *Home Office Computing*, October 2000, 86; *Family PC*, March 2000, cover.

60 See, example, Arthur J. Polis, *American Design Ethic: A History of Industrial Design* (Cambridge: MIT, 1986); Adrian Forte, *Objects of Desire: Design and Society from Wedgewood to IBM* (New York: Pantheon, 1986); Leo Marx, *The Machine in the Garden: Technology and the Pastoral Ideal in America* (New York: Oxford, 1965).

61 Carol Weber Thomas, "This Old House Is Really New," *Broadband House*, Winter 2001–2002, 74–81.

62 Ruth Schwartz Cowan, *More Work for Mother: The Ironies of Household Technology from the Open Hearth to the Microwave* (New York: Basic Books, 1983); Michael

Bittman, James Mahmud Rice, Judy Wajcman, "Appliances and Their Impact: The Ownership of Domestic Technology and Time Spent on Household Work," *The British Journal of Sociology* 55, no. 3 (September 2004): 401.

63 Moreover, in the context of the present-day aging population, demands on women to nurture extend from children to parents. Accordingly, everything from "care-bots" (robots designed to take care of children and aging parents) to experimental smart house assisted living developments (Like Georgia Tech's Aware House) promise the boomer generation that their parents are—if not loved— then at least surveyed by electronic eyes that will, for example, monitor your mother's heart rate and phone you and the doctor if something goes wrong.

64 Elaine Lally, *At Home with Computers*, (Oxford: Berg, 2002), 159.

65 Catherine Burke, "Women, Guilt, and Home Computers," in *The Wired Homestead: An MIT Sourcebook on the Internet and the Family*, ed. Joseph Turow and Andrea L. Kavanaugh (Cambridge, MA: MIT Press, 2003), 332–33.

66 Cited in Burke, "Women, Guilt, and Home Computers," 332–33.

67 David M. Frohlich, Susan Dray, and Amy Silverman, "Breaking Up Is Hard to Do: Family Perspectives on the Future of the Home PC," in *The Wired Homestead*, ed. Turow and Kavanaugh, 305–306.

68 Ibid., 306.

69 Ibid., 314.

70 U.S. Census Bureau, No. 980 "Home Remodeling—Work Done and Amount Spent: 2002," *Statistical Abstract of the United States, 2003*, 632.

71 Christina E. Nippert-Eng, *Home and Work: Negotiating Boundaries through Everyday Life* (Chicago: University of Chicago Press, 1995).

72 For examples of images like this see Emily Fridlander, "Surf and Sweat," *Family PC*, March 2000, 37; *Electronic House*, December 2003, 8, 47; *Electronic House*, January 2003, 9. There are some images of women at play, but typically these show them in a family group and not playing alone.

73 *Home Office Computing*, November 2000, 36.

74 These images recall similar depictions of male domesticity found in advice literature aimed at men at the turn of the nineteenth century. As Margaret Marsh argues, these turn-of-the-nineteenth-century men's magazines suggested that men's participation in the family might help to ease their sense of powerlessness in the increasingly bureaucratic workforce. So too, the advice literature of that time emphasized men's roles as "chum" to the children, stressing men's participation in family leisure and play. Contemporary ads combine the family man image with images of executive class masculinity tailored for today's lifestyles. Margaret Marsh, *Suburban Lives* (New Brunswick, N.J.: Rutgers University Press, 1990).

75 Cited in Lisa Montgomery, "High-Speed Home Office," *Electronic House*, December 2003, 73.

76 Angus Wilkie, "Live/Work," *Elle Décor*, February/March 1999, 138–41. While the man featured in the photo essay admits he that he finds the absence of

socializing hard, he nevertheless boasts about his mobile lifestyle, emphasizing that he has no "specific routine" as he ambles around his large loft with cell phone in hand.

77 Adi Shamir Zion discusses the nostalgia for wood and other natural materials in Bill Gates's digital home. See his, "New Modern: Architecture in the Age of Digital Technology," *Assemblage* 35 (1998): 65.

78 Lytle, "House," 78.

79 Betty Friedan, *The Feminine Mystique* (New York: Dell, 1963).

80 See iaaa.nl/hh/div/robotrights.html; see also jon.werborg.net/photos/robotrights. For more on ethnical issues and/or robot-human relations see Hayles, *How We Became Posthuman;* Rodney Brooks, *Flesh and Machines: How Robots Will Change Us* (New York: Pantheon, 2002).

81 See ASPCR.com.

82 See jon.werborg.net/photos/robotrights.

83 In his essay "The Uncanny," Freud argues that fantasies about automatons are rooted in sexual difference, which is also the source of the "uncanny" sensibility they evoke. Tracing the derivation of the word "uncanny" (in German, "Unheimlich," roughly translated as "unhomey"), Freud shows that the word itself is characterized by a turning onto its opposite. What was once entirely familiar is strange; what was once homey becomes unhomey, what seems inanimate becomes animate. Reading Hoffman's tale "The Sandman," which deals with a boy who is in love with an automaton, Freud argues that the sense of the uncanny that the tale provokes is rooted in repressed anxieties and the fear of castration—in other words in male anxiety about women and the mother's womb (the child's first home, which later becomes a source of fear and dread). Whether or not we take Freud's analysis as truth about human psychology, as a piece of literary analysis his essay sheds light on stories about technology, humans, and the idea of home, stories that are ultimately connected to male anxieties about women and sexual difference. See Sigmund Freud, "The Uncanny," *Studies in Parapsychology* (New York: Collier, 1971), 19–62.

84 Philip Wylie, *Generation of Vipers* (1942; New York: Holt, Reinhart and Winston, 1955).

85 Morley, *Home Territories*.

86 bell hooks, *Black Looks: Race and Representation* (Boston: South End Press, 1992), 165–78; Janet Wolff, "On the Road Again: Metaphors of Travel in Cultural Criticism," *Cultural Studies* 7, no. 2 (1993): 235.

87 Donna J. Haraway, "Manifesto for Cyborgs: Science, Technology, and Socialist Feminism in the 1980s," *Socialist Review* 80 (1985): 65–108.

PART II

Electronic Publics

5

New Documentary in China:

Public Space, Public Television

How should we understand the connection between the virtual topographies produced by the media—the electronic elsewheres of this book—and the idea of the public? In his original work on the public sphere, Jürgen Habermas saw the classic public sphere as physical spaces where actual people met and debated, and he was dubious about the impact of mediation on the quality of the public sphere. However, this distinction has been lost in much media studies debate, which discusses the public sphere as a product of mediation. To explore these issues further, this chapter turns to the People's Republic of China and the worlds of new television and independent video documentary. What kinds of public are these electronic elsewheres producing? How can our efforts to investigate them enable us to question the assumptions underlying much of our existing discourse and enable us to formulate a more rigorous understanding of electronic elsewheres as public spaces?

In 2001, Chinese feature filmmaker Jia Zhangke contributed a short documentary to a three-part digital video film sponsored by South Korea's Jeonju International Film Festival. The English-language title in the subtitles is *In Public*, but the original Chinese title, *Gonggong Changsuo*, can be translated more literally as "public place" or "public arena." In this chapter the title is translated as *Public Space*, and the film acts as a counterpoint to the two main projects of the chapter. First, this chapter tries to delineate the role of new documentary film, video, and television in the production of electronic elsewheres as new publics and new public spaces in contemporary Chinese culture. Second, it asks what this can tell us about theorizing and analyzing public spaces as kinds of electronic elsewheres.

The documentary *Public Space* shares much with Jia's earlier feature films *Xiao Wu* (a.k.a. *The Pickpocket*, 1997) and *Platform* (*Zhantai*, 2000), as well as *Unknown Pleasures* (*Ren Xiao Yao*, 2002), which he was shooting at the same time he made *Public Space*. All these films are set in the small-town northern China in which Jia was brought up. They also deploy his usual long take, long shot technique. *Public Space* has only thirty-one shots in its thirty-two-minute length. Nothing much happens. Or to be more precise, lots of actions occur but they do not add up to a coherent narrative. The film is divided into five scenes: the combined ticket hall and waiting room of a small railway station at night; a bus stop during the day; on a bus during the day; a restaurant at night; and a combined pool hall and dance hall during the daytime. Various people stand around and move about. Sometimes they talk, but the heavy local accent and ambient noise from the road or railway make it impossible to hear anything but snatches of conversation. No characters are named or carry over from one scene to the next. We never discover where they are going, how they are related, or anything else that might bind the disparate events into narrative. Bérénice Reynaud sums up the film when she writes that it captures "the gap between 'life's slowness and hope's violence' (Apollinaire), between the ennui, backwardness, and dreary atmosphere of a small town, and the impatience, hidden desire and private concerns of its inhabitants, that create as many enigmatic narrative vignettes."[1]

Documentary film and video materials, from feature-length theatrical films such as Michael Moore's *Fahrenheit 911* (2004) to segments on television magazine shows such as *60 Minutes*, are conventionally seen as valuable contributors to and promoters of the liberal ideals of public debate and public culture as realms of rational and progressive community-building. Jia Zhangke's *Public Space* seems like mordant satire of not only that liberal ideal of meaningful activity, but possibly also of socialist modernity's vision of the public as mobilized masses. The electronic elsewhere *Public Space* produces prompts us to ask what public space means in postsocialist China today.[2] This chapter begins to answer that question by introducing and examining new kinds of television and independent documentary production in the People's Republic. It considers them as electronic elsewheres that have already begun to produce public spaces and cultures very different from the old socialist culture.

Many commentators have assumed that divergence from the old "totalitarian" model means movement toward an idealized "Western" model of a "free" "public sphere" operating in "civil society" separate from the state. Others apply the same standard, but question how far change has gone. Yet another group of writers doubts whether this "Western" model is appropriate for the Chinese context. This chapter does not want to confine the critique to cultural appropriateness. It argues that subscribing to such an idealized and ideological model as the public sphere blinds us to the complexity and range of publics and public spaces in general—in the Western just as much as in the Chinese context. Furthermore, it also binds us into an Orientalist posture in which China's efforts to "catch up" confirm the West—where it is assumed that such a thing as the "public sphere" exists—as a model for all to follow. The public sphere model's equation of freedom with the removal of state power is too simple. Instead, this chapter argues for replacing the idea of the kind of mediated (and often electronic) elsewhere we call the "public sphere" with a concept of public space. Drawing from Foucault's idea of productive power, it argues that public spaces are not only multiple and varied but also positively produced and shaped externally and internally by configurations of power. With this approach, we can begin both to grasp the specificity of postsocialist public space as a particular electronic elsewhere in China and also to avoid any assumption that its appearance must indicate Westernization.

New Documentary—TV

Chinese documentary has undergone transformation since the early 1990s. With this change, the types of public and public space it anticipates have also shifted. Before that date, a pedagogical style of illustrated lecture, in what Bill Nichols calls the "expository mode," dominated.[3] Since then a more spontaneous form characterized by on-the-spot footage and free-flowing interviews has become the new norm. In Chinese, the particular form of realism underlying this new form is known as *jishizhuyi*, and the term is also applied to realist feature films and literature with a similar on-the-spot feel. Documentary has two main variants: television documentary (including magazine show segments), and independent documentary, ranging from early 16 mm and Betacam films by trained filmmakers to the more recent emergence of amateur and digital video forms.[4]

To begin with television, this was an underemphasized medium in the People's Republic from its 1958 birth until the early 1980s. Film and radio were the dominant media of the socialist heyday. Television was completely funded and controlled by the central government, and because television receivers were few and often installed in public halls, the audience literally gathered in public spaces to constitute themselves as viewing publics. The format for documentary programming was the "*zhuanti pian*," or "special topic program," resembling an illustrated lecture. This format imagined its audience as eager pupils—Chairman Mao's famous "blank piece of paper," waiting to be written upon.[5] Rather than the independently active and questioning public composed of disparate and debating individuals imagined by the public sphere model, this is the public as unified masses mobilized according to the needs of the Party and state.

Since the mid-1980s, Chinese television has been undergoing structural transformation and a great boom. To give just a few statistics, only 925,000 television receivers were manufactured between 1958 and Mao's death in 1976, but annual output had reached 27.67 million as early as 1989.[6] In 1978 there was less than one television receiver per one hundred people, and only ten million out of a population of nearly one billion, or less than 1 percent, had access to television. By 1996, there was a television receiver for every four persons, and one billion had access.[7] By 2000, this figure had risen to 1.19 billion, representing 92 percent of the population, and cable television was bringing a wider range of channels to 85.3 percent of the population in the relatively wealthy ten largest cities.[8]

This huge growth has been fueled by economic change. Once Chinese television stations were not only state-owned—as they continue to be—but also state-funded. Now advertising supplies as much as 99 percent of income for Chinese television, and only 0.5 percent of national broadcaster China Central Television (CCTV)'s income still comes from the government—less than it pays back in tax.[9] Ratings are provided by ACNeilsen and CVSC-Sofres Media Peoplemeters, and television's share of all expenditures on advertising rose in the 1990s from 27.7 percent at the beginning of the decade to 72.9 percent in 1997.[10] This in itself represents a significant change in how television imagines its public. Instead of—or maybe as well as, if we allow for overlap and contradiction—an electronic elsewhere constructed as the national classroom in the past, CCTV and its provincial and municipal counterparts now think of the public as an electronic elsewhere in the form of markets, and audiences have become product to be sold to advertisers.[11]

Chris Berry

Documentary programming in various forms has played an important role in this transformation. According to Li Xiaoping, the show that powered the takeoff in advertising was a daytime documentary newsmagazine show on CCTV called *Oriental Horizon (Dongfang Shikong)*.[12] Modeled somewhat on the investigative segments that make up CBS's *Sixty Minutes* and debuting in 1993, *Oriental Horizon's* combination of actuality materials with the exposure of social issues not usually aired on Chinese television represented something very new in Chinese television and in Chinese documentary in general. *Oriental Horizon* was an experiment. After its huge success with the public and acceptance by the political establishment, CCTV went on to launch the even more successful evening show *Focus (Jiaodian)* in 1994. Airing for thirteen minutes every weekday after the evening news, the program regularly gets a 20 to 25 percent rating—that is, between 200 and 250 million viewers—and it is popular with national leaders.[13] This huge success has inspired many copies: by the end of the 1990s there were already more than sixty similar television programs around the country as well as numerous newspaper watchdog journalism columns inspired by it.[14] As well as newsmagazine shows, Chinese television also has a wide range of longer documentary programming.[15]

Fifty-minute features and newsmagazine segments are not always seen as part of a single larger category called television documentary. But what binds these and other types of programming together in China as new television documentary is a set of defining rhetorical features. These can be summed up as on-the-spot spontaneity. A mixture of voice-over narration, on-the-spot interviews, and recording of events as they happen has replaced the old lecture-style mode. This new realist mode in television is known in Chinese as *jishizhuyi* (as opposed to the old socialist realist mode of *xianshizhuyi*). It has been facilitated by new lightweight technology and can be recognized both in terms of the profilmic event—what happens in front of the camera—and the style of program making. The spontaneous quality of the profilmic is signified by the sometimes stumbling delivery of thoughts in interviews along with tears and other emotions as uncontrolled and unrehearsed event. In program style, spontaneity is signified by the use of handheld cameras, the inclusion of moments of what would be considered technically unacceptable lighting and sound (but only in ways that do not detract from our understanding), and characters moving in and out of frame or acting in other ways that signify the unexpected or contingent.

What kind of public does this imply? Although the voice-over narration is scripted, there is a further and very significant change in this aspect of the new programming. In the past, the narrator spoke directly as the voice of the state and the Party. Now, this rhetoric has disappeared, and the reporter speaks in her or his own voice. This implies the media as an independent, or at least autonomous, body—maybe even a fourth estate. Newsmagazine and even hour-long documentary programs often present social issues or problems, and investigative reporting occurs now. This new rhetoric not only suggests that the media are autonomous but also that they can represent the public as ordinary citizenry in their search for justice—be it against corrupt officials, bullying and cheating entrepreneurs, or whatever larger force they have problems with. Reports of people lining up at CCTV to try and persuade *Focus* to cover their problem indicate that it acquired this status in the minds of many citizens.[16]

Independent Documentary

For the vast majority of Chinese, television documentary is the primary place in which they might encounter the new spontaneous *jishizhuyi* form. However, it also appears in another new media form that has sprung up since the 1990s—independent documentary. The author of the definitive Chinese-language book on the topic before the full emergence of digital video, Lu Xinyu, has called this a "new documentary movement" because of its distinctive form and practice, marked out by a self-conscious rejection of the old *zhuanti pian* illustrated lecture mode.[17] The documentary makers often have a background in Chinese television, such as Wu Wenguang and Duan Jinchuan, who are now internationally known. Many still work for Chinese television stations, but also make independent films. However, opinions differ on whether or not an "independent" can also work for television.[18]

Given this shared background in television, it is not surprising that the spontaneous style of the television documentary programming that began in 1993 was preceded slightly by independent documentaries, sometimes shot on film and sometimes on video. Wu Wenguang's *Bumming in Beijing: The Last Dreamers (Liulang Beijing,* 1990) was first shown outside China at the Hong Kong International Film Festival in 1991, and then traveled the world. This video consists of five vignettes about five artists living in Beijing and working, like Wu himself, outside the state-run system. Shooting began in mid-1988 and ended in late 1990.[19] We observe the independent artists' difficult living conditions, and their despair. By the end of the documentary, all but one have married foreigners and are preparing to leave or have left China. The artist who remains in China, a theater director called Mou Sen, was the focus of another early documentary, *The Other Bank* (*Bi'an*, 1995), by Jiang Yue. That video follows Mou Sen's eponymous experimental theater workshop, which attracts youngsters from a range of backgrounds and all over the country. What appears at first as an exemplary empowering exercise in democratic participation ultimately neglects to offer any practical help beyond the experience of the modernist experimental workshop itself. Xinyu opens her book with an extended discussion of this film, which she sees as representative of the fall away from utopianism and the emergence of self-criticism among the former avant-garde at the heart of new documentary.[20]

Neither *Bumming in Beijing* nor *The Other Bank* directly addresses the 1989 Tiananmen Square massacre and the associated dashing of ideals. But they resonate with its absence. Without any other reason offered for the overwhelming atmosphere of hopelessness and the desire to leave the country that is depicted in *Bumming in Beijing*, Tiananmen is most likely understood as accounting for both. In *The Other Bank*, the parallels between this event where young people respond to a call for action and gather in the hope of transformation and the event in Tiananmen is only too clear and painful. Indeed, the lack of discussion of the incident in both films may imply that it is too dangerous to mention and effectively communicates the conditions producing the mood of the interviewees and the documentary itself. Of course, neither film has ever been broadcast in its entirety in China. *Bumming in Beijing* provoked the same excited response that the feature film *Yellow Earth* (1984) did when it screened in Hong Kong in 1985.[21] Bérénice Reynaud speaks of "the feeling that a new chapter of the history of representation was being written in front of my eyes."[22] Lu Xinyu, author of *The New Documentary Movement in China*, also traces the first manifestations of that "movement" to this film.[23]

Newer generations of independent documentarians have been inspired to start making films by seeing earlier documentaries such as these, not on television but in clubs and at college screenings. With the availability of small digital video cameras since the late 1990s, training in professional television or access to television station equipment is no longer so necessary to start making documentaries, and the practice has both mushroomed and diversified. If videos such as *Bumming in Beijing* and *The Other Bank* were on topics very close to the urban and middle-class home territory of the filmmakers, more recent films have moved toward both the geographic and social margins of the People's Republic.

For example, Tibet has been a consistent site for independent documentary on the geographic margins. Since the mid-1980s, Tibet has functioned as an inspiration for alienated artists and intellectuals in China—a place for them to drop out and get in touch with themselves, perhaps. Duan Jinchuan established his reputation with a trilogy of films about Tibet. One of these, *No. 16 Barkhor Street South (Bakuo Nan Jie 16 Hao)*, won the first major international prize for a Chinese documentary, the Grand Prix at the Cinéma du Réel festival in Paris in 1997. The title refers to the address of a local government office and police station on the octagonal road in central Lhasa, where pilgrims come to circumambulate and occasional anti-Chinese protests have been held. The film observes activities in the offices. Other films based in Tibet and neighboring Qinghai Province have included many videos on Tibetan religion and culture by Wen Pulin, a Beijing-based and trained Manchu videomaker and author devoted to Tibet. Similarly, Ji Dan and her partner Sha Qing have spent many years off the beaten track in Tibet documenting traditional life there. Her videos include *Gongbo's Happy Life (Gongbu de Xingfu Shenghuo,* 1999), which shows that being without the conveniences of modernity does not preclude contentment. Together, they also made *The Elders (Laorenmen)* in 1999, another film about traditional village life.

Other documentaries have covered a huge range of the otherwise invisible dwellers on China's social margins. In 1997, Li Hong from CCTV completed a film called *Out of Phoenix Village (Hui Dao Fenghuang Qiao)* about the young women who come up from Anhui to work as maids in Beijing. Living with them in a cold and cramped shack, she captured conditions that are all the more shocking to the middle classes when the women proclaim their time in Beijing as the best years of their lives. Internal migration is a major feature of China's recent social and economic transformation. Other films on this topic include Zhou Hao's *Houjie Township (Houjie,* 2002) Wu Wenguang's *Dance with Farmers (He Mingong Yiqi Tiaowu,* 2001), Ning Ying's *Railroad of Hope (Xiwang zhi Lü,* 2001), and Du Haibin's *Under the Skyscraper (Gaolou Xiaomian,* 2002). Du previously filmed the even more marginalized homeless scavengers who live *Along the Railway (Tielu Yanxian,* 2001).

Since then, he has joined other filmmakers working another popular theme, the LGBTQ community, by making *Beautiful Men* about drag queens *(Ren Mian Taohua,* 2005).[24] Other films in this vein include various films by Cui Zi'en, an experimental filmmaker whose works combine elements ranging from science fiction to on-the-spot documentary. Two of his films with the highest amount of documentary footage, *Feeding Boys, Ayaya* (*Aiyaya, Qu Buru*, 2003) and *Night Scene* (*Ye Jing*, 2003), are set among Beijing's male sex workers.[25] In 2001, Echo Y Windy (Ying Weiwei) made a documentary about a lesbian couple. Because their apartment was the only place where they could really function as a couple, it was called *The Box* (*Hezi*). Other overlooked groups included in documentary include the elderly in Lina Yang (Yang Tianyi)'s video *Old Men* (*Lao Tou*, 1999), which focuses on the lives of the old men in her neighborhood, and Beijing's drugs and rock music scene in Zhao Liang's *Paper Airplane* (*Zhi Feiji*, 2000).

The rhetoric and style of independent documentary is in the same on-the-spot spontaneous mode as its television counterpart. However, it varies in one significant way. The new television documentary still uses a lot of narration from the reporter, but this is more rare in the new documentary. Many of these films eschew all forms of narration, for example Duan Jinchuan's Tibet trilogy and Wu Wenguang's films. Others, like Li Hong's *Out of Phoenix Bridge*, reduce the narration to a scene-setting minimum. The inspiration for this is the tradition of observational documentary, which had a huge impact on Wu Wenguang and Duan Jinchuan. While Duan followed the American mode of fly-on-the-wall direct cinema, Wu's films have been more in the Jean Rouche mode of *cinéma vérité*, in which the filmmaker interacts with his or her subjects even though the films include no narration.[26] Although strict observational filmmaking is on the decline and more narration appears today, it is still rarer than on television.

This independent mode is therefore more open than the new television documentaries. Absence of direct address means that different viewers will make quite different decisions about what they think the topics of the documentaries are, never mind what they think the filmmaker's "message" is. This has an obvious utility in the political environment of the People's Republic, making it difficult for the authorities to claim that the films definitely constitute social critique. In regard to questions of audience, the frequent focus on what would be understood as social issues and the construction of the geographic and social margins of the People's Republic in the films assumes the perspective of an urban, middle-class, and educated public, or what in Chinese might be called "intellectuals" (*zhishifenzi*). The absence of address also means that this public is assumed to be critically active when it comes to interpretation and also diverse, in contrast to the "masses" of the socialist realist documentary. The public spaces produced by both television and independent documentary are clearly very different kinds of electronic elsewheres from the national classroom of the past, but do they constitute public spheres or civil society?

A Chinese Civil Society? A Chinese Public Sphere?

As discussed previously, a common characteristic linking both the television and independent forms of the *jishizhuyi* spontaneous documentary is a rhetorical stance of autonomy from the state. This has created great excitement among the public and intellectuals inside and outside China, because this kind of actuality material was unknown during the socialist heyday when the media was a mouthpiece of the Party–state apparatus. As such, the new documentary joins a host of other economic, social, and cultural phenomena that have sprung up with the rollback of the state in the People's Republic after Deng Xiaoping's rise to power in 1979. What concepts are appropriate to understand the spaces produced by these electronic elsewheres?

Scholars and commentators alike have turned repeatedly to the social model that celebrates the separation of state and society—liberal capital-ist democracy—in their search for appropriate concepts. "Civil society," "the public sphere," and "freedom of the press" are all invoked frequently in discussions of general social change and transformation of the media and culture. However historically circumscribed they may have been in their original delineation, what the contemporary invocation of these concepts shares is an opposition between state and society, whereby freedom is believed to prosper as the separation between the two grows and the role of the state is minimized. A comprehensive description of the debates around these ideas and their application in a Chinese context is impossible within the space constraints of this chapter. But a sense of their breadth and complexity can be gleaned from He Baogang's summary of the discussions around civil society alone:

> The conceptualization of civil society is diverse and complex in Chinese studies. So far, five major competing models have been employed; namely the Gramscian model (Thomas Gold, Barret McCormick, Timothy Cheek, and Sarah Pfizner), the Kantian model (Madsen, 1993), the Habermasian model (David Strand, William Rowe, and Craig Calhoun), the Communi-tarian model (Chamberlain, 1993) and the Rousseauvian model (Lawrence Sullivan, 1990).[27]

However, three main positions have developed across these debates. Some believe that China is moving in the direction of these various models, others disagree, and a third group argues that China is too different for the application of these foreign ideas. It is important to note that there is no chronological progression from the first to the third of these positions. Indeed, as Timothy Brook and Michael B. Frolic note, initial interest in the application of these concepts in the Chinese context accelerated rapidly in a skeptical mode post-1989.[28] Prior to the 1989 Tiananmen Square massacre of students and workers demonstrating for democracy, it had seemed that China, Eastern Europe, and the Soviet Union were all moving along the same path toward some version of liberal democracy. But the events of 1989 seemed to mark China as an "exception" that needed its own special analysis. A limited amount of earlier 1980s scholarship had focused less on the contemporary era—which then seemed relatively unproblematic—and more on the late Qing dynasty. The growth of commerce in that period roughly contemporary with the era in which Habermas located the development of the bourgeois public sphere had prompted scholars to ask if something like a Chinese bourgeois public sphere was emerging then.[29] The post-1989 boom was also stimulated by the belated 1989 publication of the English translation of Habermas's seminal 1962 work, *The Structural Transformation of the Public Sphere*.[30]

Although scholarship skeptical about the public sphere in China flourished after 1989, much commentary on the development of the Chinese media continues to assume and celebrate a movement in that direction. For example, Terence Graham's 2003 paper on Chinese television opens with the bold prediction that, "In 10 years, China's TV industry will become more like the rest of the world. It is moving from a world of control and subsidies to one of greater experimentation and freedom, where money far outweighs other considerations. The Propaganda Department of the Chinese Communist Party (CCP) might still view TV as the Party's mouthpiece, but business people are now running the 'Show.'"[31] First, Graham mistakes the United States for the "rest of the world" beyond China, assuming that all non-Chinese television is commercial. In fact, public television is still important on a global scale. Second, he equates a television system "where business people are now running the 'Show'" with "experimentation and freedom."

More modulated but along the same lines is the conclusion of former executive producer for the CCTV newsmagazine shows *Focus* and *Oriental Horizon*, Li Xiaoping. Li argues that, "Chinese television has gained much more freedom and independence," and *Focus* "helps galvanize more public debate and subsequently pressure on government to tackle the problem

. . . media plays the role of a campaigner for social justice."[32] Why are many Chinese researchers also willing to apply Western models in China? Guobin Yang notes that although this always runs the risk of inciting nationalist backlash, it can operate strategically to pressure local authorities for change.[33]

Li Xiaoping qualifies her optimism by noting the continued importance of the state. On the same basis, many others question whether separation between state and society is really occurring in China. Some believe that nothing has really changed and that "the Chinese propaganda authorities have not relinquished their control over television," as Yong Zhong puts it. In his essay on the apparent public sphere of debating contests on CCTV, he finds numerous ideological controls.[34] Studying *Focus*—the program that underpins Li Xiaoping's optimism—Alex Chan's content analysis leads him to argue that criticism is limited and subordinated to the needs of the Party and state apparatus. As a result, he believes the program is not radical but "conservative," operating as a "safety valve" only.[35]

Others believe that the Chinese context is so fundamentally different from the west that ideas like civil society cannot be usefully transferred across to China without a lot of qualification and careful reconsideration. Michael Keane's scholarship on Chinese television policy is exemplary in this regard. Keane points out that "Whereas citizens in liberal democracies seek to influence the formulation of policy by force of ideas, by interest group activities and ultimately through the ballot box. . . . Under the Chinese socialist tradition, we find . . . the balance shifts towards interpretation of policy."[36] As Keane explains, in Western societies policy is manifested and enforced as law, which is inflexible. In China, the tendency is for regulation, which is not ironclad law but subject to negotiation. In other words, Keane doubts whether anything approaching a civil society or a public sphere exists in regard to media policy formation in China. However, he also demonstrates the overall difference in the structure of the polity that does produce other areas and mechanisms empowering citizens and stakeholders in ways that models like "civil society" and "the public sphere" are blind to.

A Problem with "Freedom"

Insights such as Keane's into the inadequacies of models like civil society, the public sphere, and freedom of expression in the Chinese context are worth pursuing further. What are the implications and consequences of accepting such a model as a standard against which to measure developments in China? First, using these models assumes an East–West binarism that almost automatically perpetuates Orientalism, because they measure China against a Western standard that is assumed to be an ideal one, find it lacking, and therefore affirm Western superiority. Said notes this narcissistic feature of Orientalism: "In a quite constant way, Orientalism depends for its strategy on this flexible *positional* superiority, which puts the Westerner in a whole series of possible relationships with the Orient without ever losing him the relative upper hand."[37] Even arguments that China is too different to apply ideas like the public sphere and civil society can slide all too easily into a framework that interprets alterity as lack—as suggesting not merely that China has failed to "catch up" but that it is fundamentally incapable of doing so.

Yang Guobin has noted that "it seems [China] researchers are now careful to avoid the explicit use of the concept of public sphere. . . . Instead more value-neutral terms such as 'social space' and 'public space' are frequently used. Even where the 'public sphere' is used explicitly, its definition is loosened ."[38] Self-defensive avoidance is understandable, but does not amount to rigorous thought. We need to grasp exactly why concepts like civil society and the public sphere do not work and then adequately theorize new terms like public space to make them operable concepts—not only in China, but everywhere.

Orientalism is not the only problem with using concepts like the public sphere and civil society in a Chinese context. A second problem is that it assumes they apply anywhere, including in the West. In fact, the Habermasian bourgeois public sphere was only open to a very particular segment of the population, excluding those without property, women, people of color, those who could not read and write, and so forth.[39] Others have spoken of the formation of "counter-publics" where proletarians and others come together to organize and strategize.[40] Important though these critiques unquestionably are, they are largely reformist in spirit, implying that the notion of the public sphere itself as a zone of free discourse defined by separation from the state is still a useful concept.

A more fundamental problem lies in the concept of freedom at work here. Underlying this structure is a negative concept of power as solely oppressive and exclusively possessed by the state. Therefore, if the state is removed, power is removed, and freedom results. Of course, Habermas himself is very aware that the rise of huge corporations has undermined the public sphere as he originally conceived of it, and this seems to have been the original trigger for his research. But does this simply mean that removing corporate as well as state power will restore or produce the ideal of civil society and the public sphere?

In rethinking the concept of power as productive as well as repressive, Foucault's work has been central.[41] This idea of productiveness does not necessarily mean that power is good, but that it is active and shapes activities and conditions. If we transfer such an understanding to ideas of the public and civil society, how does this change our understanding? The famous First Amendment of the American constitution that guarantees freedom of speech might seem like a good example of the idea of power as productive and one in which the state helps to produce civil society. However, a performative paradox is at work here. On one hand, the rhetoric of "freedom" is still defined only as absence of the state, because what this amendment guarantees is that the state cannot censor speech. But on the other hand, it is state power that guarantees and maintains this power.

Furthermore, such an example does not think about power beyond the state. In other words, it does not allow that other social actors—including corporations, individuals, associations, political parties, and so forth—also exert power and produce, constrain, and shape public space and activity as well as civil society. It does not recognize that power continues to operate in the zones where unregulated speech occurs. Although state intervention may be prohibited, a host of other factors shape speech in these public spaces. These factors include agreed protocols of speech (for example, not interrupting, not speaking about personal matters, agreeing that logic has precedence in argument, and so forth), different technologies and access to them (from loudspeakers to printing presses, television stations, and Web sites), ownership and editorial control of media, and so forth. With this understanding of power as a practice of contestation and persuasion among various collective social actors, we may be closer to Gramsci's idea of hegemony.[42]

In the last paragraph, the term "public sphere" disappeared and "public space" and "public activity" took its place. The idea of the public sphere is not only inadequate to accommodate this new understanding of publicness, but its impossible ideality makes it an ideological lure rather than a concept with analytical value. If public space is theorized in contrast to the public sphere as produced by power relationships among multiple social actors and multiple in its variations, then we may have a more precise way of describing different types of public space and public activity than the either/or impossible standard of the public sphere.

Public Space, Public Television

Used in the Chinese context, such an understanding of public space also avoids the Orientalist pitfall of using a supposed Western public sphere as a gold standard against which to measure change in China. Indeed, something that immediately comes to mind is that the growing convergence of state and corporate interests is a feature of both Chinese and Western society, politics, and also media. The kind of thinking in both China and the West that automatically assumed an opposition between the state and the markets up until the 1990s no longer applies, as governments depend upon corporate funds and support just as corporations depend upon state laws and regulations. However, if we are to begin to really think about public spaces and the dispositions of power that produce and sustain them, we need a more sophisticated analysis.

In an effort to grasp what are the additional variables we need to introduce into the equation to understand the public spaces produced by electronic elsewheres, this final section returns to the independent documentary scene (*Public Space*) and documentary on state-owned television (public television) as a kind of case study. At first sight, both of these practices might seem to be evidence of an emergent public sphere in China. However, there is no possibility of apprehending either the specificity of the Chinese situation (as it differs from other countries) or the differences between these two Chinese practices of the public with such an approach. But with a public space model, we can develop a series of additional questions beyond, "state control, yes or no?"

Perhaps we can begin to get a sense of what this might mean if we try to contrast the public spaces of television documentary and independent documentary in China. The slightly different rhetorical systems of television and independent documentary have already been detailed, with the latter described as a more "open" mode because of its less pronounced use of narration. In other words, independent documentary's rhetorical protocols call upon the audience to be more active and allow for more open interpretation. But the real distinctions between the two kinds of public space are to be observed less in the rhetoric of the discourse and more in the networks of power shaping them, and the scope or range of the public spaces resulting, and the characteristics of the interactions in these spaces.

To some extent, the networks of power shaping television documentary's public space can be thought of in terms of what Media Studies usually refers to as "gatekeepers." In the Chinese case, television documentary's public space is heavily shaped by the forces of the state and the market. From conception to broadcast, all programming has to be approved by various station executives who are concerned both with avoiding offending the sensitivities of propaganda bureaus at all levels from local to national and also with maximizing ratings possibilities. These two forces operate in different directions, as the more unusual the kind of social problem or degree of corruption exposed, the higher the ratings but the more likely the censors are to be offended. As a result, producers are constantly either looking for safe but popular formats—animal documentaries, for example—or pushing the envelope. This is a distinctively Chinese situation in terms of lack of separation between Party/state and television. But in other ways, it runs parallel to the efforts of, for example, American television to juggle the demands of advertisers and the FCC.

Because independent documentaries are rarely broadcast or screened commercially, the power of the Party/state and the market are greatly minimized and they do not act as gatekeepers. In China, video work is only subject to direct censorship when it is broadcast. If it is to be screened without charge in a university class, or a cafe, the authorities may decide to intervene and close down the event for other reasons, but there is no procedure of submitting the work for approval and/or classification. In these circumstances, independents will still be aware of the need to avoid inciting state intervention—for example, by making anything that could be deemed "counter-revolutionary" or a betrayal of "state secrets." But beyond this, they can touch on topics too sensitive for television and make the films in styles unlikely to appeal to wide audiences—for example, the three-part, nine-hour epic length of Wang Bing's *West of the Tracks*. Gatekeepers are much more localized, such as those who control access to individual venues. And if a particular venue is unwilling to screen a particular film, the filmmaker can try going elsewhere. This Chinese independent documentary scene is unlike that of liberal democracies. First, it is relatively noncommercial (although this may change). Second, the general background of the Chinese political system is different, with limited legal rights or possibilities for appeal when problems do occur. And third, unlike the independent documentary system in liberal democracies, television is not an important screening outlet for most of the Chinese independent documentary makers.

The scope or range of the public spaces of television documentary and independent documentary in China are also very different. Television documentary's public spaces are constituted by the broadcasting range of individual stations. As many local stations are now picked up via satellite and made available in other parts of the country, and stations may also run webcasts, television documentary's public space may be the national or even global Chinese-speaking public. On the other hand, independent documentary circulates mostly by physical screenings in particular spaces, as mentioned above. The kinds of cafes and university classes that screen these materials are located in a relatively small number of large cities. In other words, the range of these public spaces is very tiny. In this regard, the similarities with the public spaces constituted by analogous practices in liberal democracies are considerable.

Finally, resulting from all these circumstances is a third area of important difference between the independent documentary and the television documentary public spaces. Television producers and documentary makers tell me that they get feedback from the public in the form of letters, e-mails, and telephone calls, as well as by going out to the public and talking to them in forums. Often this feedback suggests topics for future documentaries. But at best, this feedback is deferred, and most members of the audience are constituted as relatively passive viewers in this public space, with little direct input into what is made or what happens beyond the decision to switch channels. This is the same as in the liberal democracies.

On the other hand, the viewers of independent documentary meet each other in the public spaces where the documentaries are screened. In a space like a cafe or a classroom, it is assumed that they will probably not leave immediately after the screening and that they will discuss the film with each other. Furthermore, the filmmakers often travel with their films, so not only is the response collective and face-to-face, but it also is often a direct and immediate exchange with the documentarians themselves. These audiences are the cultural and intellectual young elite of China, a country where still relatively few people are able to go on to tertiary education of any kind, and it may be that their future impact will be greater than that of many other citizens. This quality of interaction in the public space of the independent documentary is much more intense than in the liberal democracies, where television remains the primary outlet for independent documentary filmmakers.

Reviewing this material, we might reach the surprising result that the independent Chinese documentary scene runs closer to the Habermasian ideal public sphere than any other documentary practice in China, or the established documentary practices in the liberal democracies. However, rather than returning to this impossible ideal, I hope that this chapter has demonstrated that the full range of public spaces and the differences constituting them can only be grasped by a multidimensional understanding of public space and the variety of forces producing it. By adopting such an approach, it may not only be possible to grasp the full range of differences distinguishing the public spaces produced by different electronic elsewheres. It may also be more possible to resist the kind of binary and ideologically invested thinking that results in the stigmatizing of one society as "free" and others as "not free," so commonly associated with the discourse around the "public sphere."

Notes

1 Bérénice Reynaud, "Cutting Edge and Missed Encounters—Digital Short Films by Three Filmmakers," *Senses of Cinema*, May 2002, http://www.sensesofcinema. com/contents/o2/20/tsai_digital.html (22 May 2002). The other two parts of the whole film are by John Akomfrah and Tsai Ming-Liang, and Reynaud discusses them here, too.

2 By "postsocialist," I mean China's specific postmodern condition, where everything new develops in the shadow of the socialist grand narrative of modernity that few believe in anymore. For further discussion, see Chris Berry, *Postsocialist Cinema in Post-Mao China: The Cultural Revolution after the Cultural Revolution* (New York: Routledge, 2004), 13–14.

3 Bill Nichols, *Introduction to Documentary* (Bloomington: Indiana University Press, 2001), 105–09.

4 On DV and the amateur aesthetic, see Yiman Wang, "The Amateur's Lightning Rod: DV Documentary in Postsocialist China," *Film Quarterly* 58, no. 4 (2005): 16–26.

5 Mao Zedong, "On the Ten Major Relationships," *Selected Works*, Volume V (Beijing: Foreign Languages Press, 1977), 306.

6 Yu Huang, "Peaceful Evolution: The case of television reform in post-Mao China," *Media, Culture & Society* 16 (1994), 217.

7 Todd Hazelbarth, *The Chinese Media: More Autonomous and Diverse—Within Limits* (CIA Center for the Study of Intelligence Monograph, September 1997), 1.

8 Li Xiaoping, *Significant Changes in the Chinese Television Industry and Their Impact in the PRC: An Insider's Perspective* (Washington DC: Working Paper of the Center for Northeast Asian Policy Studies, the Brookings Institution, August 2001). Available at Columbia International Affairs Online, http://www.ciaonet.org/ wps/lix01, downloaded 10 September 2002.

9 Ibid.

10 *Broadcasting & Cable's TV International* 7, no. 21 (1 November 1999): 5.

11 This new situation is nicely captured in the title of Zhao Bin's essay, "Mouth-piece of Money-Spinner: The Double Life of Chinese Television in the late 1990s," *International Journal of Cultural Studies* 2, no. 3: (1999): 291–305.

12 Li Xiaoping, 2001. The rather quaint English title is not my translation, but the official English title of the show.

13 Li Xiaoping, "'Focus' (*Jiaodian Fangtan*) and the Changes in the Chinese Television Industry," *Journal of Contemporary China* 11, no. 30 (2002): 22–23.

14 Alex Chan, "From Propaganda to Hegemony: *Jiaodian Fangtan* and China's Media Policy," *Journal of Contemporary China* 11, no. 30 (2002): 39. Synopses of a year's worth of programming can be found in Liang Jianzeng, ed., *Jiaodian Dang'an 2002 [Focus Cases, 2002]* (Beijing: Wenhua Yishu Chubanshe, 2002).

15 Although beyond the scope of this chapter, another new genre that has attracted attention from those interested in civil society is the talk show, which debuted in 1996 with *Tell It Like It Is (Shi Hua Shi Shuo)*, modeled on *The Oprah Winfrey Show*: Bian Yi, "Talk Shows 'Tell It as It Is'," *China Daily* (8 March 2001), http://www. chinadaily.com.cn/cndydb/2001/03/d9-1show.309.html (10 March 2001).

16 Li Xiaoping (2002), 24.

17 Lu Xinyu, *Jilü Zhongguo: Dangdai Zhongguo Xin Jilü Yundong* [Documentary China: Contemporary China's New Documentary Movement] (Beijing: Sanlian Shudian, 2003).

18 For further discussion, see Chris Berry, "Independently Chinese: Duan Jinchuan, Jiang Yue and Chinese Documentary," in *From Underground to Independent: Alternative Film Culture in Contemporary China*, ed. Paul Pickowicz and Yingjin Zhang, 109–22 (Lanham, MD: Rowman and Littlefield, 2006).

19 Wu Wenguang, "*Bumming in Beijing—The Last Dreamers*," in *The 20th Hong Kong International Film Festival*, ed. The Urban Council, (Hong Kong: The Urban Council, 1996), 130.

20 Lu Xinyu, 1–4.

21 According to Tony Rayns, the occasion, which he finds "tempting" to date as the birth of the "New Chinese Cinema," "was received with something like collective rapture"; "Chinese Vocabulary: An Introduction to *King of the Children and the New Chinese Cinema*," in *King of the Children and the new Chinese Cinema*, Chen Kaige and Tony Rayns (London: Faber and Faber, 1989), 1.

22 Bérénice Reynaud, "New Visions/New Chinas: Video—Art, Documentation, and the Chinese Modernity in Question," in *Resolutions: Contemporary Video Practices*, ed. Michael Renov and Erika Suderburg (Minneapolis: University of Minnesota Press, 1996), 235.

23 Lu Xinyu, 5.

24 For an excellent overview and analysis of the independent documentary movement, including the focus on the "other," see Bérénice Reynaud, "Dancing with Myself, Drifting with My Camera: The Emotional Vagabonds of China's

New Documentary," *Senses of Cinema* no. 28 (2003), http://www.sensesofcinema. com/contents/03/28/chinas_new_documentary/html (13 May 2004). See also Chris Berry, "Getting Real: Chinese Documentaries, Chinese Postsocialism," in Zhang Zhen, ed., *China's Urban Generation* (Durham, N.C.: Duke University Press, 2007), 115–134.

25 For an introduction to Cui's film and video works, see Chris Berry, "The Sacred, the Profane, and the Domestic: Locating the Cinema of Cui Zi'en," *Positions* 12, no. 1 (2004): 195–202.

26 For further discussion of these two modes of observational documentary, see Keith Beattie, "The Truth of the Matter: Cinema Verite and Direct Cinema," in *Documentary Screens: Nonfiction Film and Television,* 83–104 (New York: Palgrave Macmillan, 2004).

27 He Baogang, *The Democratic Implications of Civil Society in China* (New York: St. Martin's Press, 1997), 5. The works referred to are: Thomas B. Gold, "The Resurgence of Civil Society in China," *Journal of Democracy* 1, no. 1 (1990): 18–31; Barret McCormick, Su Shaozhi and Xiao Xiaoming, "The 1989 Democracy Movement: A Review of the Prospects for Civil Society in China," *Pacific Affairs* 65, no. 2 (1992): 182–201; Timothy Cheek, "From Priests to Professionals: Intellectuals and the State under the CCP," in *Popular Protest and Political Culture in Modern China,* ed. Jeffrey N. Wasserstrom and Elizabeth J. Perry, 124–45 (Boulder, Colo.: Westview Press, 1992); Sarah Pfizner, "Politics in Command: Debunking Economic Rationalism in Contemporary China. The Case of Guangdong," paper presented at 1995 APSA Conference, University of Melbourne, 28 September 1995; Richard Madsen, "The Public Sphere, Civil Society and Moral Community: A Research Agenda for Contemporary China Studies," *Modern China* 19, no. 2 (1993): 183–98; David Strand, "Protest in Beijing: Civil Society and Public Sphere in China," *Problems of Communism,* no. 39 (1990): 1–19; William T. Rowe, "The Problem of 'Civil Society' in Late Imperial China," *Modern China,* 19, no. 2 (1993): 139–57; Craig Calhoun, *Neither Gods nor Emperors: The Struggle for Democracy in China* (Berkeley: University of California Press, 1994); Heath B. Chamberlain, "On the Search for Civil Society in China," *Modern China* 19, no. 2 (1993): 199–215; and Lawrence Sullivan, "The Emergence of Civil Society in China, Spring 1989," in *The Chinese People's Movement: Perspectives on Spring 1989,* ed. Tony Saich, 129–44 (Armonk, N.Y.: M.E. Sharpe, 1990). For a discussion of the situation in China, see Ma Shu-Yun, "The Chinese Discourse on Civil Society," *China Quarterly* no. 137 (1994): 180–93, and He Baogang, "The Ideas of Civil Society in Mainland China and Taiwan," *Issues and Studies* 31, no. 6 (1995): 24–64.

28 Timothy Brook and B. Michael Frolic, "The Ambiguous Challenge of Civil Society," in *Civil Society in China,* ed. Timothy Brook and B. Michael Frolic, 3–4 (Armonk, N.Y.: M.E. Sharpe, 1997).

29 Jürgen Habermas, *The Structural Transformation of the Public Sphere: An Inquiry into a Category of Bourgeois Society,* trans. Thomas Burger (Cambridge, Mass.: MIT

Press, 1989), 14–25; William T. Rowe, *Hankow: Commerce and Society in a Chinese City, 1796–1889* (Stanford: Stanford University Press, 1984); and Mary Backus Rankin, *Elite Activism and Political Transformation in China: Zhejiang Province, 1865–1911* (Stanford: Stanford University Press, 1986). Rowe's work is focused on civil society, and Rankin uses the term "public sphere" extensively in her book.

30 For a good example of the post-1989 critique of the direct use of ideas like the public sphere and civil society in both Qing and contemporary China, see Philip C. C. Huang, "'Public Sphere'/'Civil Society' in China? The Third Realm between State and Society," *Modern China* 19, no. 2 (1993): 216–40. However, it should be noted that others, such as Richard Madsen (1993), believed that these concepts should be used to research contemporary developments in China.

31 Terence Graham, "The Future of TV in China," (Hong Kong: Telecommunications Research Project, Centre for Asian Studies, University of Hong Kong, 2003): 1. Available online at http:www.trp.hku.hk/papers/2003/tv_china_wp.pdf (8 August 2005).

32 Li Xiaoping (2002), 18, 26. See also Xu Hua, "Morality Discourse in the Marketplace: Narratives in the Chinese Television News Magazine *Oriental Horizon*," *Journalism Studies* 1, no. 4 (2000): 637–47.

33 Guobin Yang, "Civil Society in China: A Dynamic Field of Study," *China Review International* 9, no. 1 (2002): 4–5.

34 Yong Zhong, "Debating with Muzzled Mouths: A Case Analysis of How Control Works in a Chinese Television Debate Used for Educating Youths," *Media, Culture & Society* 24, no. 1 (2002): 27. See also Zhong's earlier essays, "Popular Family Television and Party Ideology: The Spring Festival Eve Happy Gathering," *Media, Culture & Society* 20, no. 1 (1998): 43–58; "Mass of Master's Medium? A Case Study of Chinese Talk Shows," *Asia Pacific Media Educator* no. 5 (1998): 92–102; and "The Other Edge of Commercialisation: Enhancing CCTV's Propaganda," *Media International Australia* no. 100 (2001): 167–80.

35 Alex Chan, "From Propaganda to Hegemony," 37.

36 Michael Keane, "Broadcasting Policy, Creative Compliance and the Myth of Civil Society in China," *Media, Culture & Society* 23, no. 6 (2001): 783. See also Michael Keane, "Civil Society, Regulatory Space and Cultural Authority in China's Television Industry," in *Television, Regulation and Civil Society in Asia*, ed. Philip Kitley, 69–187 (London: Routledge, 2003).

37 Edward Said, *Orientalism* (London: Routledge and Kegan Paul, 1978), 7.

38 Guobin Yang, 6.

39 Nancy Fraser, "Rethinking the Public Sphere: A Contribution to the Critique of Actually Existing Democracy," in *Habermas and the Public Sphere*, ed. Craig Calhoun, 109–42 (Cambridge, Mass.: MIT Press, 1992). Fraser's main focus is on gender. David Morley writes about the "the whiteness of the public sphere" in *Home Territories: Media, Mobility and Identity* (London: Routledge, 2000), 118–124.

40 Oskar Negt and Alexander Kluge, *Public Sphere and Experience: Toward an Analysis of the Bourgeois and Proletarian Public Sphere*, trans. Peter Labanyi et al. (Minneapolis: University of Minnesota Press, 1993).

41 Foucault differentiates the productive power of modernity from the repressive power of the ancien regime in Europe. He distinguishes between external forms of productive power, or disciplines, and the internalization of productive power in such forms as identity. For the former, see Michel Foucault, *Discipline and Punish: The Birth of the Prison* (Harmondsworth: Penguin Books, 1977). For the latter, see Michel Foucault, *The History of Sexuality, Volume 1: An Introduction* (Harmondsworth: Penguin Books, 1976).

42 This concept is elaborated at various points through his *Selections from the Prison Notebooks* (London: Lawrence and Wishart, 1971). A detailed analysis is provided by Carl Cuneo, "Hegemony in Gramsci's Original Prison Notebooks," http://socserv2.mcmaster.ca/soc/courses/soc2r3/gramsci/gramheg.htm, downloaded 6 August 2006.

Ratiba Hadj-Moussa

6

The Undecidable and the Irreversible:

Satellite Television in the Algerian Public Arena

The introduction of new communication technologies in nondemocratic societies poses an interesting problem to those scholars who want to understand their significance for and effect in public life. In practice, not only are the media foundational to the emergence of the nation–state,[1] but they are also the pillars of democratic expression. How are these new public forms situated in nondemocratic or authoritarian societies, such as Maghrebian societies, or where people have lived in the tatters of civil war, as in Algerian society?

In this chapter, I will limit my focus to satellite television, disregarding other forms of communication, such as the Internet, that are spreading despite the logics of containment at work in all the countries of the Maghreb. I also limit my analysis to a few sites in public space, particularly to those incorporated into the everyday practices of social actors and situated in horizontal forms of sociability, such as the family, the house and the neighborhood.[2] Although it is necessary to understand the vertical mechanisms generated by the state that lead to the acceptance of satellite television, it is also important to examine how these technologies are adopted and reconfigured by men and women, the public actors who decide what is at stake in these technologies.

I am interested in understanding how satellite television transforms public and domestic life, assuming that it is located at the junction of the two. How does it express the social positions of men and women, not only in domestic space but also in the neighborhood and other shared contexts? How does it allow for the expression of singularity and individuality? And finally, how do viewers' practices generated by satellite television displace the notion of the political?

These questions are predicated on particular conceptions of public space and politics. I draw on Jocelyne Dakhlia's and Hamadi Redissi's work, in which both authors examine the existence of the political and the mediation of the public space in the Islamic world (from the eighth to thirteenth centuries in the Middle East and North Africa), demystifying the relation between religion and politics in Islamic societies.[3] As a counterpoint to this, Catherine Neveu offers new ways of thinking about the political in contemporary France, in which, although the political appears disconnected from marginalized segments of that society, they in fact rearticulate it in novel ways.[4]

In addition to the previously mentioned case specific to democratic France, several studies that are devoted to Arab and/or Muslim countries take as examples the same social actors, the poor among the poor, in the urban neighborhoods of Cairo, Tehran, or more recently in various Muslim countries.[5] These works question the predominance of the notion of representation in politics and the participation of excluded social actors in politics. They also emphasize new forms of participation that do not necessarily follow established formulas and are defined and experienced in different social and political contexts. Philippe Lucas replaces the notion of civil society with that of "civil stakes" that mediate the relations between society and political society. The excluded may not be part of "civil society," but what remains crucial are the issues and stakes that refer to the "becoming civil" in which the State does not have a dominant role.[6]

In considering what is at stake regarding the struggle for public space, it is important to briefly investigate the notion of public space. Who can make a space public? Anne Querrien argues that the formation of public space is processual. Public space is not a preformed space and is not constituted on the basis of agreement as the theory of representation claims. She uses the term *raccord* to describe the particular way she understands public space to be constituted. Public space consists of articulating practices of "self-affirmation" in the social field, which are emerging. Also, a public space is prefigured each time actors produce collective practices, and form what Querrien calls "a minimal public space."[7] The latter takes into account the manner in which a collective addresses precarious social or political conditions. Querrien's approach best approximates my own perspective, which attempts to displace the dominant terms that define public space. Moreover, this approach refers to experiences that permit us to consider the practices produced by satellite television as at least a minimal public space. Indeed, viewing practices established on the basis of connections between different locations (home, neighborhood, cafes, stores, *hammam*), and between different media (radio, print press, national television) are competing with other dominant practices.

These approaches, which refashion dominant notions of politics and public space into more inclusive models, allow us to reflect on phenomena that are situated at the margins of (but are not marginal to) politics that serve to challenge public institutions.

They also allow us to formulate the "mass of viewers" differently. What do these viewers represent? How does a *weak* mediation (that is, a mediation through television) pose crucial questions about modes of being viewers, including those who do not have satellite television? How can "isolated" practices within the home interact with relations of sociability outside it? How can these relations of sociability facilitate a self-reflection that disrupts the order of the acceptable, especially within gender relations?

I respond to these questions by briefly describing the context and the conditions under which satellite television appeared in the audiovisual landscape of Algeria. I then examine the stake raised by the technology while linking it to other dimensions of the social and political field. In particular, I discuss how social entities such as the family and the neighborhood (*houma*), which are not usually seen as political, can affect the ways in which Algerian society is organized politically and socially. I will show how the family is mediating public and domestic space through the uses of satellite television. In doing so, my analysis of the family introduces certain shifts in rearticulating it to the political. The *houma* and the family are constantly interacting, and this interaction is affected by the redefinitions generated by the new media—in particular, real and symbolic spaces related to gender.

El Houbel Meets the Dish: Elements of Context

At the beginning of the 1980s, an American-type shopping mall, a part of the architectural ensemble of the Park of Victory (*Ryad el Feth*), still unique in its style, was built in the neighborhood of East Algiers, as an early but nonetheless visible sign of the passage from "specific socialism"[8] to the market economy. Contraband products (or *trabendo* in Algerian dialect) from Europe mixed with local ones, juxtaposed with cinemas and cafes unaffordable to children from the surrounding neighborhoods. This

ensemble has a monument dedicated to the martyrs of the war of liberation with an immense sculpture in the shape of three leaves, symbolizing
the three revolutions (agrarian, industrial, and cultural), and representing
the achievements of an independent Algeria. In keeping with their famous
biting humor, the neighborhood children renamed the three branches
of the sculpture *el Houbel*, referring to pre-Islamic idols.[9] My choice of *el
Houbel*, as an example of modern Algeria, is not neutral. Indeed, the first
satellite dish made its appearance in The Park of Victory. The chairman of
the park, a military officer, introduced the *parabole* (dish) that was eventually adopted by the majority of Algerians.[10] The coastal Algerian population had used regular antennas to illegally "pull in" European programs in
good weather since the early 1980s, but the first dish still jarred Algeria's
audiovisual landscape. There was no law that sanctioned its use. A law
passed in 1990 permits the privatization of audiovisual communication,
but no operator has ever received authorization to broadcast programs
in Algerian territory. As a result, the private sector has no choice but to
broadcast from abroad using satellites.[11]

During the same decade the International Monetary Fund (IMF) and
the World Bank dictated a regime of progressive liberalization in Algeria.
The contradictions of this liberalization translated into the events of
October 1988, one of the largest popular uprisings Algeria has known
since its independence in 1962. The first agenda of economic liberalization
already announced by the Park of Victory was accelerated, and political
measures advocating a "democratic opening" were put into place by the
government. To make concrete this "democratic opening," the right to
form associations and parties, and the freedom of the written press were
implemented by the Constitution of 1989. The reasons for this economic
liberalization are complex. Simultaneously, endogenous and exogenous,
they explain the advent of the "dish."[12] But the dish remained limited to
a few privileged nomenklatura until the end of the 1980s. It then became
popular very quickly, and extended beyond Algerian representatives of
the regime, becoming a central piece in a struggle between social forces,
among them the Islamists.

Passages . . .

I will now examine how the "minimal public space" related to satellite
television is shaped in the context of Algeria. I have shown elsewhere
(Hadj-Moussa, 1996, 2003) how the introduction of satellite television is
conditioned by three key elements: the State, the opposition (notably the

Islamists), and the television spectators who may or may not have adopted satellite television.

First, since its inception, the State has made the only state-controlled national channel its own instrument. Political debates were nonexistent, and the news programs were a vehicle for State propaganda until the events of October 1988. With the "democratic opening," television became the medium through which the majority of Algerians could be reached.

Second, television was coveted by the Islamists, who understood its importance for their movement. Several works on Arab and Muslim countries have shown that the Islamists have used older forms of media, such as booklets and written media,[13] as well as new media such as audiovisual and electronic forms of communication, to enhance their ability to persuade their compatriots in authoritarian regimes.[14] The Islamists in Algeria did not stop there—they also knew how to use satellite channels. As Mustapha Al Ahnaf et al.[15] contend, for Islamists, information, like education, lies at the heart of the struggle for public space. Their project is traversed by great contradictions and it uses satellite television in very conflicting ways. They attack the dish in their preaching, as was reported to me by my research participants, but they were still the first to take advantage of it. The struggle for public space became more intense when the Islamist political party was banned in 1992, and its religious associations were forced to work underground after the military stopped the legislative election in 1992. The struggle over public space was radicalized, and two important signs emerged: the satellite dish and the mosque.

Finally, having understood that satellite television offered more appealing programs, television spectators adopted a position in regard to television watching that denies the legitimacy of national television programming and State power. Algerian national television experienced its "democratic opening" in the late 1980s. Political programs of a new type were aired, in which political opponents were invited to express their views. Between 1988 and 1992, the national channel echoed the debates among Algerians on taboo subjects, such as corruption and bad administration, which were silenced not long ago. At the same time, the Algerian geopolitical space was enlarged through the interweaving of national and international media. Thanks to the French channels, Algerians were able to see their exiled opposition leaders for the first time. Disgusted by the media silence about their everyday life, Algerians have turned in massive numbers to satellite television programming, thirsty not only for political information—which they certainly crave[16]—but also for sports, films, and children's shows. For them, satellite television represents "an alternative" to national television.

By introducing incremental change into Algerians' daily lives, satellite television has prompted new behaviors and ways of being among Algerian viewers. Many observers of Algerian society have noticed the political enthusiasm generated by the development of associations following the events of October 1988 and the subsequent "democratic opening." However, few have highlighted television spectators' self-affirmative practices within the informal "associations" created by satellite television viewers. I have already described how the emergence of satellite television produced an autonomous grassroots mode of organization.[17] Certainly, these informal associations were motivated by television viewers' desire to watch programs other than those of the national channel and to escape a difficult everyday life, but they also generate new practices that, although not recognized officially, nevertheless structure life in the local neighborhood. For example, in the first decade of satellite television, most of the dishes were managed collectively. In some neighborhoods, up to 200 families teamed up to acquire a satellite dish. They also discussed regularly the channels that they wished to add to the initial package offered by satellite connections. The novelty of these informal collective organizations should be seen as an indication of change and "as an appropriation of culture resources arising from the broader struggle for the social control of historicity."[18]

In the process of acquiring a satellite dish, the initial decision is, in my opinion, the most important moment. It presupposes that viewers have already negotiated the introduction of the satellite dish into their home, warding off the "dangers" to "tradition" brought by the dish. In addition to raising moral issues, satellite dishes highlight the divisions between classes, genders, and rural and urban spaces. In effect, the choice of the dish, and subsequently the extra channels, appears more difficult in rural than in urban areas.

As Djamel, a research participant, explains, the difference between rural and urban areas is that most urbanites have "traveled and know Europe," but for residents of smaller interior cities "this is not the case for everyone." He omits to mention that those urbanites who "know Europe" are mostly executives or members of middle-class liberal professions. For example, the channel Arte, a French–German channel that focuses on art and culture and offers good quality programming, is more or less unknown in both the peripheral cities and the suburbs of the big cities. Antar, a research participant, who lives outside the capital and is renowned for his cultural achievements, told me that, "you would have to move heaven and earth to have *Arte* selected. I was the only one who wanted *Arte* [in my neighborhood]. We discussed it for a long time. I had to comply with the choice of the majority. The rest [of the channels] were French channels and MBC for the women."[19]

As indicated by Antar, from the outset, with the decision about having a satellite dish, the "question" of women's viewing is salient for male viewers, because "Algerian women" tend to prefer the "Arab serials" and the *telenovelas* aired on Arab channels like MBC, Orbit, ART, EDTV (Emirates Dubai Television), and MBC, judged by viewers as "unthreatening to tradition." Women may not participate directly in collective discussions about the dish, but they still have a role, because the choice of Arab satellite channels is fundamentally, although not exclusively, justified by the existence of a female audience.

Although these collective practices generated by the acquisition of the dish are not performed under established political motifs, they nonetheless produce a chronotope and new networks of information beyond the control of the State. The existence of these networks poses theoretical problems that exceed the scope of this chapter, like the observation of the growing dissociation between State and society. But here this dissociation demands that we understand how parallel networks of communication, animated by national and supranational communication technologies, interact through experience.

The process of constituting television audiences is never politically neutral. It becomes even more charged politically when it includes gender and generational differences. Two principal social sites give the contours of this process, at the least at the micro level: the family and the neighborhood (*Houma*), including cafes, street corners, men's boutiques, public baths, and women's hair salons. The *houma* is vital to urban life. Omar Carlier, in his influential book on the sociopolitical history of colonial Algeria, indicates its importance.[20] As a "central unified point of reference," the *houma* was a centralized space in which a national Algerian consciousness emerged.[21] Today it remains an important political enclave. The significance of the *houma* has been strategically identified by Islamists, whose activities spread from another central social space: the mosque. The latter has become a space of refuge and compensation for the "multidimensional frustration" of youth (above all men, but also women) excluded at all levels (mainly from work and housing), and unable to start a family. Carlier explains the resurgence in the 1980s of the mosque this way:

> The stadium has lost its function of regulating the energy of the youth, the cinema has lost its power of escapism and of transferring dreams, the political area and unions have not preserved their function of the seventies, much less the vitality of the thirties and forties. The mosque, on the other hand, has once again found its central role in the conflict of society, but the sacred space, if it is old and authentic, acquires a logistic and strategic dimension without historical precedent.[22]

The public spaces that constitute the *houma* are places *par excellence* for the deployment of masculinity. Here, affiliations involving the symbolic carving up of territory, possessions, and people, are both made and undone. It is also here that with a sense of mission, men, notably young unemployed men, populate the streets night and day, gauge the arrival of "strangers," and prevent them from "invading" their *houma*. The space of the *houma* is increasingly infused with emerging financial and commercial practices, such as *trabendo* and the "D system."[23] Satellite television has reconfigured the space of the *houma*, which has been an almost exclusive place for men, especially young men. It has isolated them, detaching them from their peer groups and redirecting them toward the interior of their homes, where they spend more and more time watching television. Although these activities may have been encouraged by the state of siege that lasted until 1998 in the *willayas* (administrative units) of Central Algeria, satellite television cannot be ignored as a powerful attraction for young Algerian men.

This movement toward the home—the traditional place of women—and the presence of television in the *houma* provoke critical debate among viewers. This new forum is at the junction of what the readers/viewers learned from the Algerian press (where the rate of readership is very high[24]), hearsay, and satellite television. It is also at this junction that one uncovers the hidden side of the regime that, in one participant's words only "shows what it wants."

What happens inside the houses? How do women position themselves with the arrival of the satellite dish? How do they occupy physical space? To answer these questions, we must examine how men and women (re) define their place in the family and in the *houma*.

Like the *houma*, the family plays a mediating role between domestic and public spaces. It links the *houma* with satellite television, not only in discussions between men, but also in the diverse exchanges between women in the public bath, the hair salon, and even at school. The *houma* and the family are thus not separate entities. They are both affected by what I argue is a new and important change: the incursion of men into women's space. The explanations for this incursion cannot be limited to satellite television, but must also extend to structural transformations in the family and Algerian society more generally. First caused by colonization, these transformations showed the disintegration of the relationship between rural communities and their lands, which primarily defines the group's identity.[25] During the post independence period, modernization and the wholesale entry of the first generations of girls into the school system defused the authority of the father to the benefit of state institutions.[26] For the first time, an intruder, in the form of the (Algerian) state, was competing with fathers in family issues. Demographic evidence shows how certain indicators, such as "the free choice of marriage on the basis of chance meeting"[27] or later first marriages for men and women,[28] have become entrenched in social life. Despite these transformations and the retreat of the state during recent crises, the family still occupies the role of mediator.

Classical and contemporary political theorists have not usually considered the role played by the family in the formation of civil society in Western societies. The family is considered to be insulated from public space. Although many scholars are now recognizing the role of the family in the development of civic virtues, such as the socialization and shaping of good citizens, and thus recognizing its impact on the foundation of the polity, they feel the family still has to guarantee the principle of equality of all its members.[29] Indeed, in many instances, the family has to address the lack of equality among its members. This issue seems even more pressing for families and women who do not live in "modern democratic" societies.[30] Theories that describe the formal conditions in which politics and public space are formed thus exclude the family as both historical fact and one of these constitutive conditions. Therefore, they cannot adequately account for situations that break down and challenge these exclusions. In the Algerian case, the family mediates the introduction of the dish as *an object*, and also negotiates it in political terms. People who own the dish say that they "bring in" satellite television. The research participants never used this expression for Algerian terrestrial television. What meaning is given to this expression? To answer this question, I will return to my reflections on the exclusion and mediating position of the family as welfare system.

"Bringing in the dish" refers to the social, rather than monetary, price paid by the family installing the "dish." The negotiations among the viewers about the acquisition of the dish are multiple. They exceed the family circle when the choice of owning a dish is made collectively, and they are internal to the family when the choice is made either collectively or individually. To monetary considerations are added discussions in each family regarding the "consequences" of the choice of the "dish" on the family. In effect, the introduction of the "dish" is not easy, because it requires the reformulation and the adjustment of family viewing and normative practices. The retreat of men into the houses, which challenges the sexual division of space, is translated into multiple strategies. Hence, adjustments and agreements are made in the family regarding watching satellite programs so that "customs and tradition" are not unsettled. These "customs" are based on the codification of people's behaviors according to sex, generation, and the set of rules of modesty that sanction collective and individual viewing for women and children. The popular expression used by Algerians to describe the "immoral" images brought by satellite television is "the scenes." "The scenes" of kissing, nude bodies, underwear, and making love are condemned by the majority of the viewers and are strictly avoided by the family. In the context of the family, some people only watch Algerian television, following the dictates of "custom and tradition." Those who have only one television set often choose to implicitly schedule viewing for women and men according to men's availability; that is, the time they are back at home and wish to relax. Those viewers who are well off and have more space often own several televisions. In more liberal families, satellite programming is sometimes watched together, but the most common practice is to watch the same program separately because there is always a danger of an unpredictable image. In some cases, men of the same generation even refuse to watch television in the presence of younger or older siblings, because they may become embarrassed by a kiss or a commercial for underwear.

Watching television becomes an issue about how to view the body. When forbidden physical contacts or "scenes" are inadvertently watched, some of the viewers subsequently perform ablutions to purify themselves of these "satanic images."

In this culture, where bodily and sexual relations must be secluded from the public gaze, the limits imposed on television target specifically women and children.

If the house is small, a certain violence is exercised. For example, one participant reminisced about her sister, divorced and living with her son, who vacated her only room to spend the evenings in the courtyard so that her son could watch satellite programming. This self-exclusion is less common than the eviction of women from the television room. When women are forced to leave their place at the television when men come in, they often use "tricks."[31] Women will gather in large groups in the room with the television so that the male "intruders" are discouraged, or at least made to feel guilty for entering female space. This tactic draws on customary notions of the sexual separation of space and *el h'ya*, the modesty men and women must show toward each other. Hence, norms of decency are closely allied to a soft version of the authority that men sometimes exercise over women, especially as regards the time allocated to television viewing. Thus, women watch television until mid-evening, and they are followed by men, in general by the younger men in the family.

However, in relation to watching satellite programs, the demonstration of modesty is not systematic and is accompanied and counterbalanced with heterodox phenomena that affect the sacredness[32] of the house and the relations between generations. When I asked Nassim, a twenty-three-year-old man, if it disturbs him that his father knows that he watches erotic films, he replied "Personally, I know that my dad knows that I watch them. He knows . . . There was a period when my dad left the room even though I did not have the desire to watch [them]."

Notions of what is socially acceptable, informed by modesty, are modified by an unspoken knowledge of sex and the body whose opacity allows practices that counterbalance customary relations between father and son, and mother and son, and the deference and respect that the younger must show to the older. As the unacceptable—watching an erotic film in the house—is actualized by young men, a new normativity is emerging. Throughout my fieldwork, the reference to erotic films has underlain research participants' reservations about satellite television. More than certain "scenes," these films totally depart from the rules. It was said that a number of family dramas had occurred because of the negative impact of foreign (that is, Western) programs. Sexuality and eroticism should not be banned—some women acknowledged that they have watched these films with their husbands and benefited from them, and Islam celebrates sexual pleasure—but at the same time, sexuality and eroticism should not appear in public and must remain within the confines of marriage. The advent of satellite television images within the sacred space of the family raises several questions, because of these contradictions surrounding the relationships to the body, as well as the types of interpersonal relations occurring between the family members. The latter are in fact unprecedented. The knowledge that family members have about what is viewed is at the same time deliberately erased and, therefore, not processed.

The Undecidable and the Irreversible

Within the new social situation, young men's dominance is affirmed: new practices are introduced within the walls of the home that were *unimaginable* until quite recently, and larger relations of authority are put into question. Women, and in particular young women, are subjected to prohibitions on viewing. The prescriptions and practices of conformity that women have to respect are not confined to the anthropological, if we mean by this elements that explain *a culture* (by definition "traditional" as Algerian culture could be seen!). These practices also have a political meaning in the sense that public display of sexuality means rendering visible what was hidden from view and allowing it to be acted upon, in other words, to be made public. The dominant mise-en-scene of the body and sexuality, which locates women in the shadow, frames their presence in the public space as well as the domestic space. Thanks to television, among other things, these two spaces are being brought together. Changes in gender and generational relations are what appear to be fundamentally at stake in the introduction of satellite television in Algeria.

The important economic role played by women to sustain the family's welfare puts into question theoretical approaches that render women absent in public space. This role is reframed by women's position in "culture" and political culture, which expresses the condition that shapes public space. What is observed in the house in regard to viewing practices and beyond communicates the way in which women are positioned politically.

In order to discuss this connection, I will examine the problem posed by the politics of language in Algeria, and then link it with satellite television and public space. The task is to understand how the languages of selected channels or satellites (French and Arabic) coincide with state politics that designate women as the "guardians of immutable Arab–Muslim values," according to the official expression popular in Algeria since Algerian independence.

According to certain authors, one of the reasons for the rise of terror in Algeria was the support of Arabist cohorts frustrated by their exclusion from the system of production.[33] Embracing the strand of Islamist thought popular in the 1980s and early 1990s was a way of accessing the benefits then exclusively available to high position francophones in the public administration. For many Western media, the corresponding linguistic division became the cliché explaining the Algerian civil war. However, in regard to satellite channels, this linguistic division is not amongst men, but *between men and women*. The majority of interviewed young men—Arabophones between 18 and 25 years of age who understood French, but had not mastered it—preferred that their female family members, especially their sisters, do not watch Western (essentially French) satellite channels. These men preferred their sisters to watch Arabic channels, such as El Arabia, Abu Dhabi, and MBC, to spare themselves the embarrassment of being exposed to "dangers imported" by Western television stations. However, these young men were not drawn to the Arab satellite channels themselves, except to watch the news and sports, because— although more sophisticated and better financed—they resemble too closely the Algerian channel.

The Algerian channel broadcasts soap operas, *telenovelas*, and musical programming that "attracts women." Why do women watch Arabic channels and conform to what is expected of them or, perhaps more importantly, why do men educated in Arabic turn to Western programming? To be sure, women like the Arab channels and programs, but they also like French channels that inspire a sense of fashion and home décor. Yet, the fact that women are attracted to Arab channels seems to reassert social conformity. Symbolic violence is inscribed not only in the normative structure but is also embodied by the women themselves. "After all, we are Arabs," young Naima said to me. However, this violence does not explain the conformity to the norms and it is sometimes subverted, as I will show later.

As opposed to women, young men prefer Western channels, although since the second Palestinian Intifadha, they also watch more and more Arabic channels such as El Djazeera and El Arabia. I contend that young men still do not prefer Arab channels, because, as one participant explains it, "[t]hey are uninterested in films spoken in classical Arabic or Egyptian [a term used to designate all Middle-Eastern languages]. These men are horrified by Egyptian serials, more so than women who stay at home." When I reminded the participant that the youths are educated in Arabic, he added, "that doesn't mean anything. The street was stronger [*la rue était plus forte*]. It is true that they [Arab channels] have an audience and fans, [but] they are not as important as the French channels. Even the power relations are not the same, and the influence is not the same. The proof: [The Islamists] have done everything to cut the umbilical relation between Algeria and the West—they tried to cut the satellite antennae during the terror—but you see, the people keep them collectively and individually."

This participant had reason to emphasize the influence that makes certain masculine spectators feel obliged to watch "with a dictionary in hand to learn the French language [even] when the program was useless."

I have noted that Algerian women and men criticize the censorship of national television programming, the lack of means and the paucity of its programs, its ideological orientations and above all, its failure to show the reality of Algerian everyday life. Satellite television brings another culture and transmits knowledge *through the French language,* the most commonly spoken foreign language in Algeria.

On one hand, French satellite channels can be seen as a block of *masculine* television, open to the world, to science and knowledge. This television stimulates the spirit of critique and reflection as suggested by participants: "The children pose good questions, questions to reflect on." Television spectators also use it to compare their political situation with democratic countries such as France or England. Furthermore, the problems created by the "scenes" are compensated for by the debate and polemics, not to mention the entertainment. Satellite television constitutes the crossroads where different forms of liberty are expressed, freedom of expression and freedom to inform.[34] On the other hand, in watching Arab channels, women are mainly limited to the terrain of the already known and seen. They allow the fiction of Arabness to function because they are assigned the role of guardian of the threshold. In this sense, the division of the channels by language coincides with an essential element of political discourse in Algeria on women, for which they represent and embody the "profound values" and the essence of Algeria. The inclusion of women in the project of modernization, and their presence in the streets, schools, and factories, are articulated by the implicit and latent opposition between the fathers and the state.[35]

With satellite television, the frontier between the collective and the domestic becomes even more blurred. Satellite television reconfigures the house so that the structure defining the major relations in the society is the least affected. Practices of containment around women's viewing and the appropriation of the television and its accessories, like the remote control and the menu, become more pronounced. This containment, practiced by male Arabic and French-speaking television viewers, *concurs with the prohibitions advocated by the Islamists.* Indeed, the different social discourses converge when it comes to women. What is at stake in this convergence is the participation of women in public space. If women represent immutable values, how can they be a vehicle for the changes in public space? The dynamic of viewing put into play by satellite television touches all social discourses. A recent survey of primary school male teachers showed that they are very critical about the attacks on individual freedoms and human rights, but remain "laconic" about the rights of women.[36] Satellite television produces practices that maintain intertextual relations with other social realities such as political discourses. What is at stake is less the instrumentalization of language than the position of women and the emergence of a singular voice in public space.

One could object that my argument about the consequences of languages for making the public needs to be more nuanced considering certain channels like el Djazeera. El Djazeera is, in my opinion, the exception that confirms the rule. Arab populations encountered el Djazeera well before the events of 11 September 2001. The freedom that characterizes the channel is surprising for an Arab channel that was supported by an oil monarchy, Qatar. El Djazeera is the only Arab channel classified as "independent"; all others are "private" or "public."[37] Without "danger" for family or collective viewing, it can be watched by men and women, yet it is primarily men who watch it. El Djazeera is watched publicly in cafes and electronics stores. It is watched for politics and for the debates and polemics that are considered taboo in the Arab world, such as inviting members of the political opposition or dissidents to appear and speak. With the example of el Djazeera, the line that is formed between men and women is political.

Is this to say that women are forever confined by the limits imposed by the social structure? Are there other elements that complicate this interpretation? First, women are not categorically barred from watching all European satellite programming. In addition, as other authors have shown, the medium—itself an object of modernity—presupposes a knowledgeable audience, all the more so because it opens the community to other realities.[38] In his research on the transformation of Belcourt, a neighborhood in the east end of Algiers known for its Islamist allegiances, Shams Benghribil points to the new phenomenon of young girls called "papichettes,"[39] who adopt styles of dress and behavior from television which defy all expectation. He writes that "[t]he cultural universe of this generation (16–25) is marked by the advent of the dish at the end of the 1980s."[40]

For women, television is "the window on the world," and also a social opening; they "go to great lengths to watch satellite television. They . . . gather penny after penny. They are not indifferent to what is being said or who says it" (Lilia, age 42). "They turn it on [the television] and see things, people who think" (Hakima, age 46). In addition to this opening, the Lebanese, Egyptian, Mexican, and Brazilian series broadcast daily on national television and satellite tackle subjects that are not discussed in the public arena. Abortion, incest, illegitimate children, and unmarried couples are not subjects to which women are "indifferent." However, women were most sensitive to the subjects, such as love and individualization, that single them out, and which most undermine the social structure. Young participants told me that they agreed with and are similar to the young runaways of a French series because "they are not obliged to follow [the desires of] their parents." In doing so, they show a form of self-affirmation, which doesn't express itself in a social movement, but which ceaselessly and gradually creates new spaces for them. As Charlotte Brundson has remarked, research on agency has been decisive for feminist studies on audiences.[41] I would add that agency is informed by the historicity and the struggles, often undeclared and invisible, that shape it. In other words, women's "art of saying"[42] is supported by an "art of doing." The two render visible micropractices that are absent in dominant discourses. Moreover, the individualization and singularity to which women aspire in general, and which cannot be limited to television viewing and practices, refer to the phenomenon of *differentiation* that has characterized public space and contemporary Algerian history. This *differentiation* is a bête noir that does not adhere to official slogans on the "fraternity of brothers" and the ideological discourse of "unity" and "national features." It is because women are the potential bearers of this differentiation that against all expectations they represent the society against community, and this is why it is necessary to be attentive to micropractices, such as those involved in television viewing, that seem far from public space yet are at its core.

Conclusion

Satellite television raises fundamental questions for Algerian society. Although satellite television is most commonly viewed as an innocuous form of entertainment, it has an impact on the redefinition of public space. The form of entertainment that satellite television involves must be understood in its etymological sense—"to turn away, to be different"—because it modifies how audiences are situated in the discursive relations that govern them. Yet television does not comprise all of public space; without neglecting its impact as the most accessible medium in Algeria, it needs to be situated in the whole of public space and linked with other media, like the press. Satellite television shows the "tension between culture and institutions" in Avritzer's terms, between hybrid forms of culture in mutation and fixed forms of political and administrative institutions.[43] Satellite television also raises the question of freedom. As summarized by one of the participants, Bakir (22 years old), democracy allows people "to speak and let speak." According to Hannah Arendt, freedom, more than fraternity and equality, makes a person "a somebody."[44] To the prohibitions (*l'interdit*) of Islamists and the political regime, television spectators oppose the shared word (*l'inter-dit*), the word in circulation, the mediation necessary for speech. Satellite television makes the problem of differentiation, embodied by women, and the danger it poses to the political and cultural system, equally visible.[45] Finally, satellite television registers deeply what remains undecidable and difficult to think—the place of women in public space in Algerian society—all the while signaling the emergence of the irreversible—the gains women have made in public space.

Notes

1 Philip Schlesinger, *"The Nation and Communicative Space,"* in *Media Power, Professionals, and Policies,* ed. Howard Tumber (New York: Routledge, 2000).

2 This paper is part of a larger project on public space and new media in North Africa. I draw my interpretations from several fieldwork trips (1994, 1995, 1996, 1999, 2001) that I have undertaken mainly in Central Algeria. I interviewed 66 participants and had many other informal discussions with viewers at different settings.

3 Jocelyne Dakhlia, *Le divan des rois: Le politique et le religieux dans l'Islam* (Paris: Aubier, 1998); Hamadi Redissi, *Les politiques en Islam: Le Prophète, le roi et le savant* (Paris: L'Harmattan, 1998).

4 Catherine Neveu, "Anthropologie de la citoyenneté," in *Anthropologie du Politique,* ed. M. Abélès and H. P. Jeudy, 69–99 (Paris: Armand Colin, 1997).

5 Diane Singerman, *Avenues of Participation: Family, Politics, and Networks in Urban Quarters in Cairo* (Princeton: University Press of New Jersey, 1995); Asef Bayet, *Street Politics: Poor Peoples Movements in Iran* (New York: Columbia University Press, 1997); and Olivier Fillieule and Mounia Bennani-Chraibi, *Résistances et Protestations dans les Sociétiés Musulmanes* (Paris: Press de Sciences Po, 2003).

6 Philippe Lucas, "Après la citoyenneté les multi-citoyennetés," *Cahiers Internationaux de Sociologie LXXIX* (1985): 251.

7 Anne Querrien, "Un art des centres et des banlieux," *Hermès* 10 (1999): 85–93.

8 This official expression was popular in the 1970s, and amalgamated socialism and Arabic–Islamism values in a demagogic way.

9 Idols were combated by Islam because they were multiple and humanly conceived, while Allah is unique and nonrepresentational.

10 Eighty-one per cent, according to Eutelsat sources. Naomi Sakr, *Satellite Realms: Transnational Television, Globalization, and the Middle East* (London and New York: Tauris, 2001), 114.

11 For this reason, the launching of the Khalifa Group of KTV and K News occurred in the summer of 2002 from Europe.

12 Yahia H. Zoubir, "State and Civil Society in Algeria," in *North Africa in Transition: State Society, and Economic Transformation in the 1900s* (Gainesville: University Press of Florida, 1998), 35–36.

13 Yves Gonzalez-Quijano, *Les Gens du Livre: Edition et Champ Intellectuel dans l'Égypte Républicaine* (Paris: CNRS, 1998); Dale Eikelman and Jon Anderson, "Print, Islam and the Prospects for Civic Pluralism: New Religious Writings and Their Audiences," *Journal of Islamic Studies* 8, no. 1 (1997): 43–62.

14 Dale Eickelman and Jon Anderson, *New Media in the Muslim World: The Emerging Public Sphere* (Bloomington & Indianapolis: Indiana University Press, 1999); Charles Hirschkind, "Civic Virtue and Religious Reason: An Islamic Counterpublic," *Cultural Anthropology* 16, no. 1 (2001): 3–34.

15 Mustapha Al Ahnaf, Bernard Botiveau, and Franck Frégosi, *L'Algérie par ses oislamistes* (Paris: Karthala, 1991), 207.

16 One of the participants said that since 1988 "a political culture has developed in Algeria. You have an extremist political culture on the left, the right, the nationalists, the populists. . . . All Algerians speak of politics. Political instability, the crisis that Algeria lives, is first of all, a political problem. As a result, even the laborer, the unemployed, the manager, those in school and in high school, women who do not work, everyone talks about politics. Even if in some cases, they do not conceptualize or theorize it."

17 Ratiba Hadj-Moussa, "New Media, Community and Politics in Algeria," *Media, Culture and Society* 25, no. 4 (2003): 451–69.

18 Lois McNay, "Subject, Psyche and Agency: The Work of Judith Butler," *Theory, Culture, and Society* 16, no. 2 (2000): 175–93.

19 MBC: The Middle East Broadcasting Centre. The Saudi-owned organization was launched on 18 September 1991, becoming the first independent Arabic language satellite station.

20 Omar Carlier, *Entre nation et jihad: Histoire sociale des radicalismes Algériens* (Paris: Presses de Sciences Po, 1995).

21 Ibid., 33.

22 Ibid., 24.

23 "D system," a French expression, refers to the first letter of the French word *débrouillardise*, or resourcefulness, which a person resorts to when facing a difficult situation.

24 M'hamed Rebah, *La presse algérienne: Journal d'un défi* (Algiers: Chihab, 2002), 213.

25 Pierre Bourdieu and Sayad Abdelmalek, *Le déracinement* (Paris: Minuit, 1964); Mohamed Kerrou and Mostapha Kharoufi, "Maghreb: Familles, valeurs et changements sociaux," *Monde Arabe Maghreb Machrek* 144 (1994): 26–39.

26 Gilbert Guillaume, "Père subvertis, Langage interdits," *Peuples Méditerranéens* 3 (1985): 163–82.

27 Kamel Kateb, *La fin du marriage traditional en Algérie?: Une exigence d'égalité des sexes* (Paris: Bouchene, 2001), 89.

28 Aziz Ajbilou, *Analyse de la variabilité spatio-temporelle de la primo-nuptialité au Maghreb* (Bruxels and Paris: Academia-Bruylant and L'Harmattan, 1998), 103.

29 Cohen and Arato, discussed by Emirbayer, Mostapha, and Mimi Scheller, "Publics in History," *Theory and Society* 28, no. 1 (1999): 145–97.

30 Jenny White, *Civic Culture and Islam in Urban Turkey* (New York: Routledge, 1996), 143–54.

31 *"Ruser pour user"*: The expression was used by a participant when he explained how he tried to thwart the ban on satellite television by armed groups during the first years of civil war (1991–1996).

32 The house is designated by the term *harem*, which means "sacred" or the forbidden space to "foreigners."

33 Algeria made its politics of Arabization official in the early 1970s as Gilbert Grandguillaume demonstrates in *Arabisation et politique linguistique au Maghreb* (Paris: Maisonneuve and Larose, 1983), Ch. 5, 95–134. Arabization was a politics of affirmation and reappropriation of Algerian identity. It was a measure against a law passed in 1938 that declared Arabic a foreign language (98). However, this political claim was made at the expense of other languages, such as Algerian Arabic dialects and Berber languages.

34 This applies to the majority of the Arab countries as noted by Mark Lynch who writes, "These new Arab media have created a new rich information environment that directly challenges the state-controlled domestic media. . . . Those newspapers and stations that were perceived as independent of state control and adopted an Arabist perspective tended to stand out the most." (62) ("Beyond the Arab Street: Iraq and the Public Sphere," *Politics and Society* 31, no. 1, [2003]: 55–91).

35 Ratiba Hadj-Moussa, *Le corps, l'histoire, le territoire: Les rapports de genre dans le cinéma algérien* (Paris and Montreal: PubliSud and Balzac, 1994).

36 Thaâlbi in Nourredine Toualbi, *L'identité au Magreb: L'Errance* (Algiers: Casbah, 2000).

37 Sakr, *Satellite Realms*.

38 Purnima Mankekar, *Screening Culture, Viewing Politics: An Ethnography of Television, Womanhood, and Nation in Postcolonial India* (Durham, N.C.: Duke University Press, 1999); Lila Abu-Lughod, "The Objects of Soap Opera: Egyptian Television and the Cultural Politics of Modernity," in *Worlds Apart: Modernity Through the Prism of the Local*, ed. Daniel Miller, 190–210 (London: Routledge, 1995).

39 He writes that they are the equivalent to *"hittistes,"* the young men who neither work nor go to school who lean against walls (*h'it*) all day. It is said that they "hold up the wall"—I have interviewed a good number of them.

40 Shams Benghribil, "La décomposition du djihad dans un quartier populaire d'Alger," *Annuaire de l'Afrique du Nord XXXVII* (1999): 145.

41 Charlotte Brunsdon, *The Feminist, the Housewife, and the Soap Opera* (Oxford: Clarendon Press), 19–36.

42 Isabelle Berry-Chikhaoui, "Mobilisation des habitants et construction du Voisi-nage," in *La compétence des citadins dans le Monde Arabe*, ed. Isabelle Berry-Chikhaoui (Paris: Kathala, 2000), 155–82.

43 Avritzer argues that, in Latin America, one of the problems "for establishing democratic institutions outside of the centers of modernity is . . . from the very moment of their formation, Latin American societies had to face the tension between their liberal normative horizon and their impossibility of applying liberalism to their existing structures." Leonardo Avritzer, *Democracy and the Public Space in Latin America* (Princeton, N.J.: Princeton University Press, 2002), 70–71.

44 Françoise Collin, *L'Homme est-il devenu superflu? Hannah Arendt* (Paris: Odile Jacob, 1999).

45 This question deserves more thought. The direction that I have taken does not permit me to address it here. For a psychoanalytic perspective see Fethi Benslama, *La psychanalyse à l'épreuve de l'Islam* (Paris: Aubie, 2002).

Tamar Liebes-Plesner

7

The Voice of Jacob:

Radio's Role in Reviving a Nation

No other nation has as strong a need as our nation for the medium of radio; as if it were created in the six days of creation in order to bridge between one Diaspora and another, and between them and the homeland, gradually being built.

—Y. M., *Davar*, 4 June 1947

The medium typically associated with nation building, in the case of new nations established in the twentieth century, is television.[1] In the founding of the Jewish state, radio was the instrument charged with the project of integrating the immigrants from the various diasporas. Television was introduced only two decades later and even then for the wrong reasons.[2] Israel's Radio made its first steps twelve years prior to the establishment of the state as the "Hebrew Hour" of the British Mandatory government channel, titled *The Voice of Jerusalem*.[3] During Israel's formative decade, radio turned out to be the central site for negotiating the ideological and cultural identity of the future nation. The *Yishuv*, the organized Zionist entity in British Mandatory Palestine, made use of the daily broadcasts for inventing modern Hebrew and a civic culture, and for experimenting with acoustic formats and practices for the ritual and functional needs of the nascent society. These were in place when the Hebrew Hour reemerged in 1948 as "The Voice of Israel," charged with nothing less than the forging of a national culture from the remnants of two thousand years of dispersion.

Privileging Voice over Image: The Hebrews and the Greeks

Although radio played an important part in the public life of Western nations, it was particularly compatible with the culture of the Jewish state. Unlike the Greeks, Judaism favors the voice over the picture, and the sense of hearing over seeing. To quote cultural historian Martin Jay, "it is generally agreed that classical Greece privileged sight over the other senses, a judgment lent special weight by the contrast often posited with its more verbally oriented Hebraic competitor."[4] Thus, mind for the Greeks serves as an absorber of images; hence, the word "theory" (which shares its root with "theatre") means "to *look* attentively and to behold," and knowledge in the Greek epistemology is "the state of having seen."[5] This visual bias, says Hans Jonas emphasizes the unchanging eternal presence as against the fleeting succession of temporality. "If the Jews could begin their most heartfelt prayer, 'Hear, O Israel,' says Jay, "the Greek philosophers were in effect urging, 'See, O Hellas.'"[6] The primordial centrality of the voice rather than the image, of hearing rather than seeing, is evidenced throughout the biblical text, in which God is revealed as a voice. First heard from in the creation of the physical world, God's voice reverberates in the negotiations with the central characters of Genesis, and again with the Jewish people at Mount Sinai, who suddenly "saw the voices" and promised, in response, to act and to listen. In later times, too, talk is the medium that best characterizes the most vital genres of Talmudic disputation in the *yeshivot*, and the sermonizing in the synagogues.[7]

Heinrich Graetz, a most influential historian of Judaism, has argued that the voice is directly relevant to the religious heritage, to the Jewish national movement, and, in particular, to the centrality of the voice at Mount Sinai, the founding moment of the Jewish People. Graetz sees the superiority of the voice over the image as an essential characteristic of Judaism, the one that distinguishes it from Paganism. Whereas pagan religions worship nature, and, at the same time are steeped in it, their gods, just as much as men, are oppressed by its rules. In Judaism God is separated from nature and frees man from it. Accordingly, the Greeks are oriented toward visual art, which personifies gods in the shape of men by making them into sculptures. Judaism, in which God's spiritual appearance is formed in the human consciousness, is oriented to poetry, which can connect with God only by the word.

The Relevance of Primordial Culture to Nationalism

On what grounds can a nation's primordial roots be relevant for contemporary nationalist movements, the nation–states that they found, and the media that act as their mouthpiece? As for the Jews, Graetz makes the connection between the idea of a monotheism and modern Jewish nationalism by anchoring God in historic action. He sees Judaism not as a religion of individuals but of the collective. Jewish life, accordingly, turns around religious truth and the social good; Judaism is both church and state. Thus, Benedict Anderson's imagined communities entail imagining the nation as connected with the collective past as well as with a continuing future.[8] It is wrong to conceive of nationalism as a conscious ideology, says Anderson. Rather, similarly to the way in which we think of "family relationship," nationalism should be seen as a cultural system, created vis a vis, and in opposition to, religious community and kingdom. With the loss of religion, and, with it, the loss of the comfort in the idea of redemption, it is nationalism that is expected to fulfill the promises of continuity and meaning. The nation-states, "widely considered to be 'new' and 'historic,'" cannot do it by themselves. Therefore, "the nations to which they give political expression always loom out an of immemorial past, and . . . glide into a limitless future." Thus, "it is the magic of nationalism to turn chance into destiny."[9]

The tie between Judaism and Zionism is particularly problematic inasmuch as the Zionist national movement was founded by Jews who broke away from religion, into modernism, enlightenment, and socialism. After realizing that the emancipation gained by nineteenth-century Jews in Europe was leading to a new vicious form of anti-Semitism, the Zionists adopted the idea of nationalism. At the same time they also realized that in order to mobilize a national movement they needed to appeal to the largely religious communities with whom they had only little in common. This tension between the secular Zionist idea and its primordial base was experienced from the outset and continues with the contemporary debate over whether to treat religion as part of the state's cultural heritage. A clue to the secular acknowledgement of the shared past is the case of *The Voice of Israel* which (to this day) continues the ancient ritual of opening its broadcasts with a ceremonial reading of "Hear, O Israel," in which a deep male voice, with an unmistakable Yemenite Hebrew accent, leads a collective prayer to God for the majority of (nonobservant) Israelis. By invoking the ancient voice, it also leans on the compatibility of radio, rather than television, to this heritage. Thus, ironically, whereas the voice was preserved throughout the generations by the written scrolls, radio's transmission by the voice is closer to the original.

The Voice and the Word: in Print and on Radio

The voice cannot be separated from the word it carries unless it is a cry of joy or agony, that is, a purely expressive utterance.[10] In the spirit of McLuhan's brilliant insight, according to which each mass medium becomes the content of the medium that follows in its wake, radio is the medium for which the voice is the content, with the voice itself serving as medium for the word, the medium for conveying meaning. But the linear succession of media and content is not as neat as McLuhan would have it. It may be more precise to argue that the pure word is mass-diffused by two kinds of media. One is the older medium of the printed text (be it scrolls, books, pamphlets, or newspapers), which mediates the word "cold" without the "tone" or "mood" of its expression (sometimes supplementing it with a verbal description—"angrily," "smilingly"). Seen from the perspective of communication technology—print mutes the voice, and packages the message, robbing it of being heard in real time, and emphasizing its cognitive, organized, controlled aspects. But when the genres of writing, and the ways in which the text is read, are taken into account, not all is dead. The most prominent example of a written text designed to evoke the speaking voice are Plato's dialogues, intended to overcome the closed finality of the text (which cannot be argued with) by inserting performative elements—a "live" debate among "real" fictional characters. Other texts are written as scripts to be acted. As for variations in the reading, and in the context of reception, consider the Biblical text, read aloud, in public, in synagogue, its intensity and earthiness reinstated.

The newer medium of radio lifts the voice from the page, resurrects its texture, diffusing it simultaneously, or by simulating simultaneity. Radio is also more directly focused than television's mix of icons and words. Listening means concentrating on the message, not being sidetracked by visual details that may be peripheral, or irrelevant for the meaning conveyed by a speaker. There is, however, another possibility. Whereas the texture and "purity" of the spoken word give it focus and authenticity, directing the listener to meaning, the style of delivery leaves room for variation and manipulation. Presenters may address listeners as individuals, conveying intimacy and/or spontaneity, or address the community or the public, conveying ritualistic formality (recall the BBC model of news reading compared to the presenters' style on commercial radio and television).[11]

The fact that radio exercised a formative influence on the renascent Israeli culture is not a coincidence of history. Just as television in the 1970s was central to the establishment of the third-world nations, and printed pamphlets were the central medium of the American revolution, so radio was the only accessible electronic medium in the 1940s, in British Mandatory Palestine.[12] Nevertheless, there is no doubt that its power was enhanced by its compatibility with the culture of the voice and the word, as the medium that characterized the various genres of Jewish talk. The fact that radio was an active preference, rather than just an economic or a technological necessity, is evidenced in the political establishment's strong opposition to introducing television for the first two decades of the State's existence. Politicians feared that television would displace reading, Americanize the culture, promote consumerism, undermine the diffusion of the Hebrew language and culture, and personalize and deideologize politics.[13] When television was finally approved, it was slipped in through the back door, and for misguided reasons.

Given these initial fears, it is no small paradox that both television and radio were founded, or rather, rushed into being, for external political reasons. In the case of television, the push came in the wake of the Six Day War of 1967, when Israel (following an attack by Egypt, Syria, and Jordan) found itself a conqueror, and with the somewhat naïve idea of having to "balance" Arab propaganda with "truth" and with positive images of coexistence. Similarly, *The Voice of Jerusalem* was established by the British as an arena in which the Arab and the Jewish communities could let off steam and act less violently. Instead, the Hebrew Hour—as the space allotted to the *Yishuv*—became the unlikely rallying site, in which and around which the Zionist revolutionary movement consolidated its ideological and cultural togetherness.[14]

Live Radio versus Live Television: The Voice of Trauma, the Site of Ceremony

The Israeli case suggests that radio and television specialize in different types of dramatic genres. In the era at which radio reigned alone (that is, in the pre-state era of the British Mandate and in the first two decades of the state), radio broadcasting of public events was associated with moments of crisis and fear, sometimes of existential anxiety. By contrast, Israelis remember the great events of television for the performance of ceremonial events.[15] This division of labor has to do both with the different technologies as well as with the changing economic, ideological, and cultural contexts associated with each.

The events characterizing the years of radio, even those that should have been, or ended in, ceremonial moments, began as traumatic, anxiety-arousing events, often taking the listeners by surprise. Their outcomes were uncertain, sometimes clandestine, always in the shadow of risk and failure. Such fateful events, via radio, were followed with trepidation by listener/witnesses waiting for the verdict. Unlike today's image of radio as an intimate companion in the quiet of a car, or in bed at night, Israeli radio's heyday was a time of collective audiences. At critical moments in the nation's history, people streamed into the streets to listen together, gathering around public loudspeakers, or car transistors, or within earshot of their neighbors' radios.

The most memorable example of such a fateful event was the live broadcast of the UN roll-call vote on the partition of Palestine into two states. In 1947, for the Jewish inhabitants of mandatory Palestine—most of whom had escaped from their countries of origin—this meant finally having a state of their own. Years later, people recall the experience of this broadcast, at midnight Israeli time. They remember where, and with whom, they were at the time, how they kept their own count of the votes while they were being announced, the point at which they knew the resolution would pass, and the spontaneous dancing that broke out once it was announced. Movingly documented in the autobiographical novel by Amos Oz,[16] this was a transformative moment, fraught with collective anxiety, at the end of which, a neighborhood community of (mostly) World War II refugees felt a surge of relief, joy, and a new sense of belonging. The recollection of this moment is commonly visualized in the form of a dense mass of heads crowding around the radio set.

The next in the chain of open-ended landmarks in the history of nation building events was the declaration of independence six months later. Unlike the UN vote, in which the time of the event was known but the outcome was not, the Declaration of Independence was expected, but the timing remained uncertain. Indeed, neither the society nor the paramilitary armed forces had much advance notice of the decision. The reason, as many knew, was that the announcement would almost certainly be followed by the frightening prospect of a full-fledged war, inasmuch as the Arabs, who had made no secret of their objection to the division of

Palestine into two states, and their competing claim to the whole of the territory, had already started violent insurgency to prevent its implementation. The transmission of the broadcast itself was poor, and heard by some to the sound of shooting.[17] Far from a ceremonial event, the poor semiclandestine broadcast of the Declaration of Independence was part of the larger drama of British forces leaving, Arab states invading, and Jewish World War II refugees streaming in. PM Ben Gurion's decisive (surprisingly high) voice, infiltrating the chaos, was the signal for the beginning of a battle. Only the consequences of the war would determine whether this was the birth of a state.

The third memorable broadcast, typically listened to in public, was the live transmission of the Adolph Eichmann trial in Jerusalem, following his capture in Argentina in 1961 (Eichmann was the senior Nazi bureaucrat in charge of transporting the Jews to the death camps).[18] The trial marked a transformation in the way in which the first generation of native-born Israelis, in particular, perceived their relationship with the holocaust, and with its Jewish survivors. For the native born, the Zionist ethos was intended to distance the "diasporic" Jewish existence. The dominant ideology focused on the new Jew—the pioneer, working the land, and defending himself against his enemies. For young Israelis, and for thousands of Jewish immigrants from Arab countries who had little acquaintance with the history of European Jewry, the trial was a first confrontation with the collective trauma in which the majority of the Jewish communities in Europe had perished. The voice of the holocaust remained mute in the daily life of the Israeli survivors until then. The history books were still unwritten. For some, the holocaust was seen in the image of half-crazed survivors, wandering the streets.[19] Ironically, the Eichmann trial was conducted with an eye to the world outside, to show that Israel can conduct a fair and dignified trial against a senior Nazi war criminal. The major impact on the society in Israel came as a surprise to the organizers, who had not even planned in advance to broadcast the trial live. But from the first day, people huddled around the voices that emerged from radio sets in public buses, children gathered around loudspeakers in school classes and school yards, and families gathered at home around the one radio set to relive the incongruously tragic common past.[20] Listening to the voices of the survivors, in their role of witnesses, recalling their life histories, had a shattering effect.

Why were the organizers surprised after the impact of these live broadcasts? Perhaps their failure to anticipate radio's power in this case was rooted in the widely held belief among contemporaries that radio, a form of mediation, would only be a poor substitute for actual presence at the place in which the event was happening. Ascending to Jerusalem (as to the temple in ancient times), demonstrated motivation, and a willingness to make an effort, and "being there" meant exposure to the event in its unique, authentic, context. Thus, little thought was given to the live broadcasting of the Eichmann trial, even if much effort was invested in finding and rehabilitating a hall large enough to contain the audience that was expected to come to Jerusalem for the trial.

Indeed, in the era of radio, the major ceremonial events, notably the military parades of Independence Day, were organized to encourage in-person participation, echoing the ancient ritual of festive pilgrimage. The descriptions in the newspapers focused on the masses that were gathered along the route. Radio's attempts to conduct vox pop interviews in the streets sound dull, awkward, uninspired, even pompous, and fail to convey the audience excitement, or the mood of folksy celebration. Ironically, these anniversary parades were discontinued after the introduction of television, following the only victory parade, broadcast live, in 1968.

Yet another aspect of radio's poor performance in mediating establishment ceremonies may be the dissonance between the extravagance of public celebrations and the ascetic attitude that characterized Israel's early years. The dominant value was one of austerity. Indeed, *Davar*, the daily of Israel's yet undefeated Labor party, took pride in the policy of playing down ceremonies, especially the ones that encourage a cult of leadership. One self-congratulatory report (25 January 1950) quotes the amazement expressed by *A Zaiad*, a Lebanese newspaper, over the simplicity with which Israeli radio had reported the reception given to Israel's ailing president Haim Weizman on his return from medical treatment abroad. Unsurprisingly, it is difficult to distinguish between the simplicity of the ceremony itself and of its report on radio. Headlined "Such Wonders!," *A Zaiad* continues:

> The State that was just established in the East reports its ceremonies in a most simple form. We did not hear any inflated titles, nor did we hear about decorations and tributes in celebrating the arrival of this great man. The announcer did not pour on words of prayer, or of thanks, nor did he express happiness over this celebrity's convalescence. . . . We should not forget either that this is the man who brought back to the promised land the people, who had departed, and were dispersed for 2000 years, from all ends of the world, and laid the foundation for a homeland and a government. How ungrateful of Israel, yet how wise.

Thus, live radio in its heyday is remembered for its transmission of uncertain, often traumatic events. Unlike radio, the historic moments of television, during the two decades in which one monopoly channel acted as tribal bonfire, are best remembered for the live broadcasts of preplanned, ceremonial, "media events" such as Egyptian President Sadat's visit to Jerusalem, followed by the signing of the peace treaty on the White House lawn. Such ceremonial events, viewed on television, lacked the suspense and anxiety of the fateful events transmitted by radio in its great moments.[21]

The Integrative Role of Radio

The centrality of radio in the pre-state life of the Jewish community, and in the first formative years of the state, is evident in the large space devoted to it in the daily printed press. The way in which journalists saw radio can be demonstrated by the following commentary in Davar (10 October 1948): "Radio is a tremendous instrument, which, if you will, largely determines the soul of the nation . . . it is endowed with the tasks of educating to citizenship the hundreds of thousands of immigrants coming in, and creating connections with the diaspora." The paper concludes with the romantic expectation that "the airwaves should also infiltrate waves of love and affection to the state."

Commentators, radio critics, and intellectuals expressed profound belief in radio's ability to reinforce (and even to invent) the central aspects of national and cultural identity. They argued about the goals of radio, and how well these were being accomplished in light of the various perceptions of the governing principles of the new state. Proposals for improving the performance of the new medium ranged from the way it treated the most fundamental cultural issues to reprimanding announcers for the mistaken use of a Hebrew word, or for mispronouncing it, or even for using the wrong (mostly "too high") register. The heated debates on programming reflected the conflicting views on the ideological, political and cultural dilemmas facing the new nation, and the high expectations that radio, as the only medium accessible to the mass of Israelis, would play a major part in the diffusion of the language and cultural riches considered essential for the new Israelis.

Radio was indeed a central actor in the major issues of identity formation.[22] Anticipating a model of public broadcasting, paternalistic from the outset, the guiding value was to give equal access to cultural heritage and ceremony.[23] Functionally, access meant first teaching Hebrew to new immigrants, and continuing with "improving their tastes and values" (*Davar*, 10 October 1948). In spite of the wish to promote cultural unity, in broadcasting to a society of immigrants from various cultural backgrounds, and to Jews and Arabs, radio broadcasters faced the classic dilemma of the extent to which to allow for segmented multiculturalism. Should radio allocate separate channels to cultural minorities? How many cultural and linguistic slots should it allocate to the various groups on the one mainstream channel?[24] In spite of the elitist Ashkenazi bias, the predominant voice of both policy makers and public opinion recognized the need for a balance between "high" culture (complete with classical music, literature, and art) imported by immigrants from Europe, and oriental/folk/popular culture of the Jewish immigration from Arab countries on the shared mainstream channel. A partially overlapping dilemma faced by radio broadcasters, regarding themselves as the voice of a liberal, secular, socialist society, was finding ways in which to incorporate religion as cultural heritage rather than normative codes.[25] There was unanimous agreement, in the spirit of Zionism, about daily readings of a chapter from the Bible, but a bitter continual argument about the identity of the commentators. To the orthodox community, literary historical interpretation was seen as a threat. Another basic dilemma that arose in the debate over public broadcasting everywhere was the balance between education and entertainment. Typical of the Israeli anomaly was the constant demand of Kibbutz members to have classical music in the evening instead of "salon dancing" music to entertain cafe goers in Tel Aviv, who could look after themselves by employing local musicians. Even where there was agreement, the attempt to carry out the various tasks within the limited time of daily broadcasting, mostly on the one channel, entailed impossible choices, such as the one attacked in a furious *Davar* column criticizing radio's substitution of "Hebrew/ Jewish music" with "gymnastic lessons for the workers" at 7:30 in the morning.

Radio's immediate tasks included bringing home the formative (and transformative) historic moments—the events that led to the founding of Israel, and its first stormy decades—including wars, political crises, and ceremonial events. Often, as in Ben Gurion's tense Declaration of Independence, heard to the sound of shooting, and a sadness over the knowledge of the looming war, ceremony and crisis were mixed. Serving as the real time announcer of history in the making, a courier for mobilizing the troops, and a babysitter for the home front, radio lived up to its role of instructing civilians in emergencies. Even in the era of television it remained the medium to turn to in immediate crisis. The slogan "Yellow cheese" broke the traditional media silence of Yom Kippur in 1973 and put the reserve army on its way. "Viper Snake" interrupted the broadcast at the start of the first Gulf War, assembling Israelis in the "sealed room" to defend themselves against Saddam Hussein's chemical missiles.

Hebrew Radio Talking Yiddish to World War II Jewish Survivors

Whereas radio broadcasters struggled with answering all these needs and values, the most crucial, difficult, and miraculously successful task undertaken by radio was that of reviving the Hebrew language, accompanied by its fight against the Yiddish that symbolized life in the diaspora.

Radio's need to undertake the task of reviving, updating, and giving voice to the ancient Hebrew language was the result of 2000 years of diasporic existence, which it had survived mostly as the written language of prayer and study. Yiddish was the vernacular for the masses of Jews in Eastern Europe. Radio rose to the challenge of impressing Hebrew on large sections of the multicultural population of immigrants to Israel, the majority of whom had to learn it from scratch (by the daily repeated routines, direct teaching, programs in "easy Hebrew," and slowing down the speed of reading news).

However, the irony of history dictated that following World War II, the assignment of reviving Hebrew had to be postponed. Before mobilizing the broadcasts for the Zionist revolution, the most urgent task faced by the Hebrew Hour was creating contact with that part of the Jewish people in Europe who survived the war, the predominant language of whom was Yiddish. These refugees were now dispersed in displaced camps throughout Europe. This attempt to call the survivors and to listen to their voices was crucial for the luckier refugees who had managed to escape to Palestine before the war, and were desperately trying to establish contact with their loved ones. Regarding itself as "a homeland in process," (*Davar*, 4 June 1947), the community in British Palestine acted in the spirit of the Jewish principle of mutual responsibility, extending the boundaries of the imagined community to give preference to Jews in distress wherever they were. Broadcasting in Yiddish, the language spoken by the masses of the Jews in Eastern Europe, was done in direct contradiction to the ideological principles of the *Yishuv*. As literary scholar Dan Miron convincingly argues, the adoption of Hebrew—the ancient language of the Hebrews in the Land of the Israelites—was the symbol of the clear divide between the experience and the way of life of Jewish nonrevolutionary existence "in exile," and that of the born again life in *Eretz Yisrael*.[26] Miron argues that separation between the Yiddish and the Hebrew was crucial for serving the goals of the Zionist Hebrew culture because Yiddish was the most commonly used language throughout the generations in spite of the continuous struggle against it. It was especially important, as a large part of life in pre-Israel Palestine was also marked by Jewish "exile-like" culture, not fully internalizing that they are "the last generation of slavery, and the first of redemption."

But once the war was won, ideologies had to wait, and the *Hebrew Hour*, stretching far beyond the geographic and the linguistic boundaries of the *Yishuv* set out to search for remnants of the Jewish communities in Europe. One obvious way to discover which of them were still alive was to send greetings by short wave radio to "the Jewish communities where-ever they may be" (*Davar*, 22 June 1947) and to pray for signs of life. These voices transmitting greetings from Palestine, perhaps only by talking into thin air, were sometimes miraculously answered by transmissions received from radio Lublin, Stockholm, and Warsaw.

One section of the nation-to-be, still waiting behind fences, were the homeless refugees, who, following the war, tried to make their way to Palestine. Regardless of the decision taken by the British, according to which Palestine was declared national home for the Jewish people, these displaced persons were arrested by the British at sea, or on disembarking on the shores of Tel Aviv. Thus, as reported by *HaZofe* (27 August 1948), broadcasts to the illegal immigrants imprisoned in Cyprus were intended to "allow them to listen to the voice of the homeland." The demand for special programs in Yiddish had first come from the camp residents themselves (titled by the paper "the Cyprus diaspora") who asked "to be brought closer to the life of the state and its problems by broadcasting news, commentary, and light talks in a language which is familiar to most of them." One program titled *"zabar,"* addressed to the new Jewish immigrants on their way to Palestine, was devoted to explaining, "what is 'exile' and what is the '*Yishuv*,' in a (rather naïve) effort to turn the newcomers into 'real' native '*Yishuvniks*'" (16 August 1945, *HaAretz*).

Closer to home, the most urgent need following the defeat of the Nazis, for many Jews in Palestine, was the possibility of creating contact with the Jewish soldiers who had taken part in the war. There was particular concern for the fate of the Brigade of Jewish soldiers from Mandatory Palestine, who had volunteered to join the British army and were stationed in Europe (*HaZofe*, 9 April 1945). For this task, the Hebrew press encountered only little enthusiasm in its struggle to convince British officials in Palestine to allocate the short waves that had served for anti-Nazi propaganda to the Middle Eastern countries (*HaMashkif*, 30 January 1945; *Davar*, 4 February 1945). One strategy of persuasion was to remind the British that the Hebrew (Palestinian) soldiers were prevented from contact with the homeland—a contact that "every nation tries to keep with its soldiers." Using the occasion of the celebration of Passover, the paper urged, "not to impose this exclusion from the *Voice of Jerusalem* on our soldiers and on the diasporic communities in exile" (*Davar*, 27 March 1945). A few months later the short wave transmission began broadcasting to the Jewish Brigade.

A glimpse at the papers of this period indicates a collaboration between the BBC and the Hebrew radio in bringing home voices of Jewish soldiers. For example, the BBC recorded a prayer for Jewish soldiers in a London synagogue for the *Hebrew Hour* (*Davar*, 15 August 1945), conducted interviews with Jewish soldiers who were imprisoned in Germany (*HaMashkif*, 12 August 1945), and initiated "greetings from the *Gola* (exile)" twice a week. Note that it was the participation of volunteer Jewish soldiers from Palestine in the British army that gave legitimacy to the *Yishuv's* claim to broadcast to Europe, and in turn to serve as a channel for contacting displaced Jewish survivors.

Radio and the Revival of the Hebrew Language

Before reestablishing itself as the daily spoken language within the first and second-generation immigrants to Palestine, Hebrew had been preserved through the generations in the various Jewish diasporas only as the language of prayer and religious study. Daily life within the community was conducted in Yiddish, and the lingua franca was used in contacts with the rest of the society. Moreover, the choice of Hebrew as Israel's official language was far from self-evident for some of the first Zionist leaders. As Zionism in Western Europe arose as a national movement within the climate of enlightenment and emancipation, its leaders had broken away from religion, and from the language associated with it. Theodor Herzl, the movement's undisputed leader, was an assimilated journalist, who grew up with German and Hungarian, and later acquired English and French. He set out at the latter part of the nineteenth century to solve the Jewish problem (defined as the poverty and persecution of the East European Jews, and the rise of a new kind of anti-Semitism at the onset of emancipation and enlightenment in West Europe). He envisioned a multicultural state, one in which the Jews from the East and the West would continue to speak in their own languages. He, for one, was convinced that he would continue to speak German. Once Hebrew was decided on, its diffusion became the radio's greatest challenge. Dr. Z. M. (*Davar*, 12 November 1948) expresses the expectations from the miraculous new medium in the following words:

> Radio . . . is conquering the world, unlimited in its influence and power. . . . And if this is true for the world's nations, all the more so in our case. . . . It is a national educational instrument of the first order, and we have to prepare in time so that we will not miss its potential. The Hebrew language is the first and foremost element. The rest of the world's nations takes this element for granted, which it is by no means the case here. And as the language is so central, it has to be carefully nurtured . . . both in terms of the culture of speech, and in terms of access to the mechanical voice that reaches every ear.

The obsession with teaching Hebrew was accompanied by unrelenting criticism of broadcasting in Yiddish. A forceful example is A. Ramba (*HaMashkif*, 20 February 1949), who reprimands Kol Yisrael for broadcasting in Yiddish. Even after the camp in Cyprus was dismantled, says Ramba, its Yiddish broadcasts continued "under the guise of broadcasting to Europe":

> The Yiddish supporters should not come to us with demagogic arguments about the tens of thousands of new immigrants who do not understand Hebrew, and the idea that their lives and absorption will be made easier by not leaving them deaf and dumb. There must not be two languages for the Hebrew people in its state. A broadcast in Yiddish, a paper, even theatre, all disturb the process of making Hebrew speakers of the new state's citizens. If they can find media in their own language, the language of exile, why should they bother to learn a new language when they are grownup or old? The only task that lies ahead is to use all the possible means in the search for adequate methods for teaching Hebrew to all the immigrants, the young and the old, men, women and babies.

In the relentless fight against Yiddish on radio, the article uses another powerful argument. Favoritism of Yiddish speakers means discrimination against the rest of the new immigrants. What about the thousands who speak other languages such as *spaniolit* (a dialect of Spanish), Hungarian, Polish and English, French and Romanian? "We dearly love all the Israelites. Will we build a new 'Tower of Babel' and broadcast in all the languages still prevalent in our country?" The drive of universalizing Hebrew was so extreme that even broadcasting to the Yemenite Jewish community, whose Hebrew pronunciation was considered the most authentic, in their "particular Hebrew dialect" was considered counterproductive from the perspective of "inculcating the (Hebrew) language" (*Al HaMishmar*, 20 September 1954).

Forming Hebrew Speech: Register, Invention, Pronunciation

As a mass medium, radio could address various groups of the population, feature special programs for new immigrants in "easy Hebrew," and develop a common standard for spoken Hebrew by adopting the "right" register for speaking, deciding on the "right" pronunciation, inventing new words (often in collaboration with the Academy for the Hebrew Language) to cover modern concepts and new technologies, and translating necessary words (mostly from the English). Such decisions were carefully considered and often furiously attacked by the daily press. Listeners criticized the radio's use of too high a register, sometimes incorrectly. Others requested a slowing of the reading pace of the news (*Haaretz*, 3 April 1949, *Haboker*, 3 April 1949).

Two examples are significant for demonstrating radio's attempts to invoke the authentic sounds and rhythms of ancient Hebrew. One is the decision to adopt the Oriental (Yemenite) pronunciation, considered to be closest to the original, in its preservation of the subtle distinctions between ostensibly similar letters. It was a romantic and heroic attempt, and doomed in advance. Long erased in the Ashkenazi pronunciation of Hebrew, there was no way the bulk of Ashkenazi Zionists could adopt this pronunciation. But it was seriously attempted. Interestingly, it was probably a unique case in which the political and educated elite made an attempt to adopt the accent and pronunciation of a low class, uneducated, group. This meant that the majority of (Ashkenazi) radio announcers had to learn and practice the right way of speaking Hebrew. The tradition was upheld until the decline of public broadcasting and the rise of commercial broadcasting. By then announcers used the universally spoken Hebrew, its richness flattened, the distinctions between similar letters (*Tet* and *Tav*, *Alef* and *Ayin*) abandoned. Its collapse, ironically, coincided with the rise of multiculturalism, and the takeover of (second generation) popular *Misrachi* singers.

Another attempt at resurrecting the sound of spoken Biblical Hebrew was the station's choice of a musical ID, meant to invoke the ancient cantillation of public reading from the Torah. For the vast majority of Jews, the language of the Bible lasted throughout the diaspora as the language of prayer only. The choice of the musical theme was another way of demonstrating the strong Zionist motivation to connect with the common religious roots, even if only in the form of "cultural heritage." The choice of the sounds that allude to the ancient intonation of the Biblical text in the synagogue, for summoning listeners to tune in, and stay with the station, strengthened the symbolic meaning of the choice of Hebrew. It could of course be argued that in making these choices, the radio programmers aimed to skip over the period of the diaspora, in connecting directly to the ancient Canaanite roots. And indeed, the choice of the signal gave rise to another heated debate. "It should be known," says Menashe Ravina (HaDor,) "that this signal is not as ancient as many believe. . . . It is well known that different ethnic groups read by different musical motifs." The author concluded that it was impossible to decide which group of tunes could be declared "the most ancient" as long as there was no authoritative committee that would support it. Nevertheless, the fact that the motif chosen was alleged to have been read aloud in synagogues for hundreds of years justified the decision to declare them uniquely Jewish.

Sounding Out a Homeland

Hebrew radio at its birth was a truly "imagined homeland," a new medium in which to try out the Zionist utopia. Unlike *Altneuland*, Herzl's utopian novel, frozen in book form, radio could experiment continuously with various genres and formats, speak in various languages, receive regular feedback from its various target audiences (mostly in the press), and report daily developments. Its imagined communities—including Jewish immigrants at home and abroad—had no continuous geographic territory. It voice was heard in a plurality of languages, by diasporic communities at home and abroad, and by Jews in the neighboring Arab countries. Thus, under the auspices of an ambivalent colonial government, Hebrew radio became the site of a state in the making, and a virtual home for the *Yishuv.*

Twenty-five years following the establishment of Hebrew radio, PM David Ben Gurion celebrated its dramatic achievement in building the cultural identity of Israelis. He underlined "the place of the broadcast Hebrew word in the miraculous act of the revival of the Hebrew language and the Hebrew speech." The biggest proof of its success, said Ben Gurion, was the paradox of how difficult it is to explain to a generation of teenagers, who had lived their whole lives in a Jewish state, that the revival of Hebrew should not be taken for granted. It would have not succeeded, said Ben Gurion, "if we did not work on this revival with all our hearts every day. . . . What few can imagine that each step of talking Hebrew was a deed of a new creation, a conquest."

Looking at the linguistic transformations that accompanied Zionism, literary critic Dan Miron points to the phenomenon of Yiddish, the language spoken in the homes of the masses of Jews (in Europe, and after immigrating to Israel), becoming a comic language in Israel. In public life, says Miron, that is, in social meetings, in the Yiddish theatre, and on media, Yiddish is used as a language for ridiculing, for telling (and listening to) jokes. Miron sees the ideological function of this distancing as achieving one of the main targets of the Zionist Hebrew culture, that of raising a clear buffer between the primordial, noncontinuous, life of redemption in *Eretz Yisrael* and the nonrevolutionary Jewish life "in exile." The sweet revenge of Yiddish, he claims, is that for the third and fourth generation of Israelis, the pathos of the Hebrew Zionist language, as it was spoken by the founding generation, became itself an object of ridicule, turning into a second Yiddish, and "put into double quotation marks." And indeed, the Hebrew heard on Israeli media half a decade after independence is a far cry from the ideal of the Zionist founders. One television critic (*Haaretz*, 21 January 2005) counted twelve mistakes in Hebrew in songs that came first in the hit parade. Speaking from the Knesset podium (to an almost empty assembly hall), PM Sharon lamented what he saw as the deterioration of spoken Hebrew, including the fashionable use of English words. In a period at which new television channels are named "Hot" and "Yes," and "shalom," as the most common Hebrew greeting, it has been replaced by the Arabic/English "*yalla bye*," the media, as usual, represents ideological and cultural changes, and, thereby, reinforces them.

Notes

1 Elihu Katz and George Wedell, *Broadcasting in the Third World: Promise and Performance* (Cambridge, Mass.: Harvard University Press, 1977).

2 Elihu Katz, "Television Comes to the People of the Book," in *The Use and Abuse of Social Science*, ed. Irving Horowitz, 17–23 (New Brunswick, Transaction Books, 1971); Tamar Liebes, "Performing a Dream and Its Dissolution: A Social History of Broadcasting in Israel," in *De-Westernizing Media Studies*, ed. James Curran and Myung-Jin Park, 305–23 (London and New York: Routledge, 2000).

3 The name was a compromise between the British suggestion of "The Broadcasting Service of Palestine," and the Jewish leadership's "Broadcasting Service of the Land of Israel."

4 Martin Jay, *Downcast Eyes: The Denigration of Vision in 20th Century French Thought*, (Berkeley: University of California Press, 1993).

5 Ibid., 24.

6 Ibid.

7 Menahem Blondheim and Shoshana Blum-Kulka, "Literacy, Orality, Television: Mediation and Authenticity in Jewish Conversational Arguing, 1–2000 C.E.," *The Communication Review*, 4, no. 4 (2001): 511–41.

8 Benedict Anderson, *Imagined Communities: Reflections on the Origins and Spread of Nationalism* (London: Verso, 1991).

9 Ibid., 12.

10 Roman Jakobson, "Linguistics and Poetics," in *The Structuralists: From Marx to Levi-Straus*, ed. R. T. de George and F. M. De George, 73–85 (New York: Anchor Books, 1972).

11 Erving Goffman, *Forms of Talk* (Oxford: Basil Blackwell, 1972).

12 Bernard Baylin, *The Ideological Origins of the American Revolution* (Cambridge, Mass.: Belknap Press, 1978).

13 Elihu Katz, "Television Comes to the People of the Book."

14 *Ezel* and *Lechi*, the more radical anti-British Zionist underground groups, had their own pirate channels, from which they managed intermittent broadcasts.

15 Daniel Dayan and Elihu Katz, *Media Events: The Live Broadcasting of History* (Cambridge, Mass.: Harvard University Press, 1992).

16 Amos Oz, *A Tale of Love and Darkness* (Tel Aviv: Am Oved, 2004).

17 *Radio Magazine*, March 1961.

18 A more detailed description of the impact of the live broadcast of historic events may be found in Tamar Liebes' "Acoustic Space: The Role of Radio in Israeli Collective History," *Jewish History* no. 19, (2005).

19 Yossi Baylin, a former government minister, and the initiator of the Oslo agreement, spoke in a radio program produced in 2002, titled "When Eichmann Came into My Home," in which a number of prominent Israelis, teenagers at the time, described how the live broadcast changed their lives.

20 Menahem Blondheim, a communication scholar at the Hebrew University, is one of a number of people who, as children, recalls listening to the trial on radio, while having lunch, for the duration of the trial. In fact, as Ora Herman has shown, in an MA dissertation at the Hebrew University's Institute for Contemporary Judaism (2005), the trial was broadcast live on no more than 11 court meetings.

21 Dayan and Katz, *Media Events*.

22 Tamar Liebes (in James Curran and Myung-Jin Park *De-Westernizing Media Studies*) elaborates the three periods in which first radio, then one TV channel, and (from the mid-1990s) a plurality of channels, formed and reflected the dominant history of electronic media in Israel.

23 David Cardiff and Paddy Scannell, "Broadcasting and National Unity," in *Impacts and Influences: Essays on Media Power in the Twentieth Century*, ed. James

Curran, Anthony Smith, and Pauline Wingate, 157–73 (London and New York: 1987).

24 Nathan Rotenstreich, a philosophy professor, wrote an article in *Davar*, in which he strongly advocates to incorporate the Arabic broadcasts in the general Hebrew channel.

25 Theodor Herzl, *Altneuland* (Tel Aviv: Akademon Press, 1997).

26 Dan Miron, *The Dark Side of Sholom Aleichem's Laughter* (Tel Aviv: Am Oved, 2004).

8

Violence, Publicity, and Secularism:

Hindu–Muslim Riots in Gujarat

On 27 February 2002, a railway compartment on a train carrying Hindu militants caught fire in Godhra near Ahmedabad, Gujarat, killing fifty-eight people. Blaming Muslims for the violence, the state and central governments stood by as more than two thousand Muslims were slaughtered or burnt alive and hundreds of women were raped and killed.

The state government dismissed reports of the massacres as exaggerated, and blamed the English-language media for anti-Hindu and anti-Gujarati bias. Furthermore, as a run-up to the approaching state elections, the government campaigned to rally Gujarati pride and to defend their state against "demons" (Muslims) and their "pseudo-secular" allies in the English media and in the opposing Congress Party.[1] In December 2002, the Hindu nationalist party, the Bharatiya Janata Party (Indian People's Party, or BJP) was rewarded with a landslide victory at the Gujarat polls, with its highest margins in those districts where the violence had been concentrated. Analysts concurred that there was a clear majority verdict in favor of the riots against Muslims.[2]

The Gujarat riots, coming soon after the establishment of nearly a dozen 24-hour TV news channels, have been described as the first televised riots in India, acts of violence captured live. Print coverage was also copious.[3] The duration and outcome of riots increased beyond that of any earlier episodes of violence (for example, in 1985, 1969, or 1941, which marked the major previous periods of Hindu–Muslim conflict in Gujarat). Although riots typically dwindle after a few days of "police holiday," in this case they continued to erupt for more than six months.

The Idea of an Elsewhere

An "elsewhere" is distinguished against a place that we know. We travel "elsewhere" to broaden the mind, and rub away our comforting parochialism. We confront phenomena that may appear strange to us, and will tend to prefer what we think are good experiences, or good things. And when we return home, we will have our prejudices either confirmed or challenged. This will depend not only on what we encounter, but how we understand it.

To go "elsewhere" in this sense is therefore not simply an expedition in collecting information. It can also reveal the limits of our own self-knowledge and critical energy. More broadly, the conditions that make something intelligible to us, and the standards of comparison we use, are not idiosyncratic.

For the best part of a century now, nationalism has provided the approved liberal means of acknowledging and circumscribing cultural difference. Ideas and practices that seemed strange or anachronistic could be relegated to the plane of national difference, where, like variations between individuals, incommensurability and inequality could both be rendered theoretically equal, even if practically insupportable. Increasingly however, the false universalism of nationalist rhetoric, long regarded benignly as a part of the cost of decolonization, is coming under pressure, from globalization on the one hand, and on the other hand, from internal challenges to the political equilibria that have defined nationalism in most countries. Those who travel "elsewhere" today might encounter fierce denunciations of immigrants in France, of mothers who freely opt for abortion in the United States, of un-Islamic behavior in Egypt, or of troublesome Muslims in India, whereas a few decades ago, few of these issues might have surfaced. In each case, one might imagine an easy answer to the problem: issues pertaining to religious or cultural belief and identity belong in the private sphere, one might say, so that a tolerant multicultural civil society can be maintained. We should recollect however, that the time-honored method of ratifying such an answer was by pointing to countries where such a solution appeared to work. Even from the short list provided in these examples, it should be evident that this is not so easy any longer. In the post–World War II period when new nations emerged, state practices used to be able to assert a monopoly on the interpretation of political programs originating from elsewhere, whether from the United States, United Kingdom, Soviet Union, or China, as part of the authority they claimed for modernization, and adjudicating religious and cultural difference among their populations. Today ideas and images of "elsewhere" are perhaps so profuse, and so profusely reimagined, that the limits of monological methods soon become evident. An attentiveness to the method and manner of mediation, including the work of language itself, is helpful, as I will argue in this chapter.

Language, Media, and National Development

Many have assumed that communication media offer a turnkey technology of modernization that can promote prosocial and developmental values under all circumstances.[4] Rational-critical publicity is often assumed to be a scalar quantity, an absolute good resulting from the circulation of information and certainly from the growth of news media. The evidence is, however, ambivalent to say the least. In numerous cases, mass media are implicated in hate campaigns targeting minorities, for example, and become propaganda vehicles in violent and genocidal programs.[5]

Media have in fact become increasingly central in the enactment of nationalist violence, but they have not been incorporated into social scientific explanations except in instrumental terms, as either deterring or promoting violence. In India, such explanations tend to be qualified; it is the Indian language press that tends to draw most of the blame, in other words "sections of the vernacular press," as opposed to the English language press, which are considered the stalwarts of secularism. Because this view emanates from members of the English language press itself, and because English continues to be a minority language of elites in India, one moreover with a colonial history, it is insufficient and potentially misleading.

In fact, publicity works through linguistically stratified media, and does not operate in a single linguistic register. That is, the historical relations between language groups are brought into play in the dynamics of publicity, and itself becomes a political factor requiring understanding. This has long been true in the era of print dominance, but the growth of electronic media has deepened the structural rift between cosmopolitan and indigenous language cultures.

Thus, for instance, many Hindus in Gujarat believed English language press coverage of the riots was inappropriate, and that the circulation of such information was unethical. For the most part, Hindus believed their community's social dominance was just, and that violence toward the Muslim minority was reasonable, at least during the time of the riots. Briefly, Hindu nationalist identity is mapped onto a Gujarati language public, and to Gujarati identity, whereas their opponents are declared to be outsiders. Increased publicity can work, paradoxically, to deepen support for the perpetrators of violence, either as endorsing legitimate and sanctioned aggression, or as proof of outsiders victimizing natives through unfair media coverage. What we observe, I suggest, is that the expansion of communications in a multilingual society correlates with the growth of Hindu nationalist violence, other things being equal.

Rather than promote critical awareness, the media may strengthen identity formation within social groups while deepening the differences between these groups. Indeed, with the globalization of communications, numerous scholars have testified to the growth of a new politics of violence against ethnic or religious "Others" being advanced by the same groups and parties that embrace globalization in India.[6] For example, the Gujarati press participated in redirecting criticism of the anti-Muslim carnage as propaganda against Gujaratis by "outsiders." This redefinition created the space for violence to endure much longer than it might otherwise have done.

Violence and the Media

Violence is increasingly prominent as a technique of electoral democracy, where the engineering of riots can help consolidate vote-banks based on caste and religious community, at least for the short term. As individuals shift from traditional electoral affiliations, and political parties confront what has been called the "rise of the non-committed vote," political appeals are more particularistic, and campaigns tend to oppose rather than invoke the power of the secular state.[7]

But the violence in Gujarat in 2002 was, in some important respects, distinct from preceding episodes. Both central and state governments were ruled by the BJP at the time. There was widespread support and participation of ordinary Gujaratis. The BJP deflected criticism from itself onto Gujaratis as a whole, at least within Gujarat. The English language media, and secularists in particular, were accused of scapegoating an entire population and besmirching Gujarati pride, with the BJP themselves as Gujarat's righteous defenders. Critical here was the work of Gujarati language press in particular, and its normalization of violence by Hindus in relation to Muslims.

Typically, the vernacular press (as the Indian language press often tends to be called, in a term that tacitly relegates indigenous languages to a second-class status) is regarded as prejudiced and unprofessional, especially by members of the English language press. During communal violence, for example, sections of the Gujarati press become vociferously Hindu, and newspaper sales double or triple at such times. By contrast, the English press is perceived, from the vantage point of Indian language audiences, as elitist and as culturally alien; it tends to engage with issues of Hindu identity from a law-and-order perspective rather than as a cultural matter.

Religion, Secularism, and New Political Formations

Hindu nationalism was ejected from the Centre in the 2004 national elections, but was returned to power in Gujarat. Parastate agencies committed (and may continue to commit) sanctioned—or law-making—violence, implicitly redrawing the boundaries of citizenship around the Hindu community. As economic globalization further marginalizes the unprivileged, new forms of cultural identity are offered as means of empowerment—as Hindu identity emptied of caste difference. Such new artifacts emerge from a combination of political mobilization and communication technologies, and point to a relationship between state form and political culture distinct from those familiar to social scientific convention.

In the West, secularism emerged as the product of a historic compromise between church and state, in which monoethnic, monoreligious nationhood was won by dealing with minorities in nonsecular ways. The rational–critical norms inaugurated in the bourgeois public sphere following the constitution of these nation-states upheld realist conventions of truthtelling that could not reflect their own emergence from a violent historical process. In short, secularism's victory was partly due to nonsecular causes, involving forced conversions and/or expulsion, often accompanied by violence. It is this little-remembered European history that Hindu nationalists seek to reenact in India. In the treatment of the events, however, English language media have highlighted Hindu violence against Muslims as scandalous, whereas Indian language media, specifically in the case I am examining here, Gujarati language media, have been more prone to rationalize such violence.

The gap between the formal rules of constitutional politics and actual practice is witnessed more clearly in the matter of secularism than in almost any other area of life. For example, although political parties are often enjoined to be neutral in religious matters, in many countries, parties have mobilized unofficially on the basis of religious affiliation, to a greater or lesser extent. The public role of religion has grown by leaps and bounds, while secularism has become a defensive policy, or something for experts to adjudicate. It is evident that secularists assumed they had history on their side, no doubt partly because they believed they also had state power on their side.

Meanwhile, religion has proven dynamic and polymorphous. A range of classes have been quicker to perceive and respond to mobilization on religious than on, for example, economic bases. By contrast, secularism has often been a maladroit state ideology and a platitude, offering principles that appeared effete before its adversaries. Which was the opiate, religion or secularism, one might wonder.

My concern is not so much with the recrudescence of religion or of fundamentalism.[8] Such inquiries often fail to grapple adequately with the large-scale historical and social transformations of which religion is more a symptom than a cause. We can usefully compare these transformations with those in early modern Europe. The rapid growth of capitalism was due crucially to its relegation to (what became) the private sphere, a zone in which its virtues and vices both were believed to be made benign.[9] The historical lesson contained here has been repeated in the case of religion. Once relegated to the private sphere, religion largely ceased to be a topic of critical reflection except as an historical anomaly. In the process, religion itself transformed into something diffuse and wide-ranging, and largely outside the ambit of formal institutional structures.

The events in Gujarat show the maturation of historical contradictions that took shape during the decades after national independence in 1947, between secular ideals and electoral democracy. Gujarat itself has long been one of the most economically dynamic states in the country. In Gujarat, state and central governments reaped the electoral dividends from the spectacular displays of violence, and identified themselves with the Hindu nationalist aims of the perpetrators. Simultaneously, spatial strategies of ghettoizing Muslims, combined with the consolidation of Hinduized business capital, suggest a distinct emergent political geography of violence. Thus Gujarat's political culture offers important symptomatic readings of productive tensions between economic and cultural globalization.[10]

The Normalization of Violence in Gujarat

Who could digest the "poison" of the Gujarat elections without inviting instant death? According to then-Prime Minister Atal Behari Vajpayee, the BJP alone, like Lord Shiva, could partake of the venom, digest it, and remain alive.[11] In this extraordinary image, Vajpayee may have been referring to the party's electoral invulnerability, such that even the gruesome violence on and after 27 February 2002 at Godhra, could not affect the BJP's chances of victory despite all the charges of political connivance. Far from expressing regret at the death and destruction, Vajpayee appeared to be boasting of the aura it created around the party that had made it more godlike and fearsome.

Part of the dismay following the BJP's victory in the state assembly elections in Gujarat in 2002 was that despite extensive media coverage of the violence against Muslims, the party connected with the violence, namely the BJP, won comfortably. Interestingly, violence was almost exclusively limited to constituencies where the Congress had posed a threat to the BJP in the past, in North and Central Gujarat. The BJP won fifty-two of sixty-five seats in these regions, much more than elsewhere in the state. If there were any doubt of the link between the BJP's victory and the violence, a poll conducted by the Centre for the Study of Developing Societies clarified the matter.[12]

Was it the case with Gujarat that reports of violence against Muslims conveyed to many voters merely the justifiable response of a party avenging Godhra? Many anecdotal accounts did indicate that Godhra provoked a demand for revenge. Does this imply that modernization and the growth of communications has finally promoted a realist mode of perception, with the masses attributing the causes of collective action to objective events recorded in television and print news? Posing the question thus underlines the transparency accorded to publicity, and the self-evident status ascribed to facts. It is true that discussions of political news tend to be dominated by a realist frame of perception, and by a conception of the fact as something immediately verifiable. Yet publicity does not produce transparency; facts are neither self-evident nor instantly ascertainable. Vajpayee's quote, presented earlier, confirms that a naïve realism is inadequate to understand Hindutva. Certainly we did not notice a collective inclination toward realism when it came to assessing, say, claims about Ram Janmabhumi, polygamous Muslim men, or "pseudosecular" politics. The response to Godhra was indeed rationalized as a reaction to the perceived reality of an incendiary Muslim mob and what it wrought. But it does not follow that this rationalization was itself justified.

Many have assumed otherwise. One columnist wrote that the images of burnt carriages and charred bodies, beamed through the evening of 27 February and the morning after, "made it real." When it became known that twenty-six women and ten children were included in the deaths, what followed was inevitable, he said, explaining that the mobs included large numbers of new middle classes with television sets.[13] This appeal to the realism of the televisual medium, by a reluctant critic of the BJP, acknowledged in an apologetic fashion the unsustainability of older fictions that, presumably, the older middle classes could have been relied upon to keep, through their more old-fashioned and implicitly more tolerant codes of conduct.

We can tentatively call the form of realism being invoked here Hindu national realism, not to identify a fait accompli by any means, but rather to underline the fact that it is not by brute power alone that Hindutva works. A political project like the BJP's is not confined to politics narrowly understood, but is world-making in its aims, and seeks to shape the forms of knowledge emerging along with it. Modes of perception and terms of understanding corresponding to them are created, implausible to the skeptical no doubt, but providing a self-confirming universe to others. My purpose in this chapter is to locate points of contradiction in this project, and to ask how secularism, with its own more sober and distinguished truth claims, could have allowed this alternative form of realism to grow with so little hindrance.

In this respect, talking about Gujarat to people who do not identify themselves in one way or another as either supporters or opponents of any political party has been interesting. Chatting with an undergraduate of Gujarati origin, active in organizing South Asians for a South Asian studies program on the NYU campus, I asked what people had been saying about recent events in Gujarat. She had just told me that nearly half the students of South Asian origin were Gujarati, so I assumed there must have been some mention of the riots. She looked blank. "What events?" she asked. "There were many people killed," I said, not wanting to say too much. "There was an earthquake in Gujarat two years ago," she said, trying to guess what I might have in mind. "We raised some money for it," she added. This conversation occurred some months after Godhra, but in the midst of national debates on the Gujarat elections. Although the massacres that had recently occurred were extensively televised, my query evoked no recognition.

It was tempting to dismiss this as the response of an uninformed youth to a vague question. I was reminded of it a few days later, when speaking on the telephone to an elderly relative in India, S. An invalid who spent her evenings in front of the television, she had always impressed people with her recall of events, public and private. "See what they've done— they've come into a temple and killed people," she said, referring to the attack at Akshardham temple in September 2002. "But this is because of all the killings that just happened," I replied. "What killings?" she asked, sounding perplexed. "All the killings that happened earlier this year, when many people died," I said. She remained confused. "There was an earthquake sometime ago," she said, implying that was what I must be referring to. S. had not voted for decades, and took mainly a dramaturgical interest in party politics.

I do not think her failure to remember was deliberate. Violence committed by so-called Hindus did not seem to register as violence. Neither of the persons I spoke to seemed to recognize Hindu aggression; both referred instead to the earthquake, invoking a metaphoric Richter scale of destruction and tectonic shift.

Somewhat similar accounts emerged from Gujarat itself. A human rights lawyer who investigated the Gujarat killings reported that, when she asked school children what happened in the year 2002, they replied, "Godhra." Asked what else happened, the children said, "Akshardham." Pressed to indicate if anything else happened, they mentioned terrorism, implicitly of Muslim origin, in other places. Only on further coaxing did they allude to violence against Muslims, dismissing it as a reactive episode.[14]

The accounts reported here are neither specifically religious nor political. They cannot be ascribed to ignorance in any simple sense either. News about Gujarat was abundant, but absorption of their import was contingent on prevailing frames of understanding. To invoke media bias as an explanation is also unsatisfactory. The little available analysis of news coverage about Gujarat does not point to any obvious pro-BJP tilt. Thus for instance the Editors' Guild Report has concluded, after a survey of news coverage on Gujarat, that "barring some notable offenders, especially Sandesh and Gujarat Samachar and certain local cable channels," the news media played an exemplary role.[15] Siddharth Varadarajan has gone further, to say that the news media were critical in bringing the violence to an end, and that it would have gone on for longer if not for press and TV coverage. Perhaps we still have much to learn about the structures of popular perception, and cannot assume the self-evident power of a realist sensibility.

Secular Realism and a Split Public

The introduction of television provided the technical means for thinking of the nation as a unified entity across a public divided by barriers of language, literacy, and region (with nationwide broadcasting beginning in 1982), and helped precipitate identitarian modes of addressing national questions (such as of secularism). The decision in 1987 to televise Hindu epics on state-owned television, violating a decades-old taboo on religious programming, was a fateful move in this respect. The epics, widely recognized but diversely understood, presented a narrative basis for imagining national unification. It was not surprising that Hindu nationalism was the most effective at making political capital out of this opportunity, and mobilizing national sentiment on the ground. Here the incapacity of secularism as a political force was revealed. Except for a well-educated minority, secularism could not provide an efficacious identity in the contests that ensued. The socially dominant portion of this minority was English-educated, for whom class and cultural privilege were intertwined with secular identity in ways that were difficult to disentangle. As a symptom of the kinds of problems involved here, we can recall that secularism was itself an English word, for which no proper South Asian equivalent existed.[16] If secularists could often not distinguish between challenges to their politics and resentment of their cultural privilege, it was because political form and cultural privilege appeared as one.

One reporter's account on a visit to Gujarat after the riots provides an interesting example of the difficulties of engaging across linguistic and cultural divides. The columnist Tavleen Singh, when chatting with some young men at a teashop in Mogri, found that their support for Narendra Modi was quite open; for instance they told her that if the Congress was in power, half of them would be in jail because Narendra Modi could not protect them. She then asked if they thought the massacres of Muslims and the rape of young girls in Ahmedabad had been a good thing. They replied "with angry unanimity and conviction," that there had been no rapes except in Godhra, where twenty women, according to the Gujarati newspapers, had been raped. Tavleen Singh told them that this was incorrect, and that *Sandesh* and *Gujarat Samachar* had published denials. With more anger, the young men—of whom there were "thirty or forty," said

"It is the English newspapers that tell lies." As Singh insistently carried on a debate with them, the men launched into an attack against the English press that was, "so angry and so aggressive that it seemed that there could be more violence," and so she left.

Tavleen Singh does not explore this incident further. It is worth asking why, for the young men, no defense was considered necessary when it came to Gujarati newspapers, even when they contradicted Hindutva claims. Similarly, it is striking that for Tavleen Singh, the charge that English newspapers tell lies is worth repeating only as a portrait of a communal mindset. The accusation itself is so uninteresting that no rebuttal is required. It was these men, and those like them, who were under investigation; to turn the telescope around was not required.

Here we can glimpse not only the mythic world of Hindu national realism, but also the parallel universe of secular realism, in an event that, despite a serious attempt at investigative journalism, appears like a missed encounter. One way to initiate a description of it is to indicate the material bases through which secular realism is constituted, in the means of its mediation. It is appropriate that the example chosen features a print journalist, because print news culture is indeed a privileged orbit of these parallel worlds. Print helps reinforce particular forms of knowledge without disclosing the identity of those who gain most by upholding these forms of knowledge, and its public is bounded by shared recognition of a given language. We can locate Nehruvian secularism here, at the level of sociolinguistic practice, in its adherents' ability to switch between different linguistic codes and registers, specifically between English as a language of command, and indigenous languages. Performative competence in elaborated codes of the English language appears as the public secret of secular realism. That secularism was identified with English language speakers was known to all, but it could not be admitted by English language users themselves, because this would obviously compromise the position from which they defended secularism, as well as secularism itself.

What did it mean for secularists to uphold realism in a society where realist narrative tropes were evident mainly in their scarcity, where the achievement of realism proceeded unevenly and contradictorily in a nationalist project that worked through a public split by language, caste, and creed? How did realism operate across a language divide when it was always seen to be anchored in the perceptual "neutrality" and objectivity of the English language news culture, and this news culture in its turn based its authority on a state whose neutrality was hardly a general assumption? Seen from the side of indigenous languages, it could be argued, as it has been argued, by Hindu nationalism, that the state was never neutral, but passed from one form of colonialism, British-led, to another, led by a technocratic English-speaking elite. Sober realism was hardly adequate to capture the registers of responses to this new and perhaps unforeseen marginalization, that is, the cultural invisibility of the Indian language intelligentsia, despite its history of being at the forefront of the anticolonial struggle, and the demographic majority it stood for, vis-à-vis English language speakers in India.

The realist epistemology of the English language elite often appeared like a relatively painless achievement because inherited from elsewhere. To establish and inscribe a realist aesthetics for an Indian language audience and simultaneously to dethrone this sensibility as it currently existed in the English language press (which provided the access route to the English language elite), to institute a different mode of realist perception—this can be described very briefly as part of the Hindu nationalist project, although to state it in this summary fashion is already to give it a coherence that such a mammoth undertaking cannot possibly possess.

Conclusion

National Human Rights Commission Chairman J. S. Verma, speaking to Prime Minister A. B. Vajpayee, asked him to translate his rhetoric on religious intolerance into action, and pointed out that those affected by the violence in Gujarat could not return to their homes, and had lost large numbers of their kith and kin. "How is it different from war?" the former Chief Justice of the Supreme Court asked.[17]

J. S. Verma, as Chief Justice, was the author of the landmark judgment in 1996, in which he ruled that Hindutva was a way of life, and as such could not be construed as a partisan appeal to religious identity. Hence, according to the Court, the Shiv Sena had not violated campaign rules in the elections following the demolition of Babri Masjid and the tumultuous violence that rocked Bombay thereafter. Within a few years he was confronting the party that incubated Hindutva, in another state, and another assembly election, where the violence preceding the campaign had escalated beyond almost anything seen in postindependence India.

As Verma implied, there was something about the violence in Gujarat in 2002 that made it qualitatively different. Justice Verma offered a name for the events and thus, a way of seeing them. The moral economy invoked was indeed not that of crime and punishment, but of battling an enemy nation, and of giving no quarter, lest one betray one's own country.

All Muslims were, in this view, actual or potential agents of Pakistan, and Pakistan was a terrorist nation implacably hostile to India. Implicitly and explicitly, being Hindu is the condition of belonging in India, and having one's rights protected.

In one of the most widely circulated remarks exemplifying such a view, the prominent Hindu leader Ashok Singhal termed Gujarat a "successful experiment" that would be repeated all over India. "Godhra happened on 27 February and the next day, fifty *lakh* Hindus were on the streets. We were successful in our experiment of raising Hindu consciousness, which will be repeated all over the country now." Singhal also spoke glowingly of how whole villages had been "emptied of Islam," and how whole communities of Muslims had been dispatched to refugee camps. This was a victory for Hindu society, he added, a first for the religion. "People say I praise Gujarat. Yes I do," he told an appreciative, but modest audience.[18]

The announcement was a provocative one. Singhal not only refused to condemn the violence following Godhra, but also endorsed it. As a glimpse of an emergent political culture deeply dependent on the press and television, it challenged the deeply held assumption that the development of mass mediated cultures in countries like India will repeat the historical experience of the west.

Very briefly, the historical crisis of experience in the west, as registered for example in art and literature in the late nineteenth and early twentieth centuries, of the decentering of the subject of knowledge and the emergence of multiple perspectives, occurs subsequent to the formation of national cultures, and well after the consolidation of the modern state. If the experience of modern industrialized society entails sensory shock and perceptual disorientation, they occur within national contexts where individualized forms of response are preponderant, for example through consumption and lifestyle modification. The political reverberations of this crisis are thus more contained, and can be mediated by experts working within contexts where the problems can be addressed as demanding administrative and technocratic solutions.[19] By contrast, in those countries where nation building has begun recently, the destabilization of traditional forms of knowledge, and the rapid circulation of as yet only partially assimilated technologies of perception, cannot be addressed in the same ways as in older industrial countries. In new nations haunted by the specter of failure and historical marginality, individual existential crises telescope into larger crises of national existence, as changes in perception and in politics tend to be read through each other. What results is a rich field of opportunity for political mobilization, in which the longstanding liberal confidence that the balance of power lies with the demographic majority has to be posed against the increasing difficulty of attaining outcomes that reproduce older liberal outcomes.

Notes

1 S. Varadarajan, Gujarat: The Making of a Tragedy (New Delhi: Penguin, 2003).
2 Yogendra Yadav, "The Patterns and Lessons," Frontline, 19, no. 26, (21 December 2002–3 January 2003), 11.
3 Editors' Guild, Fact-Finding Mission Report on Gujarat Riots (New Delhi, May 2002).
4 Daniel Lerner, The Passing of Traditional Society (Glencoe: Free Press, 1958); Wilbur Schramm, Communication and Change in Developing Countries (Honolulu: East–West Center Press, 1967).
5 Arvind Rajagopal, Politics After Television: Hindu Nationalism and the Reshaping of the Public in India (Cambridge: Cambridge University Press, 2001).
6 Thomas Hansen, The Saffron Wave (Princeton, N.J.: Princeton University Press, 1999); Rajagopal, Politics After Television.
7 Lal Krishna Advani, interview in The Economic Times, (Bombay, 10 August 1994), 7.
8 Jose Casanova, Public Religions in the Modern World (Chicago: University of Chicago Press, 1994); Martin Marty and R. Scott Appleby, ed., Fundamentalisms Observed (Chicago: University of Chicago Press, 1991).
9 Albert O. Hirschman, The Passions and the Interests: Political Arguments for Capitalism Before Its Triumph (Princeton, N.J.: Princeton University Press, 1977).
10 Arjun Appadurai, Modernity at Large (Minneapolis: University of Minnesota Press, 1996).
11 The Hindu, 25 December 2002.
12 Yadav, "The Patterns and Lessons," 12.
13 Prem Shankar Jha, "Gujarat: A Sober Diary," Outlook Magazine (New Delhi) 22 April 2002. http://outlookindia.com/full.asp?fodname=20020422&fname=Column+Prem+%28F%29&sid=1. (20 October 2005).
14 Smita Narula, Human Rights Watch, Personal Communication, 20 March 2003.
15 Editors' Guild, Fact-Finding Mission Report on Gujarat Riots, 18.
16 Partha Chatterjee, "Secularism and Tolerance," Economic and Political Weekly, 11 June 1994, 350–51.
17 Times of India, "Match Words with Action, NHRC tells PM," 4 August 2002.
18 Indian Express, "VHP: We'll Repeat our Gujarat Experiment," 4 September 2002.
19 Jonathan Crary, Suspensions of Perception (Cambridge, Mass.: MIT Press, 1999).

9

Asu Aksoy and Kevin Robins

Turkish Satellite Television:

Toward the Demystification of Elsewhere

All across the European space now, Turkish-speaking populations are tuning in to the numerous satellite channels that are broadcasting programs from Ankara and Istanbul. Just like other migrant groups—Maghrebis, Arabs, Chinese, Indians, Afro-Caribbeans, and many more—they are now able to make use of transnational communications to gain access to media services from the country of origin. This has been an entirely new phenomenon, a development of the past decade, which has significant implications for how migrants experience their lives and for how they think and feel about their experiences. Indeed, we would regard the ability to routinely watch television from Turkey, and to be thereby in synchronized contact with everyday life and events in Turkey, as being a key innovation in the lives of Turkish migrants. Arguably, the arrival of Turkish television has made a difference—a crucial difference—for Turkish-speaking immigrants living in Europe.

But what, precisely, is the nature of the difference that television makes for those living in migrant contexts? What is the nature of Turkish migrants' engagement with the new transnational media? What are the implications—social, cultural, experiential—of having access to programming from the country of origin? Drawing on and extending research that we have been undertaking among the Turkish-speaking populations in London, we focus these questions on the particular theme of this book: the migrant relation to "elsewhere" or "elsewheres." In the case of migrant groups, the relation to "elsewhere" is generally restricted in social and cultural research to the relation to "home." Their "homeland," the homeland that has been left behind, is invariably regarded as the significant—and sometimes as the only—reference point in migrants' lives. And the underlying sentiment is that migrants are constitutively afflicted by a sense of lack or loss, and by a desire to be reconnected to their distant homeland (this trope we shall consider in the following part of this discussion). We will argue that the situation among contemporary migrants is actually more complex than these narratives of homeland, estrangement, and long-distance national attachments and belongings allow for. Migrants—and migrant television audiences—are, we suggest, actually negotiating positions between national and transnational spaces in new and significant ways. Their complex management of their relation to both proximity and distance merits reflection and, we think, revision of old orthodoxies.

In recent research in media and cultural studies, there has been considerable interest in new media and the construction of what have been called new electronic geographies, including electronic elsewheres. This interest concerns how new technologies may overcome the frictions of (physical) distance, and promote new kinds of encounter and interaction "at a distance." In the following discussion, we want to sound a note of caution in the face of this new technological emphasis. We will make two brief points here, with specific reference to our own case study material on transnational media reception. First, and perhaps it is just a minor point of qualification, we should recognize that, whereas satellite television has, of course, been crucial in mediating the relation of Turks to their country of origin, it is not only through television, and other media, that Turkish people relate to Turkey and get a sense of how it is now. As communications infrastructures have developed, and transportation (particularly air travel) has become cheaper, people frequently visit their relatives, or just go to Turkey for a holiday. They therefore have a more direct and unmediated sense of the country (and, let us emphasize here, not just of Turkey, for they also travel increasingly to visit relatives and friends in other parts of Europe). Their electronic elsewheres are only one, partial, aspect of Turks' more diverse and complex elsewhere experiences.

Our second point offers what we regard as a more significant critique and qualification of the electronic bias in much contemporary media and cultural studies research. In the case of Turkish migrants, we shall argue, the critical issue with respect to their relation to "elsewhereness" (of Turkey, but also the wider European space) is not primarily technological mediation, but, rather, the changing nature of Turkish migrant society and sociality. In other words, we adopt a social, rather than a technological, approach to the changing phenomenology of elsewhere. The findings of our research resonate strongly with those of migration researchers who have identified the formation of new "transnational communities."[1] Transnational communities are made up of the "growing number of persons who live dual lives, speaking two languages, having homes in two countries, and making a living through continuous regular contact across national borders."[2] These migrants—or transmigrants[3]—are involved in new kinds of transnational mobility and networking, developing what we might call transcultural dispositions that confound old (nation-based) models of both minority integration and transnational diaspora. Transnational migrants are actively involved in multiple linkages, and depend for their livelihoods on such linkages and networks. They therefore tend to have complex sets of affiliations. Their interests cannot be served by any single nation-state, and so there is no longer a positive incentive to invest their interests and attachments in any one national community, "home" or "away." It is consequently in their interest to remain at odds with both the host society and the society of origin. It is precisely through what might be termed strategic nonassimilation that such migrants can succeed in making a living and creating a new lifespace for themselves.

Migrants are now routinely able, then, to establish transnational communities that exist across two, or more, cultural spaces: we may speak of the enlargement of the lifespace of migrants, involving the capacity to be synchronized with lifeworlds situated elsewhere. What we want to look at, in what follows, is how these new kinds of transnational or transcultural networks and mobilities may be changing the nature or potential of migrant experience and thinking. What we will seek to draw out is what seems to us to be a growing reflexivity and lucidity with respect to collective identities, involving a significant change in the very nature of the relation that many migrants have to identity, and in the way that they think about their relation to collective communities, obligations, destinies, and so on, wherever. It is precisely this shift of experiential, intellectual, and imaginative perspective—and not the impetus of technological innovation—that we think is most significant for understanding the changing relation to "home," "homeland" and "elsewhere"—which we consider in terms of what we regard as the progressive demystification of elsewhere.

The Diasporic Paradigm and the Phantasmatic Elsewhere

Before we move on to focus on Turkish migrant contributions to understanding the changing sociology and phenomenology of elsewhere, let us first try to clarify what might be progressive (a difficult word these days) about their experiences and insights. Progressive in what sense? Progressive with respect to what? We need a reference point. And that reference point, we suggest, is what has been the prevailing way of thinking about migrants and their elsewheres until now: the diasporic paradigm. The concept of diaspora has become a favored one in social and cultural theory,[4] but a problematic one (increasingly problematic, in fact, because of its now inflated use). For what it does is to project a deterministic narrative onto the lives and motivations of migrants: a narrative concerning their belonging to a particular collective (national) culture, and concerning the implications and consequences of such a kind of attachment and belonging. "Diaspora" is preeminently a category of the national imagination. It is the kind of category that, in Anthony Cohen's terms, puts forward the proposition that the individual is "the nation writ small," and that the individual is motivated by the same logic and values as the imagined national collectivity.[5]

If we just turn to Turkish television for a moment, before moving on to cultural theory, then we can see the diasporic assumption—which we may see as a basic national assumption—in a simple, pretheoretical form. Thus, TRT, the state broadcaster, has considered Turkish populations living in Europe as "offshore" nationals. And one aspect of the TRT project has been about reaching the population of Turkish migrants in Europe, and about drawing them back into the Turkish national imaginary. As one TRT executive put it to us:

> When the Turkish population living abroad began to grow, then the fear that we might lose them came to the forefront. In Europe, and especially in Germany, it was felt that the new generation was drifting away from Turkey. In response to this, in order to strengthen people's ties with Turkey, more programs were made in the early nineties that targeted them, those living abroad.[6]

The consistent assumption has been that the Turks in Europe remain part of—that is to say, remain loyal to—this national project. The unquestioned belief, in other words, is that Turkey remains the significant elsewhere for migrant populations. In Turkish broadcasting culture (and Turkish broadcasting culture is, of course, far from unique), it is commonly asserted that Turks in Europe who watch satellite channels from Turkey are doing so because they want to be immersed in the culture of their "homeland." The commercial Turkish media, too, seem to believe that this kind of service is what they are providing. Thus, a commercial market research report concerning the consumption patterns of Turks in Germany points to the "high affinity to home [*heimatlich*] programs and to advertising on Turkish television."[7] And a marketing brochure promoting EuroD (*Reach 4.5 Million Turks in Europe*) makes the claim, with respect to European Turks, that "European television leaves them where they are: Turkish television takes them home." "In Germany," it is said,

> nearly a million televisions are turned [sic] into Turkish television by satellite during prime time every night. Turkish viewers overwhelmingly choose Turkish broadcasts whether not to forget Turkish or because they love Turkish pop-music or they find Turkish programming more meaningful. From politics to comedy, the Turks of Europe keep in touch with their roots by satellite, the only broadcast where you can really communicate with them. These viewers value Turkish television entertainment and they are willing and able to buy satellite dishes. In fact, survey results show that the loyalty of European Turks to Turkish broadcasting is unshakeable.

The discourse centers on the value of national belonging: it seems as if belonging to an imagined community—in this case the imagined community of the Turks—is the only basis on which it would be possible to make sense of viewers' engagement with the new transnational media culture. The value of Turkish media for Turkish audiences is, according to EuroD, to "keep them in touch with their homeland." The homeland is posited as their self-evidently significant and only elsewhere.

These are rather blunt (and perhaps incidental) expressions of the diasporic imagination, inspired by an unthinking national bias. The analysis of diasporas in contemporary media and cultural studies is clearly in a different league of theoretical sophistication. But we will argue that these more sophisticated theoretical discourses are actually inhabited by the same basic (national) assumptions about the imaginary location and nature of migrants' significant elsewhere. In accounts of diasporic media, what we commonly find is a concern with long-distance nationalism (long-distance imagined community). The taken-for-granted assumption is that migrant communities make use of new transnational media to maintain "bonds of cohesiveness" with the "homeland." New communications technologies are primarily understood—and valued—insofar as they work to sustain cultural cohesion and solidarity—the ties of imagined community—over 'global distances. As with the Turkish broadcasters, albeit in an entirely different register, what is presented as being most significant is the capacity of new media technologies to maintain "at-a-distance commonalities," to effect "transnational bonding," to sustain "transnations." The overriding concern and interest is with the capacity of new media technologies to connect and direct migrants back to their originary elsewhere.[8]

Let us here consider just one variant of the cultural analysis of diasporas. It is an approach that seems on the surface to be entirely at odds with the national (and sometimes nationalistic) discourses of the Turkish broadcasters. It offers a particular approach to the diasporic condition from the migrant perspective. It sets out from the observation that migration and movement from one country to another, whether in the form of economic migration or asylum seeking, has involved an experience of separation—the migrant has inevitably left behind his or her home, relatives, friends, surroundings, familiar objects, and the everyday routines of everyday life. We are concerned, then, with a particular imagination of migration in the recent literature of cultural, migration, and postcolonial studies that has taken the drama of separation and the pathos of distance from the homeland as its core issues. Migration is essentially conceived through the figures of exile, loss, and longing.

This is essentially an imagination of migration as estrangement, as Sara Ahmed makes apparent. Migration may be considered, she says, "as a process of estrangement, a process of becoming estranged from that which was inhabited at home. . . . It [involves] a process of transition, a movement from one register to another."[9] Migration involves both "spatial dislocation" and "temporal dislocation": it is about separation and distance from the homeland, and also involves the experience of discontinuity between past and present. Through the process of migration, a radical break is assumed to have taken place; and this break is associated with a sense of acute discomfort, involving "the failure to fully inhabit the present or present space"[10] Ahmed makes it clear that there are ways to redeem the sense of alienation, ways of creating new communities to substitute for the lost community. But it seems that this kind of redemption can only ever be partial, and that the original home will continue to function as a key point of reference. What migration always involves, according to Ahmed, is "a splitting of home as place of origin and home as the sensory world of everyday experience."[11]

From a somewhat different perspective—actually that of a group analyst working with Turkish-speaking immigrants in London—Seda Şengün develops a similar argument. For her, too, migration involves a process of estrangement, associated with "separation from the mother culture," as she puts it.[12] "For the immigrant things once thought to be objectively perceived are no longer so," says Şengün. "There is a completely different reality. The language one always spoke does not make sense to others. . . . Everyday things which are taken for granted are either not there any more or strongly questioned."[13] This experience of cultural dislocation is again regarded as one of discomfort (potentially it is a "traumatic experience,") we are told.[14] Like Ahmed, Şengün believes that there are ways of coping with the "anxiety of separation," but here again we find the sense of a deep, underlying antinomy of "mother culture" and "new culture."[15] "Sometimes," says Şengün, "the conflict between the new and the old culture and experiences becomes so intense and unbearable that, as a defense, strong splitting occurs."[16] Again, it is the image of splitting—this time in a more explicitly psychotherapeutic or psychoanalytical sense—that is being deployed to describe the migrant's situation "between cultures."

Estrangement from the "mother" culture, distanciation from the place of origin, processes of splitting, involving idealization of, and nostalgia for, the "homeland"—these have all by now become familiar (if not overfamiliar) themes and motifs. Although Ahmed and Şengün come out of rather different theoretical contexts and orientations—one from cultural studies, the other from transcultural psychotherapy—their concerns are remarkably similar. Both of them, in their different ways, put an emphasis on the sense of loss and consequent yearning that has seemed to be such an integral part of migrant experience. Each draws our attention to the ever-present desire to affirm, and often idealize, the culture of the homeland. This affirmation may often be simple and quotidian. Şengün tells us that the "own" culture may function "like a teddy bear during the mother's absence": "Familiar tastes, smells, tunes and gestures provide containment and comfort, reducing the anxiety of separation. When a migrant eats food which is specific to his original country, or listens to a song in his own language, he is immediately linked to his past and his own culture."[17] At other times, in other contexts, holding on to the lost culture may assume more epic and dramatic dimensions, and involve the invocation of a "mythic past," as Ahmed puts it.[18] As an example of this tendency toward mythologization, we might cite from Eva Hoffman's acclaimed autobiography, *Lost in Translation*, where the experience of separation is conceived in terms of a fall from paradise. "Loss," says Hoffman, "is a magical preservative. Time stops at the point of severance, and no subsequent impressions muddy the water you have in mind. The house, the garden, the country you have lost remain forever as you remember them. Nostalgia—that most lyrical of feelings—crystallizes around these images like amber."[19] Nostalgia is, as Vladimir Jankélévitch observes, a melancholy brought about by "awareness of something other, awareness of somewhere else, awareness of a contrast between past and present, and between present and future"—and migrations have created the conditions for its most intense and elaborated forms of expression.[20]

In this part of our argument, we have briefly addressed quite different variants of the diasporic imagination. And, of course, we acknowledge that, in many senses, there is a world of difference between the discourses of the Turkish broadcasters and those of cultural analysts like Ahmed and Şengün. But the reason for juxtaposing them is that there is also a significant underlying commonality. The diasporic imagination—in whichever variant—is, in the end, grounded in the mentality of imagined communities, cultures, and identities. And, as such, it is bound to construct a particular model of migrant culture and the migrant condition. As Roger Rouse has argued, such an imagination involves "asserting and organizing around either revalorized versions of ascribed identities or new ones that the (im)migrants develop for themselves." This is an agenda that regards individuals as socially or culturally derived and driven—an agenda that works to perpetuate the "assumption that the possession of identities and processes of identity formation are universal aspects of human experience.[21] Whether it takes a statist form (as in the pronouncements of the Turkish broadcasters) or the more romanticized cultural form of the exilic sensibility, the diasporic mentality conceives of the migrant individual as, in some way, a function of his or her collective culture and "heritage." He or she "belongs" to the imagined community; the imagined community is bound to be and remain their fundamental point of reference, interest and meaning.

And, to focus on the particular theme of the present discussion, this diasporic *imaginaire* clearly has implications for the migrant's sense of elsewhere. This particular elsewhere-orientation has two aspects that we want to draw attention to. First, elsewhere—the significant elsewhere—is always, and must always be, the "homeland." And, as such, elsewhere is a locus of collective and shared identification and imagination. "Only individual humans are real," observes Jacques Rancière, "they alone have a will and an intelligence, and the totality of the order that subjects them to humankind, to social laws and to diverse authorities, is only a creation of the imagination."[22] What the diasporic imagination does is to naturalize and sanction that "creation of the imagination" (which is, actually, *only* a creation of the imagination). Second, the elsewhere-homeland exists as a place and a community (the one true elsewhere) from which the migrant has come to be separated. Separation is the essential condition of migration. The migrant has been condemned or fated to be at a remove from where he or she really "belongs," and he or she must be acutely aware of the distance between "there" and "here," "then" and "now." The idealization of the homeland and the sense of distance and/or loss combine, we believe, to create a deeply problematic relation to (the migrant's) elsewhere. The diasporic imagination—in both nationalist and exilic forms— encourages projective mechanisms associated with the institution of what we might term an elsewhere-illusion. We would characterize the diasporic elsewhere as essentially a phantasmatic elsewhere.

A Changing Relation to Elsewhere

We have been critical of the diasporic conception of elsewhere, for we believe that it sustains a mythology (in different modalities, of course) of home and homeland. Migrants are invited to invest—intellectually, imaginatively, and emotionally—in the fiction of imagined community. Within the diasporic frame, what has been instituted is essentially a phantom elsewhere. What we now want to do is to reflect on how it might be possible to move beyond this frame. We will do this, not by engaging in theoretical and conceptual critique, but by looking at certain new developments in migrant cultures that cannot be made sense of within this diasporic cultural frame (and which may even be affecting the conditions of possibility of the diasporic imagination). We want to consider new practices that seem to open up an alternative, and potentially more creative, relation to elsewhere—a more complex relation to elsewhere.

And so we come now to our Turkish case study. Turkish populations in Europe provide an excellent example of the new kinds of developments that Portes and others characterize in terms of a new kind of transnational migrancy. The relative proximity of Turkey to western Europe, the availability of cheap and frequent flights, and the recent proliferation of new media services and communications links, are developments that are now making it possible for Turks living in Europe to achieve a new mobility across cultural spaces. In this discussion, we shall focus on what we regard as one of the key innovations in the lives of Turkish migrants, which is simply the ability to routinely watch television from Turkey, and to be thereby in synchronized contact with everyday life and events in Turkey. The arrival of Turkish television made a crucial difference for Turkish-speaking migrants living in Europe. But what precisely was the nature of that difference? What we shall argue is that the consumption of transnational media has been associated with interestingly new strategies in the management of separation and distance. And let us reiterate here that we are not putting forward some variant of technological determinism. Our argument (in line with the "transnational communities" agenda) is that something significant is happening through the emergence of transnational migrant cultures and experiences. And satellite television has provided one vital space in which that significant something is being articulated and can be discerned.

In the following discussion, then, we shall focus closely on media consumption by Turkish migrants. We shall try to identify something of the changing nature of their migrant experience—something of the way they might be rethinking their positionality between the here of their daily lives and the (various) elsewheres available to them. Of course, their behavior will always have habitual and unreflective aspects. At the same time, however, they are drawn into a constant movement between cultural positionings—being distant from what is seen on the television, being part of another life experience in another cultural setting, and yet still being connected to Turkey. Inevitably this compels reflection and thought— thought that moves across spaces, between here and elsewheres.

Fantasy and Nostalgia—And Ambivalence and Reflexivity

How does this kind of mobile thinking manifest itself? In the research that we have undertaken in London, what comes across is the way in which migrants reflect on their fantasies, reexperience their frustrations, articulate the tensions between their spontaneous and deliberative responses, and work through their complex and conflicting thoughts about their always ambivalent relationship to Turkish (television) culture. One of the ways in which migrants think about their relation to Turkish culture is through the modality of fantasy and nostalgia (we choose this example, of course, in order to engage with the melancholic variant of the diasporic imagination). They may choose to seek out those kinds of programs that convey an ideal image of Turkey and of Turkishness. "I love old Turkish films on television," said a man in his late thirties, "they take me back to Turkey."[23] "I sometimes ask myself," said another man,

> What does a person outside his country miss the most? We go out for picnics occasionally—if you can call it a picnic, since we can't find trees to sit under and we can't start our grill. It is at these moments that I start thinking

about our meadows back at home, our pine trees, our water. I'm from the Black Sea region and I remember our cool water falls, our sea. I wish my children could see the plateaux, the summer feasts, and learn about our customs and traditions. . . . I wish these were on Turkish television.[24]

Again and again, people express their heartfelt desire to see a Turkey— whether it is in nature, childhood memories, or the "old days"—that would make them happy. They look to television as the most obvious place to reflect back to them their ideal sense of Turkey—a Turkey that is longed for, desired, missed.

Sometimes fragments of this desired image of the ideal Turkey can be picked up from old movies, or from programs that celebrate special events that have shaped Turkish consciousness. What seems to appeal is a sense of purity and unity—hints of a world before degeneration had set in. A young woman, who came to Britain when she was seven, told us how these kinds of programs could carry her into "a rose-tinted world." It is possible, she said, "to become lost in dreams, imaginings . . . it gives you a very sweet sense."[25] A middle-aged woman from the Black Sea region, who has been in London for a decade, is happy to watch even the Islamic-oriented Kanal 7—and to let go of what she regards as her secularist principals—just so that she can hear Turkish folk music: "When I listen to the regional tunes I am absorbed, lost in my old days. I wish the other channels would reflect our culture. Then everybody would be happy. . . . I sit for hours watching, absorbed in my dreams."[26] "We expect Turkish television to reflect those life styles that belong to our childhood," says another focus group participant.[27] So television programs are scrutinized with this needy eye. There is this tremendous need for objects on which to project and preserve an ideal image of Turkey.

These idealizations are, indeed, a significant aspect of the migrant experience. And sometimes, it is clear, such imaginings can be overpowering. But what we have found in talking to Turkish migrants is that, even as they articulate such idealizations, they are commonly doing so in a self-aware and self-reflecting way. They are conscious of their need to elaborate compensatory mechanisms. And they know very well that their idealizations are rooted in a past that has gone, a past that can never be brought back to life. Even when they are dreaming in this way, then, they are *thinking*, and thinking critically. They are able to also stand at a critical distance from their dreaming selves. And they are able to think about the significance of this dreaming experience—to reflect on that (partial) aspect of themselves that is happy to be engaged, from time to time, with the world of phantom identities.

And they are also thinking, at the same time, about how these idealizations and fantasies relate to the actual reality of Turkey. For they generally recognize that the ideal that they sometimes invoke does not at all correspond to the Turkey that they know from personal experience. And this recognition is always a source of disappointment. "After three years being away, when I went back to Turkey I realized that it was definitely not the place that I left behind. I saw that it was not the place that I carried in my head, in my brain. . . . [I]t is not a place that I would search for, where I would desire to be."[28] It is important here to stress that it is not only through television and the media in general that Turkish people get a sense of Turkey as it is now. As communications and transportation become cheaper, people phone more, they visit their relatives, or just go to Turkey for a holiday. They have a more direct sense of it. And, paradoxically, having a more direct sense of Turkey can make these Turks more detached. "I feel like a foreigner in Turkey," says one young woman, who came to Britain ten years ago, at the age of seventeen, "I can't recognize the money, I find shopping very different—in other words I find everything different there. For this reason I'm glad to be here [in London]. I feel I've grown up here. I wouldn't think of going back. I would go for visits, but not for good."[29] First-generation migrants, as well as younger ones, carry this fear—that, if they returned to Turkey, they would no longer fit in—that they would not be able to absorb and adapt to the changes that have taken place in the country since they left. As well as having a fantasy dimension, then, the thinking of migrants about their relationship to Turkey and to Turkishness is also informed by a strong reality principle. They are moving across modalities of experiencing and of thinking about experiences.

Satellite television allows these viewers to grasp compensatory images, to think about their experiences by means of these idealized or nostalgic images, and then to go on to reflect on their thinking processes. And we should just make the point obvious here that there is a great deal more happening in the viewing practices of Turkish migrants than simply this engagement with fantasy and nostalgia. There are, of course, many other kinds of programming that they are watching, and quite other kinds of relationships with the complicated world of the screen. If Turkish migrants have a desire for fantasy, they also have an even stronger desire for actuality—for news and current affairs. And let us be clear that their mediated access to Turkish news and actuality is also very far from being a straightforward experience for them (but we will not go into this here).[30] What we see in these observations by Turkish migrants is that their Turkey is far from being the idealized homeland as conceived by the diasporic imagination. What we find are more complex and ambivalent feelings and thoughts. And we find also a relation to Turkey, and to their thoughts and feelings about Turkey, that is highly reflexive. Their mediated engagement with Turkey, in combination with their unmediated experiences, conspires to produce a disillusionment (in the positive, Winnicottian sense of that term) of their relation to elsewhere. Fantasy and nostalgia are transformed through the mental processes—the mental and imaginative optics—of ambivalence and reflexivity.

The Demythologization of Separation and Distance

Let us now consider a further way in which Turkish migrants have negotiated the condition of separation and distance from the "homeland." Watching Turkish television seems, at face value, to be about gratifying the desire to "be there": to be connected back into everyday Turkish rhythms and realities. In the frame of the diasporic cultural and media studies, the idea is put forward that new media systems can work to bridge global distances, supporting long-distance bonding with the "homeland," the maintenance of at-a-distance links with a faraway "somewhere else." At one level, this idea of electronic transmission to elsewhere may seem relatively straightforward and uncontentious. But is satellite television really taking the diaspora back home? Is it really the case that migrants are being reconnected to faraway eleswheres across the world? We should ponder on these generally taken-as-given tropes of time and space transcendence.

On the basis of our own research, we would characterize what is actually happening somewhat differently. Let us listen to what Turkish migrants have to say. As one Turkish-Cypriot man put it to us, "It [satellite television] gives you more freedom, because you don't feel so far away, because it's only six foot away from you, you don't feel so far away from it. Cyprus is like one switch of a button away, or Turkey even, mainland Turkey, you are there, aren't you?"[31] Even a young woman who migrated when she was quite young, and who is therefore not really familiar with the country, has this sense of greater proximity to the actuality of Turkey. She thinks that it is very good to be able to watch satellite television "because you too can see what's been going on in Turkey, the news. . . . I used to think that Turkey was a different kind of place. It's bringing it [Turkey] closer."[32] The key image is that of closeness: television makes a difference because it is in its nature—in the nature of television as a medium—to bring (Turkish) things closer to its viewers. The key issue concerns how transnational media can now bring Turkish cultural products and services to migrants living in London, and of how "Turkey" is consequently brought closer to them.

Two women told us of how satellite television now allows them to be synchronized with Turkish realities. "Most certainly [Turkish] television is useful for us," says one. "It's almost as if we're living in Turkey, as if nothing has really changed for us." The other confirmed this, saying that, "When you're home, you feel as if you are in Turkey. Our homes are already decorated Turkish style, everything about me is Turkish, and when I'm watching television too."[33] The key issue here has to do with the meaning of this feeling of "as if nothing has really changed for us." In the context of the diasporic agenda, this feeling of synchronization would be thought of in terms of the maintenance of at-a-distance ties—in terms of the supposed capacity of transnational media to connect migrant communities back to the cultural space of their distant "homeland." For us, in significant contrast, it is about the growing availability in London of imported things from Turkey—where we might regard the availability of television programs as being on a continuum with the (equally common) availability of food, clothes, or furnishings from Turkey. "Nothing has really changed" does not refer, then, to ethnocultural reconnection to some imagined "homeland," but simply to the possibility of having access in London now to Turkish consumer goods and the world of Turkish consumer culture. It is "almost as if we're living in Turkey" in that sense, being in a position to be Turkish in London, that is to say, and not at all in the sense of "being taken back home."

What we want to emphasize here, then, is the capacity of the reality dimension of television to undercut the abstract nostalgia of the diasporic imagination. What television does is to bring the ordinary, banal reality of Turkish life to the migrants living in London. The key to understanding transnational Turkish television is in its relation to banality. Jankélévitch notes how people who are in exile can imagine that they are living double lives, carrying around within them "inner voices . . . the voices of the past and of the distant city," while at the same time submitting to "the banal and turbulent life of everyday action."[34] This is precisely the mechanism of splitting—whereby the negativity and discomfort of the "here and now" provides the stimulus for nostalgic dreams and fantasies about the "there and then." Now, what we regard as significant about transnational television is that, as a consequence of bringing the mundane, everyday reality of Turkey "closer," it is actually working to undermine this false polarizing logic. The "here and now" reality of Turkish media culture disturbs the imagination of a "there and then" Turkey, thereby working against the romance of diaspora-as-exile, against the tendency to false idealization of the "homeland." We might say, then, that transnational Turkish television functions as an agent of cultural demythologization—the demythologization of elsewhere. The world of Turkish television is an ordinary world, and its significance resides, we suggest, in its ordinary, banal, and everyday qualities—which are qualities it has in common with countless other TV worlds. As Marisca Milikowski observes, Turkish satellite television "helps Turkish migrants, and in particular their children, to liberate themselves from certain outdated and culturally imprisoning notions of Turkishness, which had survived in the isolation of migration."[35]

The point, then, is that Turkish culture is demystified, rendered ordinary again, such that the defense of identity no longer seems the fundamental issue that it once might have. Migrants are relieved of the feeling of having to hang on defensively to a culture and identity that might be "lost." Access to the Turkish media brings with it a new experience of cultural freedom. They feel free to continue to be like ordinary human beings again, moving on in their lives. They can take Turkish culture for granted, and so they are free to get on with other things. Once migrants no longer feel disconnected from, or deprived of, Turkish culture, they can regain a sense of ease. Satellite television affords them the chance to once again make meaningful cultural and informational choices, and to feel that they are themselves in control of the choices they make.

". . . Compare, Reflect, Criticize, Understand, Combine . . ."

When cultural studies of transnational media assert that migrants want to connect back to their homeland-elsewhere, they invariably present this as a kind of identity strategy. As we have already observed, transnational media technologies, and satellite television in particular, are valued insofar as they promise to sustain identity attachments—that is to say, the bonds of imagined community—over global distances. Such an identity strategy is understood to be motivated by the migrant's sense of spatial and temporal "dislocation." And it is suggested that new transnational media might provide some kind of fix for this condition of identity dislocation. What they seem to promise is some form of compensation—albeit partial—for what Sara Ahmed characterizes in terms of a logic of "splitting" between "home as place of origin" and "home as the world of everyday experience."[36] It seems as if they might help to bridge the two worlds—the ultimately irreconcilable worlds—of then and now, of there and here.

We want to suggest that what is happening is both more complex and more pragmatic than this rather frozen and static scenario allows for. In order to understand something of this greater complexity in the migrant consumption of media, we think it is necessary to abandon the identity paradigm. In its place, we want to install the categories of "mind" and "intelligence," which are central to all human experience (let us emphasize here that this should not be read in terms of the construction of an overrationalistic model of the migrant viewer; we fully recognize that intelligence manifests itself through many different modalities of thinking, imagining, and feeling). As John Dewey once noted, "Mind in its individual aspect is shown to be the method of change and progress in the significance and values attached to things."[37] In this context, we will consider satellite and other television channels as important sources of information (among other things) for migrant viewers, allowing them to have news both from and about the various elsewheres that are significant to them. We are interested in what and how they are thinking when they select from the television channels that they watch. What are their motivations in their viewing practices? What are the implications for significance and values they attach to things?

Turkish migrants want to have as much information as possible about the events going on in the world that are of concern to them. This is captured by a young man who had been in Britain for eleven years, since the age of six. "For me," he says,

> it is important to know what's going on in the world, and Turkey is part of the world. [When you watch Turkish television] you know what's going on in Turkey, and you know what's going on around the world. If you just watch English television—because there is a lot of things which they don't tell you about abroad—they do, but they tell you the main stories, but they hardly ever occur in Turkey. . . . I find it interesting [to watch Turkish television] because you know what is going on in Turkey, and you get informed about stuff that is going on abroad.[38]

A Turkish-Cypriot man, who had been in Britain for a very long time, also emphasized the importance for him of the diversity of information sources. Having access to a variety of different sources allowed him, he said, to move across channels for news that he found interesting. "First we watch the English news," he said, "then we listen to the news about our homeland, and then, when we are bored with them, we switch over to the French or German stations, or to CNN."[39] The ability to range transnationally across channels and programs—and not just Turkish channels and programs—means being able to find information that might not be available on British television, information that may be more thorough, and that also reflects different perspectives on international events.

The demand for information becomes especially significant in times of international tension and crisis, such as in the period after 11 September 2001. During such times, there is an increased desire for more, and more diverse, sources of information—and yet we may say that this desire is complicated by a simultaneous skepticism about the reliability of these different sources. One person—the owner, at the time, of a broken-down satellite dish—expressed this combination of need and ambivalence thus:

> When there's a news item about a world event, we always look at British television as well. We compare them both [British and Turkish]. If our satellite dish were working, we would have done the same. We would have watched the news on both, to see who says what; a bit of curiosity, a desire to catch a bit more detail about something. We think that they all report in a biased way. Maybe we're mistaken, maybe what they're reporting is correct, but we're not satisfied. . . . That's why we change channels, move across different channels, to have more knowledge, to be reassured, to be better informed. . . . As long as I'm not satisfied, I look at other channels, to see what this one is saying, what that one is saying. . . . It's a kind of a small-scale research on our part.[40]

Through this mobility across channels, these transnational viewers seek out and select different elements from the various bodies of mediated evidence, as it were, in order to build up a more coherent overall picture than any single channel puts on offer. In a discussion of the 11 September events, a Kurdish man emphasizes the need for critical comparative research on the part of viewers:

> Of course there is difference [between different television stations]. Medya TV [the main Kurdish station] concentrated on the implications of these events for the Kurds. If you wanted to see things live, then you had to watch the English media, because they are more technologically advanced. They can show things at the same time as they are happening, and they could show things from different sides. This is true for channels like CNN. If you are interested in the implications of all this for us, for Turks and Kurds, then you watch Medya TV.[41]

In the aftermath of 11 September, different stations and channels were constantly being compared. Transnational viewers sifted through the information available to them, constantly making evaluations of the different channels they watched, assessing news coverage in terms of a variety of criteria—factual information, direct coverage, historical perspective, political point of view, bias, censorship, and so on.

This comparative positioning that migrant audiences find themselves in with respect to the media makes them particularly aware, then, of the limits of media in terms of being objective mediators of information. As a consequence of their experience of Turkish state media, Turks and Kurds are particularly sensitive to bias and manipulation in the media. "In general, when you look at the news, they are literally propagating views," said a Kurdish woman. "In Turkey the media are extremely controlled. This is so clear. Maybe it's because we are looking at it from afar, from the outside. I sometimes feel I am going to explode from frustration. They [Turkish media] manipulate things."[42] Another participant in the same group discussion then added that, "English media do it more professionally, more unnoticed, in ways we don't understand. In fact we are influenced by it, but we don't realize . . . very smooth. The Turkish ones are more blatant."[43] The point, then, is that there is a generalized skepticism and caution with respect to all media—they are all seen as in some way politically biased. And because they feel that they cannot trust any television channel, they become aware that they have to do the thinking for themselves. "When we watch [television] . . . we don't just accept what they're telling us," said a politically engaged young Kurdish woman. "The news that we get, we evaluate in our own heads. We don't think in the way things are presented to us."[44] And a devout Muslim man put the point to us even more forcefully (with particular reference to Turkish media): "I ask you to take this message, write this down. There are many people who think like us. When they broadcast, they shouldn't insult us. They shouldn't try to direct us or influence us when they are presenting the news. We will decide ourselves."[45] These transnational migrants want to be in a position—because they feel they now *must* be in a position—to make their own interpretations and form their own judgments about news events.

What we are saying, then, is that Turkish and Kurdish migrants are in a process of changing their relation to knowledge. In the transnational context in which they now live, they no longer take the national community—the British or the Turkish—as their natural frame of reference. Sonia Livingstone draws attention to the way in which the relation between social knowledge and audiences has been conceptualized in terms of an "interpretative community." According to this model, the media are conceived as "a resource by which, almost irrespective of their institutional purposes, meanings are circulated and reproduced according to the contextualized interests of the public. Public knowledge . . . becomes the *habitus*, the shared representations, the lived understandings of the community."[46] Livingstone recognizes that mediated knowledge is not just about recognition of the familiar and known, but also about the discovery of the new. But, even with respect to the new and unfamiliar, the point is that "we also need a ritual model to understand such knowledge in terms of local meanings and shared assumptions."[47] What we are saying with respect to transnational migrants, is that they no longer "belong" straightforwardly to any such "interpretative community"—neither British nor Turkish. The idea of "the public" and "the community" can no longer be taken for granted, that is to say. They are not buying into—and do not want to buy into—the "set of assumptions and understandings of everyday life"[48] that characterize national knowledge communities.

Turkish-speaking migrants cannot easily relate to any singular and consensual knowledge space. The trains of thought that they ride travel across frontiers, and pass through different cultural and value spaces. Their condition is one in which they are bound to be making comparisons between the different cultural systems to which they have access. And, insofar as they are making comparisons, they are, necessarily almost, aware of the constructedness, arbitrariness, and provisionality of those systems. They are more aware of the rhetorics, the ideologies, and the biases that characterize different media systems.

The complexity of perspective that characterizes many Turkish migrants comes from their condition of engagement with two (or more) cultures. But what is crucial, we think, is the particular nature of that engagement—we would characterize it in terms of an intellectual and imaginative detachment from both Turkish and British cultures. Insofar as they become mentally and imaginatively distanced from the worlds of (both British and Turkish) national commonsense, we may say that transnational viewers find themselves in an ironic stance to both cultures, an outsider stance. If irony has, as James Fernandez and Mary Taylor Huber argue, to do with the "questioning of established categories of inclusion and exclusion," then we may say that our Turkish-speaking viewers are thinking and reasoning from a perspective of ironic apprehension.[49]

Transnational media are not at all serving to connect Turkish migrant viewers to a homeland-elsewhere, then. Something more complex, and more interesting, seems to be happening. The proliferation of satellite channels has been creating a more extensive and diverse transnational media culture. And this pluralized media culture has become associated with a comparative disposition among many migrant viewers. It is akin to what Ulrich Beck calls the "dialogic imagination," in which "rival ways of life in the individual experience . . . make it a matter of fate to compare, reflect, criticize, understand, combine contradictory certainties."[50] This comparative disposition gives rise in turn to a reflexive and ironic stance. What is significant for our argument is that, as a consequence of the imperative to compare, migrant viewers become increasingly aware of the constructed—and therefore always arbitrary and provisional—nature of their "homeland" culture (as well as of British and other cultures too, of course). As a consequence, the status of the geographical homeland-elsewhere becomes recontextualized and relativized, losing much of its symbolic and emotional potency. An intuitive conclusion might be that Turkish migrants are able to be comfortably "at home" in two (media) spaces (Turkish and British) at once. The counterintuitive argument is that they are actually not at home in either space, and, moreover, that they prefer this intellectual and imaginative condition of being not-at-home. Turkish migrants have a certain freedom to think because they are not at home in two spaces at once. It is actually their experience—their double experience—of detachment that enables them to think across and between the spaces in which their lives are transacted.

Conclusion as a Possibility Space

Elsewheres are vital to the intellectual and imaginative lives of all individuals. They are a crucial aspect of what we may term mental space. A history could be written about how human societies have made use of elsewheres. And a substantial theme in such a history would be concerned with the problematic uses of elsewhere—through the colonial and orientalist imagination, for example, or what has recently been called the "tourist gaze." In this chapter, we have ventured to suggest that the diasporic imagination might also involve such a problematic relation to elsewhere. What is problematic is the way in which, in these various instances, a range of ideals, fantasies, illusions, and desires come to be projected onto the otherness of elsewhere. Elsewhere consequently ceases to a cognitive and imaginative resource, and functions simply as a projective screen. We might speak of an unproductive, because phantasmatic, relation to elsewhere. In the particular case of diasporic consciousness, elsewhere becomes suffused with the sense of loss, distance, nostalgia, melancholy, and so on.

Another, and probably less substantial, theme in the history of elsewhere would concern the ways in which it has been put to creative and productive use. For it to be productive—to serve as a possibility space—the relation to the space of elsewhere must be nonprojective. What we have argued, in the context of our discussion of transnational Turkish migrants and their consumption of satellite television, is that elements of what we might call a counterdiasporic mentality may be identified. Janké-lévitch associates the feelings of melancholy and nostalgia that we find in diasporic consciousness with the irreversibility of the diasporic condition. In the case of transnational migrants, Turkish ones at least, what we see is a constant to and fro between Europe and Turkey, and with it a less dramatic sense of what is at stake in migration. Access to transnational television channels has also made a contribution to the demythologization of the elsewhere–homeland. As Turkish media culture has become part of their everyday lives, and as they have consequently become more synchronized with Turkish realities, migrant viewers have become more intellectually and emotionally detached and more critically engaged. The Turkish elsewhere has become part of their ordinary, banal experience and reality. In the case of many Turkish migrants, then, what we see is a nonphantasmatic relation to elsewhere. We have characterized it in terms of the adoption of a comparative cultural stance toward Turkish and British (and other) realities, a stance that gives rise to a reflexive and ironic attitude. Rather than an idealization of the homeland, as we see in the diasporic consciousness, what we have is a certain lucidity, which gives rise to more ambivalent feelings and judgments about elsewheres (and heres, too). We would say, then, that the new transnational media culture, in the context of the new conditions of transnational migration, opens up significant and vital possibilities for the demystification of elsewhere.

Notes

1 Alejandro Portes, "Conclusion: Towards a New World—the Origins and Effectiveness of Transnational Activities," *Ethnic and Racial Studies*, 22: no 2 (1999): 463–77; Alejandro Portes, Luis E. Guarnizo, and Patricia Landolt, "The Study of Transnationalism: Pitfalls and Promise of an Emergent Research Field," *Ethnic and Racial Studies*, 22: no. 2 (1999): 217–37.
2 Portes, et al., "The Study of Transnationalism," 217.
3 Nina, Glick Schiller, Linda Basch, and Cristina Szanton Blanc, "From Immigrant to Transmigrant: Theorising Transnational Migration," *Anthropological Quarterly* 68, no. 1 (1995): 52.
4 Robin Cohen, *Global Diasporas: An Introduction* (London: UCL Press, 1997).
5 Anthony P. Cohen, *Self Consciousness: an Alternative Anthropology of Identity* (London: Routledge, 1994), 157.

6 Interview, Ankara, 26 November 1999.

7 IP/Turkmedia, *TiD 1996: Türken in Deutschland* (Kronberg: IP Deutschland/ TMM-Turkmedia, *1996*), 7.

8 For a fuller discussion of cultural studies of diasporic media, see Kevin Robins, and Asu Aksoy, "Parting from Phantoms: What Is at Issue in the Development of Transnational Television from Turkey," in *Worlds on the Move: Globalisation, Migration, and Cultural Security*, ed. Jonathan Friedman and Shalini Randeria, 179–206 (London: I. B. Tauris, 2004).

9 Sara, Ahmed. "Home and Away: Narratives of Migration and Estrangement," *International Journal of Cultural Studies* 2 no. 3 (1999): 343.

10 Ibid.

11 Ahmed, "Home and Away," 341.

12 Seda, Şengün, "Migration as a Transitional Space and Group Analysis," *Group Analysis* 34 no. 1 (2001): 68.

13 Şengün, "Migration as a Transitional Space and Group Analysis," 65–66.

14 Ibid., 76.

15 Ibid., 68.

16 Ibid., 69.

17 Ibid., 68.

18 Ahmed, "Home and Away: Narratives of Migration and Estrangement," 342.

19 Eva Hoffman, *Lost in Translation: Life in a New Language* (London: Minerva, 1991), 115.

20 Vladimir Jankélévitch, *L'Irréversible et la Nostalgie* (Paris: Flammarion, 1974), 346.

21 Roger Rouse, "Questions of Identity: Personhood and Collectivity in Transnational Migration to the United States," *Critique of Anthropology* 15 no. 4 (1995): 356.

22 Jacques Rancière, *The Ignorant Schoolmaster: Five Lessons in Intellectual Emancipation* (Stanford: Stanford University Press, 1991), 81.

23 Focus group, London, 3 March 2000.

24 Focus group, London, 29 April 1999.

25 Focus group, London, 3 November 1999.

26 Focus group, London, 10 February 2000.

27 Focus group, London, 10 February 2000.

28 Focus group, London, 10 February 2000.

29 Focus group, London, 18 May 1999.

30 On the viewing of news, see Asu Aksoy and Kevin Robins, "Thinking across Spaces: Transnational Television from Turkey," *European Journal of Cultural Studies* 3 no. 3 (2000): 343–65.

31 Focus group, Enfield, 21 April 2000.

32 Focus group, Islington, London, 29 March 1999.

33 Focus group, Hackney, London, 7 December 1999.

34 Jankélévitch, *L'Irréversible et la Nostalgie* (1974), 346.

35 Marisca Milikowski, "Exploring a Model of De-ethnicisation the case of Turkish Television in the Netherlands," *European Journal of Communication* 15 no. 4 (2000): 444.

36 Ahmed, "Home and Away," 341.

37 John Dewey, *Experience and Nature* (New York: Dover, 1958 [1929]), xiv.

38 Focus Group, Hackney, London, 11 December 1999.

39 Focus Group, Enfield, 18 May 1999.

40 Focus Group, Islington, London, 5 February 2002.

41 Focus Group, Hackney, London, 15 March 2002.

42 Focus Group, Hackney, London, 15 March 2002.

43 Focus Group, Hackney, London, 15 March 2002.

44 Focus Group, Hackney, London, 15 March 2002.

45 Focus Group, Hackney, London, 16 December 1999.

46 Sonia Livingstone, "Mediated Knowledge: Recognition of the Familiar, Discovery of the New," in *Television and Common Knowledge*, ed. Jostein Gripsrud (London: Routledge, 1999), 96.

47 Livingstone, "Mediated Knowledge," 96–97.

48 Livingstone, "Mediated Knowledge," 97.

49 James W. Fernandez and Mary Taylor Huber, "The Anthropology of Irony," in *Irony In Action: Anthropology, Practice, and the Moral Imagination*, ed. James W. Fernandez and Mary Taylor Huber, (Chicago: University of Chicago Press, 2001), 9.

50 Ulrich Beck, "The Cosmopolitan Society and its Enemies," *Theory, Culture and Society* 19 nos. 1–2 (2002): 18.

PART III

The Mediated City

10

Charlotte Brunsdon

The Elsewhere of the London Underground

If you access the Transport for London (TfL) Web site[1] and select "the tube," you can download the London tube maps in a range of formats including color, black and white, large print, showing disabled access, travelcard zones, and as desktop wallpaper. You can also view it in "translated versions" in Arabic, Bengali, Chinese, Greek, Gujarati, French, Hindi, Punjabi, Urdu, Turkish, Vietnamese, and Spanish. (Perhaps the Germans, Italians, Dutch, Japanese, and Scandinavians do not need translation.) If you click on "The Real Underground," you access the central section of the 2004 Underground Map, with a set of choices underneath, which permit you to move between the 2004 map, the 1933 map, and what is called the "Real Underground Map." Each map is in color, and they morph deliciously into each other as you choose between them and then play with whether to "show/hide" stations and streets.

Digital technology here promises to deliver an electronic *real* Underground to the site visitors, while also permitting play between the different diagrams through which we know the Tube. It is the latest version of the very many representations of the London Underground, and one that can be accessed from all over the world, by people who may never actually travel on the network. In this chapter I want to examine some of the earlier representations of the Underground within film and visual culture. I will suggest that the electronic "real Underground" offered by the Transport for London Web site is only one of many imaginings of a structuring "elsewhere" in the cultural geography of London, which includes, for example, "The King of the Underworld," a painting in Bhajju Shyam's series, *The London Jungle*, depicting the London Underground as a giant earthworm.[2] The earthworm is painted in stripey sections of blue and terracotta, on which appear faces—including one wearing sunglasses—a bit like passengers on the tube, and a "no smoking" sign. Shyam, a Gond artist who visited London in 2002, observes of his painting: "In Gond belief, there is another world below this one, and I discovered there is such a world in London as well, although different from the Gond one. In Gond stories, we say the world below is ruled by the earthworm. So I have thought of the earthworm as London's world below the earth, and the tube as the earthworm that rules it."[3] Shyam's painting, with its earth tones and lively wriggling snakes and worm, gives a more organic representation of the London Underground than the Transport of London Web site, but he too points to the role of the Underground network as an elsewhere to the surface city, and it is with this that this chapter will be concerned. My interest lies primarily with the way in which the London Underground features in the cinema as part of a larger project about cinematic London.[4] However the very peculiarity, materiality, and historicity of the spaces of the London Underground might have something to teach us at a point at which the new media are seen to be projecting us into an ahistorical, immaterial digital elsewhere. So I am suggesting that although the mode of delivery of the "Real Underground" promised by the Transport for London Web site is electronic and new, it is best understood historically in the context of many other imaginings and representations of the network, including the paper posters, the pocket-size maps and the "tube-map" understandings of the shape of London carried by travelers in the city, as well as organic metaphors such as the "arteries of the city" or Shyam's worm.

Within the context of this book, I aim to provide some "backstory" to the images of the remotely accessible electronic Underground, as a contribution to the argument that no electronic elsewhere can be understood without attention to its historical precedents and material bases. Thus in my choice of texts I have also wanted to emphasize another paradox of the Underground as an electronic elsewhere, which is the necessity for the production and maintenance of "the Real Underground" through arduous physical labor. It is to this end that the second part of this chapter is devoted to documentary films that follow different groups of Underground laborers. For one of my concerns is to ground the seeming increasing electronic accessibility of the Underground to computer users all over the world in the materiality of the transport system and the continuing necessity for the repetitive, dirty work of safety maintenance. Rosalind Williams, in her exploration of the imagination of the underground in literature, has pointed to the significance of the subterranean metaphor for both Marx and Freud.[5] I am not arguing that the London Underground is the "real" of the city, but I am suggesting that looking at how this urban elsewhere is imagined does indeed tell us something about the city more broadly, while also offering some intriguing relationships between the cinema and the underground.

Lynne Kirby, drawing on the work of Wolfgang Schivelbusch, has written about the relationship between early cinema and the railway, arguing that the two technologies are doubles for each other, particularly in their production of the modern subjectivity of what she calls "the spectator-passenger."[6] The underground railway, to which Kirby alludes briefly, also predates cinema, but because of its very undergroundness, there can be no analogy of panorama, view, and screen, no reciprocal formal tutoring in how to gaze. Indeed, the carriages on one of the early London lines were known as "padded cells," carpeted on floor and walls, with their tiny windows too high up to be seen through.[7] And what would one look at? Sooty pipes and wires, gnomic numerical signs, occasional arches and apertures illuminating the dark between stations. Instead one's gaze is drawn inward, to the simultaneous inspection and ignoring of fellow passengers, to reading matter and, as Marc Augé has observed, to introspection and reverie.[8] If there is a relationship to be posed between the underground and the cinema, it is not that of the window/screen and panorama, but one of public privacy.[9] In addition to this public privacy that I will discuss in more detail later, there is perhaps also a formal resonance between the two to be found in the alternation of the dark tunnels with the bright stations, so vividly rendered in the heroine's endless journeys in Amir Naderi's 2002 New York film, *Marathon*, and the way in which, in both technologies, space is transformed into time.[10]

We see already, as I draw examples from London, Paris, and New York, that there are some questions about the cinema and underground systems that are general. But we learn about these through specific instances, and there are also some very particular ways in which national subway systems are used to signify location and as the sites for particular national stories. I want to start by summoning some of the spatial contexts and iconography of the London Underground, to examine how we know this elsewhere, what Bhajju Shyam has called, "London's world below the earth."[11]

The peculiarity of the London Underground as a space is that, in a sense, it has no outside. Of course, several lines, particularly outside central London, run overground, and are thus much more akin to trains, but the core London Underground is just that: underground and hidden. Station buildings and the bar and circle roundel signify its presence in the city; lifts, stairs, and escalators lead to it; but once inside we can only know it internally—and through our imagination and current versions of its most famous representation, Harry Beck's 1933 map. Beck's diagram is an iconic image of twentieth century London, and along with the Underground roundel ("the bullseye"[12]), frequently

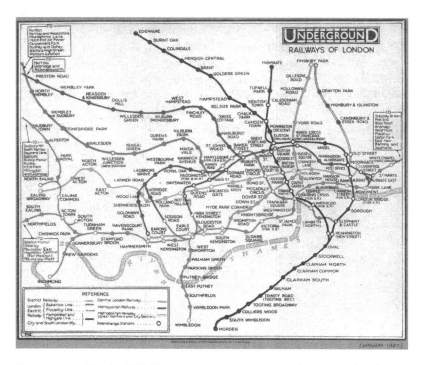

Figure 10.1.   Map by F. H. Stingemore, in use 1919–33. Courtesy of London's Transport Museum. Copyright Transport for London; used with permission.

functions as a location-setting landmark in the cinema. Its clean, clear lines, easy angles, pleasing spacing, and bright colors have ensured its longevity. As Peter Ackroyd observes, "The original Underground map bears only approximate relation to the location of lines and stations, but it is so aesthetically pleasing that its lineaments have never been changed."[13] Enormously influential internationally in the mapping of underground railways, the diagram is a key metonymic image of London, as well as a shaping of people's understanding of the spatial relations of the city.[14] Adrian Forty has shown how the map should be understood as one element in the interwar corporate design of London Transport, which contributed significantly to the sense of a modern transport "system".[15] Forty points to the radical disparity between the map's representation of distance, the ease of travel, and particularly, the ease of changing lines, in comparison with the material conditions experienced by travelers. Ken Garland's loving account of the genesis and history of the map, *Mr. Beck's Underground Map*, reveals, as does Forty, how radical, geographically, Beck's design is when compared both with predecessor maps and the physical geography of the Underground, and it is this set of relations and histories that is condensed on the TfL Web site.[16]

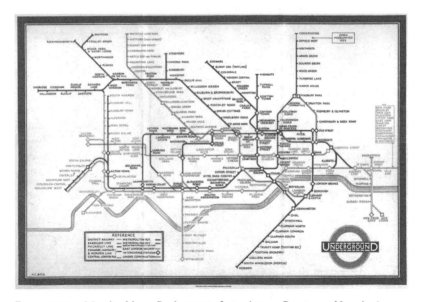

Figure 10.2.   Map by Harry Beck, 1933, first edition. Courtesy of London's Transport Museum. Copyright Transport for London; used with permission.

As John A. Walker puts it in a discussion of Beck's design: "Beck realized that clarity and geographical truth were antithetical to one another and that geographical accuracy had to be abandoned in favor of clarity."[17] Nevertheless—or consequently—it is this map that produces London as a knowable space to many people, in which the spatial relationships established here, between tube lines that you cannot see, form a kind of skeleton through which to grasp the overground.[18] Its popularity is such that the bookshop at the London Transport Museum offers versions of the map on posters, postcards, placemats, tee shirts, fridge magnets, coffee cups, mouse mats and carrier bags, while Garland's book, *Mr. Beck's Underground Map*, first published in 1994, has been reprinted in 1998 and 2003, selling 17,000 copies.[19] Both the diagram and the space of the Underground have inspired and occasioned artworks,[20] and David Pike reminds us that Eric Hobsbawm has declared that the map is "the most original work of avant-garde art in Britain between the wars."[21] Pike's discussion of the map places it convincingly within what he characterizes as a modernist conception of space, and he explores the paradoxes of the temporalities and spatialities of the Tube in a comparison of the map and the Underground:

> As a material space, the tube is not unified at all; it is quite literally Victorian, modernist, and post-war, all at the same time. . . . Aboveground, its colors and lines continue to exude the utopian modernism of its abstract, controlled and rationally organized space; below, its cramped conditions and tiny tunnels recall not the utopian Underground, but the subterranean space from which it has always striven so strenuously to escape.[22]

This vision of the Underground as partaking of several different temporalities is illuminating, and can be explored in several different ways in relation to the cinema. Pike's own concern is partly to explain the endurance and popularity of Beck's map, which he attributes mainly to the color coding of the lines, "a Victorian trace in his modernist art," which he sees as "what remains utopian about this space," thus bringing together different temporalities in the map itself.[23] However he is also concerned to explore other artistic engagements with the Underground, such as the work of Simon Patterson, which "discover what its [Beck's map] efficiency has occluded," and in this too, the cinema may prove interesting.[24]

The Underground map, as well as making spaces, is also itself placed within spaces in the cinema. As the London Transport Film Office explains on its Web site, "film-makers often use the tube to show they are in London."[25] Tube iconography can be deployed in different ways to signify location, sometimes as part of a string of landmark icons along with

Big Ben or the Houses of Parliament, sometimes, particularly in social realist cinema, as the only landmark icon, perhaps, with the flash of a red bus,
used to indicate more than local location. For example, Gary Goldman's
1997 film, *Nil By Mouth*, which is set in South London, has a sequence in
which heroin addict Billy is waiting to score outside the Elephant and
Castle tube station. A naturalist study of South London working-class
family life, which is shaped by alcoholic fathering, unemployment, and
the continual consumption of drugs and alcohol, the film is shot in a very
limited color palette, with the dim lighting of the underground tunnels
and escalator echoing the grim corridors of the block of flats in which
Billy (Charlie Creed-Miles) seeks drugs. In this scene, which takes place
about halfway through the film, when the audience is beginning to grasp
the remorselessness of the repetitions within the family, Billy emerges
from the tube and is trying to use a phone-box outside Elephant and Castle
station to make his connection. The phone-box is busy, and Billy paces
agitatedly up and down the pavement, passing the posters around the
station entrance. A busker outside the station, a young black man playing
classical violin, supplies the diegetic soundtrack to this scene. Billy crosses
and recrosses the Underground map displayed outside the station, paus-
ing by a poster exhorting the regular traveler to "save your one day travel
cards and collect dramatic savings." Here the Underground map finds
itself part of a different temporality to those Pike discusses. This is scuzzy,
down-at-heel, postcolonial South London, where the unemployed—and
unemployable—white working class frenziedly pursues oblivion. The
map and the poster also function directly as ironic mise-en-scène, in that
there is no one in the film less likely than Billy, with his £60 a day habit,
to go anywhere using the "Journey Planner" as the map is now called, just
as he will never "collect dramatic savings" by saving his old tickets. The
map and the poster both ground the film in late twentieth century London
and remind the audience, but not Billy, that there are other ways of living
and other journeys.

Everyday understandings of the city, and the role of the Underground
map in structuring London journeys, are addressed in a different way in
Helen Scalway's *Travelling Blind*. *Travelling Blind* was made in 1996 when
Scalway undertook her project "to bring to light the personal geographies
of Tube travelers whose private copings with the city's space might mingle
strangely with the authoritative suggestions of official maps."[26] Scalway's
own description of her method, which led to an Artist's Book and a 1999
Exhibition in the Cable Street Gallery, is that she "sat about on Underground station benches and asked in turn anyone who unwittingly sat

down next to me, over a hundred total strangers waiting for their trains: 'Please draw your London Underground network.'"

The Artist's Book *Travelling Blind* consists of the drawings elicited through this process, each one reproduced on heavy opaque A4[27] white manuscript paper, bound together in a landscape format, with a black and white line representation of the "true scale" of the underground network inserted as the last page.[28] The book is bound with black boards, the title embossed in black on black, and has no color pigment at all. It is a book from which the bright, meaningful colors of Beck's diagram have been excluded, as has that map itself. Drawn in the Underground, this is a ghost of a book; a book haunted by that other, colorful, diagrammatic representation of the Underground network. For if Beck's map is itself absent, it is to that map that many of the anonymous drawers address themselves, and through it—at least partly—that they understand their own journeys.

Underground London here is both private and social. What is so moving about the work is the way in which so many of these total strangers tried so very hard to respond to Scalway's request to both their own and her satisfaction. As she observes, "In every case, the line traced a thought, despite differing levels of ease with the concepts of "drawing" and "network." The book reproduces about 40 percent of the drawings as well as including two pages of brief extracts from comments made by passengers as they drew.[29] Scalway proposes that Beck's original underground map, which so dominates our sense of the spatial organization of London has its own specific, generative power: "the very spareness of the official Tube Map has freed our conceptions of our London Underground journeys from all constraints of geographical accuracy; and in doing so has opened up a different kind of space for imagination" (xvii). Although I agree about the imaginative power of the "spareness" of the Beck map, one of the things that is interesting about the drawings is the precision and the persistence with which people try to render this diagram. They inhabit, and remember, and try to reproduce, the spatial relations of the diagram. Thus, for example, most of the drawings aspire to the simplicity of line and angle that we find in the Beck map. Drawing by hand, in fineliner on paper, the bold clear colored stripes of the tube lines are unachievable, but few drawings abandon this aspiration. One marks the key line they have drawn "the blue line." Another comments, "I hate this drawing by hand stuff it makes me seem tremulous I am not a tremulous person I wish I could do this on my computer then I could use straight lines." Here, "tremulous" marks the impossible gap between the memory and knowledge of the network and the task demanded with the materials

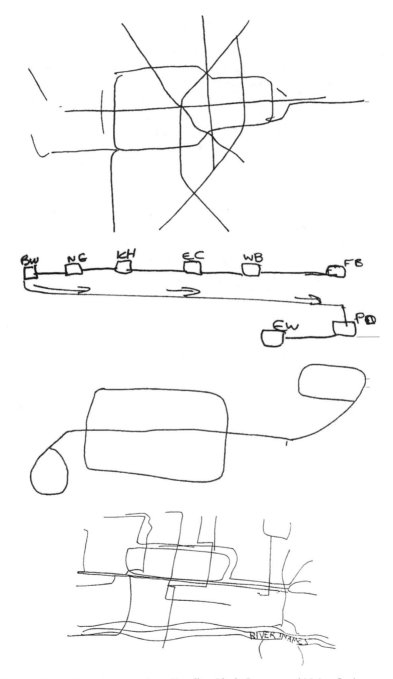

Figure 10.3. Four drawings from *Travelling Blind*. Courtesy of Helen Scalway. Copyright Helen Scalway.

at hand. Many of the maps—that were drawn in Fulham Broadway and Leytonstone—offer some kind of representation of the Circle Line as the centre of the drawing, with a spiky periphery protruding southwest.

The graphic traces of Beck's map are present in other ways, particularly in relation to the marking of stations. Most of the maps represent the Underground as a more or less complex network of free-flowing lines. Some, however, address the question—which concerned Beck greatly—of how to represent stations. One map gives the lines ends, little cross bars just like Beck's. Another draws circles round some of the interchanges, and a third maps the journey from Fulham Broadway into town with clearly initialed little oblongs to mark each station. This is a sense of the Underground as daily journey through a featureless elsewhere marked out in station names.

Scalway's question in her retrospective on the work is, "But do these drawings offer anything more than the poignant spectacle of mass misconception and the multiplicity of human isolations?" I have suggested that there are other poignancies here, poignancies measured in the very effort of so many strangers to render precisely the lines that are their journeys. But I agree with her that these line drawings also testify to the imaginative space of the "darkness of the city under the city." She suggests that we have here "a specifically London variant of the image found so often in the literature of the modern city: a shape-shifting labyrinth, shared and yet not shared. Largely shaped and misshaped by the London Underground Map, this labyrinth of the communal imagination can be seen as a space simultaneously physical, imaginary and metaphoric."[30] Scalway shows us how Beck's map is a constant presence in our understanding of the disposition of the city, but she also shows how partial, how individuated, is our relation to this spare and pleasing diagram. Not only does the Underground Map shape our understanding of our journeys, but it also shapes how we think these should be represented.

Travelling Blind is both city and site specific work. However, in their revelation of the interplay between individual memories and itineraries and Beck's map, these London drawings can be seen to harmonize with the insights of Marc Augé's ethnography of the Paris Métro.[31] Augé is concerned with "the social phenomenon of the métro," and uses the work of Mauss and Levi-Strauss to analyze behavior in the metro in terms of ritual. However there is a striking homology between his analysis of the relationship between the individual and the social on the métro and Scalway's work:

Transgressed or not, the law of the métro inscribes the individual itinerary into the comfort of collective morality, and that way it is exemplary of what might be called the ritual paradox: it is always lived individually and subjectively; only individual itineraries give a reality, and yet it is eminently social, the same for everyone, conferring on each person this minimum of collective identity through which a community is defined.[32]

Augé continues that, "for those who take it everyday, the prosaic definition of the métro: [is] collectivity without festival and solitude without isolation," and much of his analysis is concerned with the role of solitary reverie and memory for the traveler. Scalway and Augé, then, help us to develop an understanding of a relatively undiscussed aspect of the London Underground, which is its role as a paradoxically private space.

This paradox of the privacy in public of the Tube has been most substantially documented in the exceptional circumstances of the Second World War, when Underground stations were used as bomb shelters.[33] Most documentaries about the London Underground include some reference to Henry Moore's shelter drawings and his account of his accidental discovery of the shelterers in the Tube, after a dinner in town, has been reproduced in more than one version.[34] In Jill Craigie's 1944 film about the flourishing of art in London during the war, Out of Chaos, Moore is shown "wandering about" among the sleepers on the platform, taking notes and later making images. Moore has drawn attention to the relations between the "rounded perspective of the tube" and the "rows and rows of reclining figures, which has always been a favorite subject of mine," and it is clear, both in the resonance of his work and other artists such as John Farleigh and Joseph Bato and the photographer Bill Brandt, that it is the combination of the vulnerability of the (private) sleeping bodies with their massing in dramatically lit and shaped public space which is so powerful.[35] The London Blitz of the Second World War is a nodal point for twentieth century myths and icons of Englishness and Britishness, and if the Daily Mail photograph of St. Paul's rising from the smoke and flames of the Blitz is the most famous overground image,[36] this phoenix image is matched by the endurance of those of the Underground tunnel sleepers, particularly in the work of Moore and Brandt.[37]

The drama of the shelterers is recalled in a different tone in the 1943 comedy, Gert and Daisy's Weekend, which has an early scene set in a station shelter named as Goodge Street, although most of the film follows Gert (Elsie Waters) and Daisy (Doris Waters) as they care for a group of East End children evacuated to a large county house. The film is essentially a comedy of class manners, contrasting the pragmatic, earthy communality of the London shelterers with the excluding snobberies and dishonesties of those gathered at "the Hall." This contrast is principally established through the forms of entertainment in each milieu. As Gert and Daisy shelter, sitting on a bench in front of a Goodge Street sign, a group of people in evening dress dismount from a train, just like Moore and his companions returning from an evening out, and proceed to make their way through the shelterers, as Daisy says, "Gert, look at this" and Gert responds, "Oh blimey, posh." However, this evening-dressed party turns out to comprise "some West End stage stars" who have come to entertain the shelterers. This develops into a full-scale singalong, with Gert and Daisy leading a rendition of "Won't we have a party when it's over" and everyone on the platform dancing.[38] The exceptional circumstances of the war are shown here, remembering Augé's terms, to create not just a collectivity, but communal festivity under duress, and this is contrasted, later in the film, with an evening of music and song at the Hall. Here, the songs come from opera, and are presented as affected and screechy. Gert and Daisy don't enjoy the recital and try to get things going by offering "She's a lily, but only by name," a monologue with choruses. The country houseguests, though, are too stuffy to join in. At the end of the film, having helped to foil a jewelry theft, Gert and Daisy can't wait to get back to London and the Blitz—and we see exactly why they would rather be sleeping in a tube station. The alienation of the city of strangers and the barriers of class division are abolished in these images of good-hearted, ordinary Londoners singing and lying down together, the London Blitz figured, at least underground, as an opportunity for courage and conviviality.[39]

There is a strong contrast between the corporeality of the shelterers' tube and its diagrammatic presence in Beck's map and the fineliner drawings of Scalway's travelers, but together they show us the way in which this underground network is made and remade in the visual imagination, providing more than one instance of a privileged national image of London and Londoners. The London Underground begins to emerge as both an elsewhere to London and icon of it.

The Tunnel Tigers and the Good Fairies of the Underground

The *bonhomie* of the shelterers' Underground is exceptional. In fiction film, the Underground is more likely to be frightening, thrilling, or, more banally, the place for chance encounters. In each, the "underground effect" is produced through a conjunction of spatial constriction and temporal play. The most common topography is gothic, and it is most frequently within the horror genre that we find the Underground in British cinema discussed.[40] Films such as *Quatermass and the Pit* (Roy Ward Baker, 1967), *Deathline* (Gary Sherman, 1972) or *An American Werewolf in London* (John Landis, 1979) all contribute to the story about something forgotten, repressed, or unknown emerging from the dark tunnels under ground.[41] Thus we return to the complex temporalities of the Underground as a space, the way in which, as Pike suggests, different times characteristically coexist therein.

As a narrative structure, Gothic underground topographies are international, as is the second set of underground stories, narratives structured through the "too late" of closing doors, ticket barriers, and just-missed trains.[42] However, in each case, the setting in any particular underground system grounds the film nationally and locally. For London, the most obvious example of this latter type is the 1998 Gwyneth Paltrow vehicle, *Sliding Doors* (Peter Howitt, 1998), which used the device of "the train not taken" to elaborate a double "what if" time scheme for the whole film. Here, the local specificity of the Underground setting stands in for any vividness in the depiction of London as whole, for, as Mazierska and Rascaroli observe, "The fact that the characters live in London seems to have little to do with their attitudes or lifestyle."[43]

Rather than survey train chases and coincidences, I wish to turn, in the final part of the chapter, to some documentary representations of the London Underground to consider the continuity of the representational patterns observed in a genre generally thought to be governed by its relation to the real. My concerns are particularly with the articulation of public and private spaces, and with the question of what is to be found in the tunnels.

When films such as *Quatermass and the Pit* or *Deathline* show or refer to labor in the Underground, they do so generally within an aesthetic informed by key oppositions between the surface and the underground, and, symmetrically, once underground, between the safe, illuminated platforms and the dark gaping tunnels. If the Underground as a whole can be seen as an elsewhere to the surface city, within the Underground, this structure is repeated so that the unknown, inchoate tunnels are the elsewhere to the bright stations. The most dangerous thing a character can do is to stand on the edge of the platform and peer into the tunnel. The horror genre does occasionally penetrate the tunnels: in *Deathline* we do enter the dark, dank lair, decorated with suspended human limbs, where the last survivors of a nineteenth century engineering accident have lived. In documentary, however, the tunnels are treated differently. Here, they are not places of horror, but places of labor. I want to discuss this in relation to a 1965 Phillip Donnellan film, *The Irishmen*, made during the building of the Victoria Line, and in relation to a group of workers known as "Fluffers" who appear in glimpses in several documentaries about underground London.

Donnellan's film is about the lives of the Irishmen who came over to work as laborers after the Second World War. It is one of a group of films Donnellan made in the 1960s on aspects of contemporary life, the best known of which is *The Colony* (1964) about Birmingham. *The Irishmen* was made in 1965 for the BBC, although it was never shown. The immigrants are shown working on two major projects, one of which is the motorways and the other the Victoria line, London's first postwar tube line.[44] Both were built using a labor contract system called the Lump—which is non-unionized casual labor—and the film starts with men waiting to be picked up for jobs in Camden Town, and then interweaves work and leisure sequences, with one of its concerns to show the relative isolation of the laborers outside their work companionship. The canteen-like bar on site in which they are shown to drink after work in one scene is thus contrasted with the family life left behind in Ireland, while at the same time, the inevitability of exile for the young is set up early on, with a young man, whose journey we follow, musing, "What's it to be, England or America?" The film has several simultaneous temporal structures: the working day (finishing with a drink), the working week (including hurley at Wembley on a Saturday), generational migration from Ireland to England and the particular journey of one young man who arrives at a London terminal as the film finishes. The four and half minute sequence I want to analyze juxtaposes this young man's ferry trip to Holyhead with the labor of tunneling under London. As with much of the film, Donnellan uses song as his soundtrack. In this sequence, the song is not diegetic, but is used to structure both space and exposition. The intro of the fiddle begins as the traveler is shown on the deck of the ferry with the seagulls circling. This is the song of the "Tunnel Tigers," written by Ewan MacColl and Peggy Seeger, which has lyrics that counterpose the beauty and freedom of country rhythms in Ireland, the trout, the salmon, and the wild geese, with the team commands of the laborers, "Up with the shield, jack it, ram it, driving a tunnel through the London clay."[45] The juxtaposition is one of loss, the loss of the life of the countryman: the hares run free and the curragh rots because no one is there to trap and fish, to live off the land, because the men have gone to London. The song is precise in its invocation of both the plenitude of the Irish country and the locations from which the emigrants leave: Connemara, the Wicklow Mountains, Armagh, offering possibilities of identification for any migrant listener, and creates an elegiac narrative space to which the first two minutes of the sequence are cut. The montage

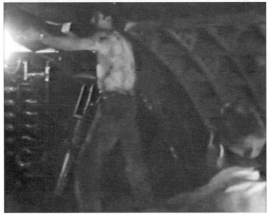

Figure 10.4.   Frame grabs from *The Irishmen*. Courtesy of Phillippa Donellan.

juxtaposes the emigrant on the boat with increasing flashes of tunnel labor contrasted with seagulls, mountains, fishing boats, and an abandoned curragh. Although it is the space of the man's journey, it is more significantly a space of exilic consciousness, the labor of the tunneling overwhelming rural origins, while the flight of wild geese are recalled while underground. The song is absent for the second part of the sequence, which is all underground with the harsh diegetic sound of tunneling. The cramped, quick shots to which we have been introduced earlier are now sustained in a way that emphasizes the constriction and heat and dirt of the labor. We see a section of tunnel roof being installed, the men working alongside the mighty shield, their sweaty skin and the whites of their eyes the lightest part of the image. The melody returns more urgently as the sequence concludes with the spoil being carried out of the excavation on a conveyor belt, and now that we understand the labor that awaits our traveler, we return to the ferry.

We have here a very particular construction of space, for although the sequence does offer quite detailed documentary footage of tunneling, of the underground as a place of work, this material is woven into an evocation of consciousness. Thus we have both a strong sense of physical labor and sense of the memories and desires—and home—of the workers. This is clearly an example of the exilic consciousness, which Hamid Naficy has shown, has its own internal elsewhere, but it is also an instance of the way in which the very cramped nature of the dark tunnels of the Underground, even as they are being built, offers a strange privacy.[46]

Donnellan's concern, in *The Irishmen*, is not with the Underground as such, although the building of the Victoria line does provide the film with its most memorable imagery, and he uses the visual contrast between the dark tunnels, the sea, and deserted rural Ireland to evoke the felt meaning of exile. His skill as a documentarist lies in the way in which he combines film footage, recorded speech, sound, and song to reveal not only what the work and the life was like, but also what it felt like. In this, I have suggested, the nature of the underground spaces is particularly amenable to the project of suggesting interiority. More commonly, the Underground features in documentary film in two formats, the "London under London," in which the Underground is featured alongside underground sites such as sewers, government bunkers, wine cellars, and silver vaults, and "London at Night," in which the focus is on the work conducted by postmen, underground cleaners, and musicians while the city sleeps.[47]

The world of each type of film is a man's world—only men are found working and it is men who act as guides to the documentarists—with two exceptions. Women working as prostitutes figure briefly—but repeatedly—sometimes just through shots of a swishing skirt above some idling high-heeled feet. Claude Goretta and Alain Tanner's 1957 short film about a night out in London, *Nice Time* concludes with the key tropes of the "London at Night" group of films: the tube closing down, the barrow boys wheeling away their barrows and only the police, some sailors and "the ladies of the night" left in Piccadilly Circus. Donovan Winter's *The Awakening Hour* (1957) also features a prostitute and then porters in Covent Garden as typical workers of the night. *City After Dark* (1955, Ian K. Barnes) has a two-shot prostitute sequence, the first shot of a high-heeled woman, standing against a shop window, tapping her foot, framed from just below her shoulders, the second of a man's legs and feet apparently approaching her. But there is also another group of women who can be found in several postwar underground documentaries, and they too have a curiously transgressive presence.

Fluffers were maintenance workers who cleaned the tube lines during its nighttime closures. They used knives, dusters, brushes, and any other suitable implements to clean, particularly, the rails and the "chairs" in which they are set, of dust, human hair, rat excrement, and other litter. The most interesting discussion of the Fluffers is given in an anonymous personal account of going out with the nighttime crews written in the 1940s, "London's Underground Army: Laying and Maintaining the Tracks":

> These pleasant happy-looking women work in pairs, collecting the dust into heaps which are shovelled into containers and taken away by a special train. . . . Work in the transport service often seems to run in families. One of the women told me her brother-in-law had been a bus-driver for fifteen years; another had her sister working there with her. . . . And all of them, of course, have domestic responsibilities. Most of them have young children. When they get home from the night's work, they have breakfast to cook, housework to do, shopping to get in. They go to bed after lunch, for before they leave home for their night's work, they have more meals to get, the children, perhaps, to put to bed, and all the small things to do which make up the housewife's round. They all seemed particularly cheerful, and there was a fine team spirit. We left these good fairies of the Underground, singing at their work.[48]

The Fluffers can also be found in *Under Night Streets* (1958), a 20-minute British Transport Film that has been selected by London's Transport Museum[49] as one of the films available to the public on its Web site, which concentrates on showing the myriad safety activities going on in the Underground "while you're pressing the mattress." Workers are shown climbing and cleaning the ventilator shafts under a deserted Piccadilly Circus station, and then the "big gang boys" undress on the platform to go down into the tunnel. The camera then switches to a group of women in overalls on the platform, and introduces them saying, "Fluffers, that's what they're called. They're VIPs, they are, for this is fire prevention work," as the women move down into the tunnels to start work. There is a hint here, in both the tone and vocabulary of this introduction, of a difficulty about the status of, and attitudes to, the Fluffers.[50] When the women are shown working in the tunnels, in the next scene, they are represented in the tradition of the representation of working class women doing manual jobs as jolly, cheeky, and potentially bawdy.[51] This is achieved through the interaction between the workingwomen and their foreman/boss who rides past them on a strange tricycle-like vehicle adapted to run along the train rails. As he glides past the women, who are brushing and scraping, he greets them familiarly and they quip back. The introduction, though, tries to set up the fluffers slightly differently. Referring to the women as "VIPs," and specifying that their labor is "fire-prevention work" (which it undoubtedly is) insists on both status and the significance of the labor in a way that amounts to a disavowal. The tone of the narrator argues against dismissing the women as insignificant, but to call them VIPs inscribes within the narration the very opposite: that these were extremely poorly paid women, working night shifts in filthy and dangerous conditions, who presumably only took the work because they also had households and families to run—and maybe even day jobs.

The Fluffers also appear in *City After Dark* (1955), a nineteen-minute film that deals with "another world" that lies "beneath the quiet paving stones of the city." Once again starting with Piccadilly Circus, this film shows nightlife closing down and then goes underground to reveal the labor of the sewage workers, underground maintenance, post office sorters, and the BBC. This film is keen to stress the precision of the timing and execution of underground maintenance work, showing the last Bakerloo tube leaving Piccadilly Circus, observing:

> A dead city needs no transport. The time is 1.32 am. But by 1.52 am, the night gangs have taken over. Every foot of every mile must be checked. The tubes never rest. Every night when the last train has passed, the ghostly tunnels witness men, and women too, checking, cleaning, tightening.

"And women too" recognizes that the employment of women in this type of work may surprise an audience, just as "the ghostly tunnels" suggests that a gothic topography haunts documentary as much as fiction film. The women are shown wearing dark overalls with their hair tied up in pale headscarves. With their sleeves rolled up to show bare arms, the women also wear earrings visible under their headscarves. Holding lamps, they wield a variety of implements to scrape and brush the line.[52]

The construction of space in this film, though, shows a very different topography of the Underground. A shot of the women working in the dark of the tunnels, the only lighting visible their individually held lamps, transforms into a very eerie view of the platform as the camera, without a cut, pans right, away from the Fluffers and up to the brightly lit, deserted station platform. The shot becomes eerie because of the revelation of concealed space and depth. While we are with the Fluffers in the tunnel, the camera is appropriately placed to allow us to observe their work. Only with the pan and tilt is the height of the platform—and our own lowly position—revealed. Whereas in horror films, the horror lurks in the tunnels, in this documentary it is the light, bright, deserted, and elevated platform that seems uncanny.

The Fluffers transform underground space again in Molly Dineen's 1989 television documentary, *The Heart of the Angel*, which was made at the Islington tube station, Angel, before it was redeveloped.[53] The Angel is the deepest station on the London underground, and was built physically so that the two lines run on either side of a central platform island, rather than in separate tunnels, which means that the underground part of the station is a unified space. The topography of the film emphasizes the verticalness of life in the station, the same faces going up and down, with nothing of the Islington outside. However, there is a horizontal dimension to space, but only deep underground. The linesmen appear on the platform from the tunnels and Dineen asks, "How far have you just walked?" "From Camden Town," comes the reply, and they are going on to Bank. But it is once again the Fluffers whose use of space is most transgressive. Unlike the 1950s representations of these workers, in which the very presence of unaccompanied women at night causes anxiety about their status and they are filmed already working, here Dineen films the women as they prepare for work, and interviews them directly. What we learn poses the question of where the women in *Under Night Streets* or *City After Dark* changed, for in *Heart of the Angel*, in 1989, the women change on the platform. We first see the Fluffers as they start to change on the deserted station platforms, stripping to their underwear to put on their overalls, using the benches daily sat on by commuters to store their clothes. In an extraordinary undoing of the daily rush hour, here the wooden benches

Figure 10.5.   Frame grabs of Fluffers from *Under Night Streets*. Courtesy of London's Transport Museum. Copyright Transport for London; used with permission.

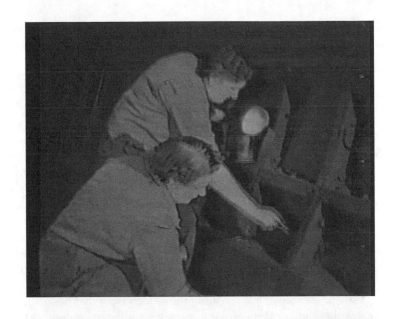

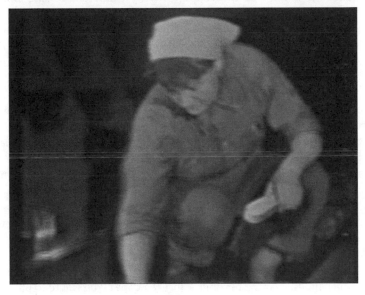

polished and worn by millions of commuting bottoms are used like bedroom chairs or dressing table stools. The empty public space of the station is rendered both intimate and unfamiliar. Their clothes neatly folded on the benches, the women climb down onto the tracks and enter the tunnels with their dusters and scrapers.

It is clearly still a filthy job—possibly filthier in 1989 than it was in 1958—and there is still something that is both incongruous and shocking about the labor of these women in the tunnels, on foot, performing a poorly paid, hidden, public housework.[54] And that is perhaps the scandal, for the work has all the attributes of housework: invisible, repetitive, directed at maintenance, not production, dealing with the detritus of everyday lives—and is, like housework, unrecognized. But it is also conducted in the middle of the night in dark tunnels, revealing the unremitting materiality of the Underground and its unknown spaces. This nightly labor of collecting up little bits of hair and epidermis and dust, both maintains and makes strange the spaces of the London Underground; it is the other side of the beauty and efficiency of Beck's map.

These documentary films, revealing the hidden labor that has built and maintains the London Underground, provide a different generic answer to the question of what lurks in the tunnel. It is not horror, or monsters, but labor, which is realized very precisely through the way in which underground space is rendered in these films. Deathline recognizes this relationship, for the cannibals who haunt the tunnels are the descendants of nineteenth century laborers, abandoned by the entrepreneurs financing the building of the Underground after a fatal accident; but the spaces and labor of the Fluffers are perhaps stranger—and maybe more uncanny—because they are less generically familiar.

So the cinematic space of the London Underground in the cinema is both a surprisingly bodily space, and also a space to which the lack of an outside or a view lends a curious privacy. It is an internationally recognizable national space that signifies London, but also an international narrative space that prefers certain kinds of stories about the forgotten, the repressed, pursuit, and chases. It is a space that is constantly made and remade in different times, and stories, and films. But perhaps the different times of the Underground are coming together in a way that forces us to recognize that this is Victorian engineering—mainly well over a century old. More frightening than monsters is the possibility that the continuing failure to properly resource the London Underground means that the skilled and semiskilled workers who can be found in the tunnels in these films are no longer there: the emptiness of the tunnels might be the most terrifying revelation of all.

Charlotte Brunsdon

Coda

This article was completed before the London bombs of 7 July 2005 and the attempted bombings of 21 July 2005. On 7 July, there were bombings on the London Underground at Aldgate, Edgware Road, and Russell Square, and on a number 30 bus in Tavistock Place. Four bombers killed themselves and fifty-two others, and many people were injured. Newspapers around the world showed mobile phone images of underground tunnels, the wrecked trains, and files of passengers walking down the tracks.[55] Much commentary after the bombs of 7 July invoked the London Blitz of the World War II. The mobile phone images of the attacks—poorly lit, obscure, and smoky—provide an unwelcome and haunting extension of the repertoire of images of the London Underground.

Notes

With thanks to Simon Murphy and Hugh Robertson of London's Transport Museum, Helen Scalway, Philippa Donnellan, Paul Long, and Tom Hughes for permissions and assistance with the illustrations.

1 Transport for London, http://www.tfl.gov.uk (21 May 2004).

2 Bhajju Shyam with Sirish Rao and Gita Wolf, *The London Jungle Book* (London: Tara Publishing in association with the Museum of London, 2004).

3 Ibid., caption to "The King of the Underworld" (book unpaginated).

4 See Charlotte Brunsdon, *London in the Cinema: The Cinematic City Since 1945* (London: British Film Institute, 2007). In Chapter Four, "Underground London," some of the material discussed here is analyzed in a different context. See also "'A Fine and Private Place': The Cinematic Spaces of the London Underground," *Screen* 47 no. 1 (2006): 1–17.

5 Rosalind Williams, *Notes on the Underground: An Essay on Technology, Society and the Imagination* (Cambridge, Mass.: MIT Press, 1990).

6 Lynne Kirby, *Parallel Tracks: The Railroad and Silent Cinema* (Exeter, University of Exeter Press: 1997).

7 City and South London line carriages, 1890, noted in Stephen Halliday, *Underground to Everywhere: London's Underground Railway in the Life of the Capital* (Stroud: Sutton Publishing in association with London's Transport Museum, 2004), 46–47.

8 Marc Augé, *In the Metro*, trans. Tom Conley (Minneapolis: University of Minnesota Press, 2002).

9 Schivelbusch discusses behavior and feeling in the railway compartment: *The Railway Journey: The Industrialization of Time and Space in the 19th Century* (Berkeley: University of California Press, 1986), Ch. 5.

10 The heroine of Naderi's film is traveling the New York subway lines doing crosswords, undertaking a marathon to better her own previous record. Thanks to Chris Gow for bringing this film to my attention and providing me with a copy.

11 Caption to "The King of the Underworld," a depiction of the London Underground as a giant earthworm in *The London Jungle* Exhibition, The Museum of London, December 2004.

12 Ken Garland, *Mr. Beck's Underground Map* (Harrow Weald, Middlesex: Capital Transport Publishing, 1994), 18.

13 Peter Ackroyd, *London: The Biography* (London: Chatto & Windus, 2000), 114.

14 Mark Ovenden, *Metro Maps of the World* (Harrow Weald, Middlesex: Capital Transport Publishing, 2003).

15 Adrian Forty, *Objects of Desire: Design and Society since 1750* (London: Thames and Hudson, 1986), 222–38.

16 Ken Garland points out, "Though not strictly speaking a map, this term is almost universally used by people referring to the London Underground diagram, hence the title of this book." Ken Garland, *Mr. Beck's Underground Map*, 3.

17 John A. Walker "The London Underground Diagram," in *Communication Design: Essays in Visual Communication*, ed. Teal Triggs (London: B. T. Batsford, 1995), 89.

18 Lynda Nead discusses the changed sense of journey produced by the building of the Underground: "Instead of traversing space by following the logic of streets and other identifiable external features, people could travel below the ground, on routes that obeyed the logic of their own lines and expediency. They could descend at one point in the city and emerge at another, with little sense of the spaces between, or the meaning of the time taken to make the journey." *Victorian Babylon: People, Streets and Images in Nineteenth-Century London* (New Haven: Yale University Press, 2000), 36.

19 Sales figures courtesy of Capital Transport Publishing, 5 December 2003.

20 The London Underground itself has a longstanding policy of artistic patronage, ranging from its famous posters, Poems on the Underground, busking sites, and many other initiatives.

21 Eric Hobsbawm, *Behind the Times: the Decline and Fall of the Twentieth-Century Avant-Gardes* (New York: Thames and Hudson, 1999) 38–39, quoted by David Pike in "Modernist Space and the Transformation of Underground London," in *Imagined Londons*, ed. Pamela K. Gilbert (Albany: State University of New York Press, 2002), 101.

22 David Pike, "Modernist Space and the Transformation of Underground London," 112.

23 Ibid., 113, 112.

24 Simon Patterson, "The Great Bear," 1992, Lithograph on paper 108.5 × 134 cm, Tate Britain, purchased 1996; David Pike, "Modernist Space and the Transformation of Underground London," 116.

25 Transport for London Web site, http://www.tfl.gov.uk/tfl accessed 21 May 2004.

26 Helen Scalway, "Traveling Blind," in *City A–Z*, ed. Steve Pile and Nigel Thrift, (London: Routledge, 2000), xvi. Scalway's previous work displays a recurring interest in place and its imagining. Other exhibitions include *Factory* (Birmingham University, 2001, in conjunction with the conference *The Performance of Place*) and *Porous* (2002, Florence Trust Gallery, London).

27 The paper is slightly larger than A4 at 21 cm × 30 cm. The maps are reproduced on both sides so that each map is always juxtaposed with another as one looks at the book.

28 This line drawing comes from Appendix H of Ken Garland's *Mr. Beck's Underground Map*, 72–73, "True scale and diagrammatic distortion: a comparison," which has a central drawing of the network in 1959. This map is pasted into Scalway's book.

29 These comments are reproduced in Scalway's account of the work in Steve Pile and Nigel Thrift. This book also uses some of the drawings on its cover.

30 Helen Scalway, "Traveling Blind," xvii.

31 Marc Augé, *In the Metro*.

32 Ibid, 30.

33 Underground stations were used in a more limited way for shelter in WWI: John Gregg, *The Shelter of the Tubes: Tube Sheltering in Wartime London* (Harrow Weald, Middlesex: Capital Transport Publishing, 2001).

34 Jill Craigie's *Out of Chaos* (1944) includes Moore with other war artists. Lee Miller's much reproduced photographs of Moore apparently sketching in the tube were taken during the shoot for this film. London Transport's celebratory *One Hundred Years Underground* (directed and narrated by John Rowdon, produced by Edgar Anstey and John Shearman). Julian Andrews, *London's War: the Shelter Drawings of Henry Moore* (Aldershot: Lund Humphries, 2002), 36–40. Andrews suggests that there is some controversy about whether Moore did or didn't sketch when actually in the shelters. In Craigie's film, Moore is shown using a notebook, but the framing is so tight that it is impossible to see whether he is in the presence of shelterers. See also John Gregg, *The Shelter of the Tubes*, 64; Peter Ackroyd, *London*, 565.

35 Moore in *One Hundred Years Underground* (British Transport Films, 1964, dir. John Rowdon, prod. Edgar Anstey and John Stearman).

36 See Stephen Daniels, "The Prince of Wales and the Shadow of St Paul's" in his *Fields of Vision*, 11–42 (Cambridge: Polity Press, 1993); Annette Kuhn, "The Phantasmagoria of Memory" in *Family Secrets* (London: Verso, 1995), 104–21.

37 A selection of Bill Brandt's shelter photographs was published in the magazine *Lilliput* with some of Moore's shelter drawings, 11: 6 (1942): 473–82.

38 The 1941 Arthur Askey film, *I Thank You* also shows morale-boosting collectivity, concluding with a singsong in the shelter/station.

39 Angus Calder does not discuss this particular film, but his *The Myth of the Blitz* (London, Pimlico, 1992) does offer some historical understanding of its

genealogy. The material conditions of the tube shelterers, and particularly the stench in the stations, are less frequently invoked.

40 Nick Freeman, "London Kills Me: The English Metropolis in British Horror Films of the 1970s," in *Shocking Cinema of the Seventies*, ed. Xavier Mendik, 193–210 (Hereford: Noir Press, 2002); Marcelle Perks, "A descent into the underworld: *Deathline*" in *British Horror Cinema*, ed. Steve Chibnall and Julian Petley 145–55 (London: Routledge, 2002). Thanks to Peter Hutchings for bringing these essays to my attention, and providing me with a copy of *Death Line*.

41 The earlier BBC serial version of *Quatermass and the Pit* (1958/9), also scripted by Nigel Kneale, does not site the current excavation at an Underground station, although an earlier extension of the tube in the 1920s is referred to.

42 David Berry, discussing the French Métro in the cinema, uses both labyrinth and maze metaphors in "Underground Cinema: French Visions of the Métro" in *Spaces in European Cinema*, ed. Myrto Konstantarakos, 8–22 (Exeter: Intellect, 2000). There is a considerable literature on the literary representation of the underworld more generally, including Rosalind Williams, *Notes on the Underground: An Essay on Technology, Society and the Imagination* (Cambridge, Mass.: MIT Press, 1990) and David Pike, *Passage through Hell: Modernists Descents, Medieval Underworlds* (Ithaca: Cornell University Press, 1997).

43 Ewa Mazierska and Laura Rascaroli, *From Moscow to Madrid: Postmodern Cities, European Cinema* (London: IB Tauris, 2003), 179. See David Martin-Jones, *Deleuze, Cinema and National Identity* (Edinburgh: Edinburgh University Press, 2006), 95–97, for a discussion of the significance of the "anywhere" of the film's London.

44 These Irish workers are part of a long tradition: the majority of laborers on Brunel's tunnel under the Thames (1825–43), the first subaqueous tunnel, were Irish. Benson Bobrick, *Labyrinths of Iron* (New York: Newsweek Books, 1981), 59.

45 The songs are credited to MacColl and Seeger as "songs to traditional Irish melodies." The credited singers are Paul Lennihan and Joe Heaney, although many individuals are featured singing diegetically. Other nondiegetic songs used include "The Rambler from Clare" and "Jack of all Trades," both of which share with the song of the Tunnel Tigers precise reference to the different parts of Ireland that might have been home to the singers or the audience. The tape editor is Charles Parker.

46 Hamid Naficy, *An Accented Cinema* (Princeton, N.J.: Princeton University Press, 2001).

47 Underground London (in general, not just the Underground) attracts passion, which is manifest in clubs, tours, books, films, and television series. Richard Trench and Ellis Hillman, *London Under London: A Subterranean Guide* (London: Murray, 1984) is one of the most thorough, whereas the most recent, Stephen Smith's *Underground London* (London: Little Brown, 2004), is wryly self-conscious about "a stripe of men—and they were predominantly men—who had a fascination with what was underground" (22). Among the

television series are *Under London Expedition* (*World About Us* tx 11 July 1971) and *Underground London* (2001).

48 "London's Underground Army: Laying and Maintaining the Tracks" (London Transport Museum Library, Document 001355 l8R6, anonymous, undated), 3.

49 The film was given a theatrical release in the West End in 1958, and the *London Transport Magazine* publicized it as "A Film You Should See," observing, "The content of facts and figures has been judged well. Not too much to overwhelm the general cinema-goer, but sufficient to hold the interest of the transport man himself." *London Transport Magazine* 12, no. 5 (1958): 16.

50 This difficulty of tone is also apparent in Trench and Hillman, who refer to the Fluffers as "that esoteric body of workers in the Underground: the fluffers. The fluffers are a small group of stalwart ladies who work in the tunnels in the small hours," (130). It is the "stalwart" in combination with the "ladies" that points to the authors' desire to be courteous despite the fact that the work is most unladylike and that few respectable women worked nights.

51 Stephen Smith, too, is unable to avoid sexual innuendo in his reference to the Fluffers, although he uses the excuse of the contemporary meaning of their name within the porn trade: "In the tunnel, Mick and I discussed the smirk-raising matter of the fluffers. Now a euphemism, or near-euphemism, for women who get male porn stars in the mood before the cameras turn, the fluffers used to be the name of the workers who had the unmirthful task of keeping the Tube tunnels clean" (274).

52 *The Museum Guide* to London's Transport Museum has a small photograph of "'Fluffers at work cleaning the tunnels of dust and debris, 1955" on page 18.

53 *The Heart of the Angel,* an Allegra Film for the BBC. Camera, Editing, and Producer: Molly Dineen. Producer for the BBC Caroline Pick. Transmitted in the *40 Minutes* slot, BBC 2, 26 November 1989. Dineen has a distinguished oeuvre of documentary portraits of people and institutions, most notably London Zoo (*The Ark,* 1993) and the army (*In the Company of Men,* 1995).

54 Halliday suggests that the Fluffers were mainly replaced in the 1970s by the "big yellow duster," a five-car cleaning train (195); clearly not at the Angel. London Transport records on this group of workers appear almost nonexistent.

55 For example, *Paris Match* printed mobile phone photographs taken by Nicolaus Thioulouse at Edgware Road (no. 2930, 13–20 July 2005, front cover and 332–35). Alexander Chadwick's mobile phone photo of the commuters walking through the tunnel site of the Russell Square/Kings Cross bomb appeared in many newspapers, including *The Independent* (8 July 2005, 9), *The Daily Telegraph* (8 July 2005, 2) and *The Sun* (8 July 2005, 9).

11

Marita Sturken

The Image at Ground Zero:

Mediating the Memory of Terrorism

Ground Zero was created in a moment on September 11, 2001, in New York City. When the towers of the World Trade Center collapsed, shockingly, into an enormous pile of rubble, spewing out a cloud of debris, the urban and aerial space that they had occupied became, quite simply, another place, one that seemed to demand a new name.[1] The name "Ground Zero" comes, of course, from history, implying both the central place of impact in nuclear destruction and, strangely, also a place of beginnings. As Amy Kaplan writes, "we often use 'ground zero' colloquially to convey the sense of starting from scratch, a clean slate, the bottom line," a meaning that she says resonates with the "often-heard claim that the world was radically altered by 9/11."[2] Thus, even in its initial naming, the space of Ground Zero was linked to a kind of exceptionalism.

Yet, what is Ground Zero as a place or a destination? It is, of course, a temporary name. Presumably when the site of Ground Zero is fully rebuilt, it will officially be called something else, the new World Trade Center perhaps. As a site that is defined as existing in between two places (the World Trade Center and its replacement) Ground Zero is more a concept than a place, a space charged with meaning, both highly overdetermined yet ephemeral.

≈ 225 ≈

Ground Zero is shaped by and experienced through media technologies, a space constantly mediated through images and "visited" through Web sites as well as in person, a space filled with photographs that is itself relentlessly photographed. Indeed, the space of Ground Zero was, from the moment of its naming, already defined through mediatization. The collapse of the World Trade Center towers was witnessed by an extraordinary number of viewers, by those standing on the rooftops and streets of Manhattan, Brooklyn, and New Jersey, by millions of television viewers throughout the United States, and by many millions of television viewers worldwide. It is now a banality to say that the terrorist attacks on New York were, in effect, a highly orchestrated media event of unimaginable scope that produced a uniquely high level of media saturation. September 11 is thus often defined as an event of the image, in which some new register of the spectacular was "achieved."

The intense networks of media that defined the events of 9/11 demonstrate the increased fluidity between what have been understood as public and private media, as mobile phone conversations and answering machine messages left by those who were trapped in the towers and on hijacked airplanes and the so-called amateur images of home video and still cameras were incorporated into the ongoing network and cable news coverage. This blurring of public and private was paralleled as well by an intermixing of old and new media (in boundary crossings that inevitably made those distinctions seem inadequate). In the age of digital technology, it is often imagined that the ether space of virtual media is just out there, without much of a technological infrastructure. Yet, when the World Trade Center towers fell, they took with them the primary antenna for network broadcasting in the region and key wireless transmitters for cell phone transmission in lower Manhattan—forcing many telecommunications companies to switch to antennas and transmitters on top of the Empire State Building.[3] It was an antenna of an older era of media, which was exalted for beaming broadcast signals in the 1970s west to New Jersey and beyond.[4] This mix of old and new media continues, as the images that circulate of 9/11 constitute television images, Web sites, and a plethora of still photographs.

In this chapter, I will look at the meanings that have been generated about Ground Zero through the practices of media and tourism. I am interested in examining how the reconfiguration and mediatization of Ground Zero as a site of cultural memory production has produced particular kinds of narratives of redemption that have an impact both on how the city will be rebuilt and how the site of Ground Zero will be deployed in the context of national politics. Thus Ground Zero exists not only as a space in lower Manhattan but as a virtual and imaginary space defined by innumerable television documentaries, replicas, tourist curios, photographs, and architectural and memorial designs.

The Spectacular

We must begin, of course by considering the role played by spectacle, as the space of Ground Zero is haunted by the spectacular images that were produced on the day of September 11, images that have been described by so many as "cinematic." It seems that so many people responded to the initial images of the planes exploding into the towers by thinking that it looked like a movie, and then catching themselves and thinking, how I can be thinking this, why do I think it looks like a movie? The television image of the towers exploding had been most prophetically imagined in flight simulator computer games, one of which, Microsoft Flight Simulator 2000, included, at the time of September 11, a joke about flying the plane into the Empire State Building.[5] This spectacular image was unbelievable yet uncanny, too familiar. The subsequent image of the towers falling, captured by the cameras of many people standing on rooftops throughout the city, is a less familiar image. The towers fell neatly inward, like a planned demolition, but the cloud of dust that they produced, which flooded the city, was dramatically otherworldly. When the towers fell, and the space of lower Manhattan was transformed from the World Trade Center to Ground Zero, the spectacle of the event was replaced by a vast pile of debris, a massive ruin that was, at least initially, off limits to cameras.

Though few would venture as far as Karlheinz Stockhausen, who declared the moment of the planes hitting the towers to be the ultimate work of art, it is now common to characterize the terrorist attacks of 9/11 as acts intended to produce not so much death as an image. As Slavoj Žižek has written, "we can perceive the collapse of the WTC towers as the climactic conclusion of twentieth-century art's 'passion for the Real'—the 'terrorists' themselves did not do it primarily to provoke real material damage but *for the spectacular effect of it.*"[6]

Žižek's rather glib pronouncement, which defines the complex politics of this event within a reductionist framework (they did it to create the image) nevertheless points to the way that the image is a central aspect of 9/11's exceptionalist discourse. Yes, it is said in this exceptionalist narrative, other violent historical events have killed more people, have destroyed cities more, have been more devastating politically, yet none has reached this level of the spectacular, none were seen live by so many millions of people, none looked like this.

Television and spectacle are defining aspects of the ways that 9/11 has been understood and consumed on a global scale, and they are defining aspects of how lower Manhattan is being reconceived. Yet, the essence of spectacle is an erasure—the awe-inspiring image of the explosion masks the bodies that are incinerated within it. In the aftermath of 9/11, these images of spectacle were countered by a proliferation of images throughout the city. The striking, clean images of the towers exploding were mediated by a profusion of amateur, street-level images, a proliferation of photographs in a vernacular intervention into the street life of the city.

The Photograph

The emergence of still photographs as a defining medium in the aftermath of the towers' destruction was almost immediate, as the city was quickly plastered with flyers for those who were missing. These missing posters, made in desperation by friends and family members, were posted near hospitals and rescue centers and on the streets of lower Manhattan, rapidly filling the visual landscape at eye level. Each of these images began as one of hope, imbued with the belief that the person would be found, would be *recognized*. Yet, within a week of the towers' fall, it became clear that there would be very few survivors, and the missing posters were transformed into images that marked, if not catalogued, the dead. Still they remained within the cityscape, tenaciously clinging to buildings and signposts, becoming increasingly faded and torn, their deterioration a kind of evocation of grief. The images on these missing posters powerfully evoked a kind of prior innocence—people smiling in vacation photos and at family gatherings, testimony to a time "before," when such a context, such an event, was unimaginable. The temporal disrupture of these images demonstrated in many ways the power of the still image to convey a mortality and finality. The identifying text, at once forensic as it noted particular physical characteristics ("eyes: blue" "eagle tattoo on right arm") and personal in its plea ("Have you seen John?") was transformed from a discourse of identification into one of fate: "1 World Trade Center, Marsh 97th Floor," "Cantor Fitzgerald," "Last seen on 102nd Floor of One World Trade Center."

The photographs in these posters were freighted with new meaning. As Marianne Hirsch writes, "Violently yanked out of one context and inserted into a totally incongruous one, they exemplify what Roland Barthes describes as the retrospective irony of looking at photographs—the viewer possesses the deadly knowledge that the subject of the image ignores."[7] This "deadly knowledge" is not simply about the fate of those imaged, but the transformation of the photograph itself—the image's change in status from casual snapshot to a talisman, to a trace that marks the absence of the dead. These photographs of people alive and naïve about events to come also acted as counterimages to the iconic images that came to define 9/11, not only the images of spectacle but also the haunting images of people falling/jumping to their deaths.

The photograph also plays a key role in mediating and negotiating a sense of loss. This was remarkably evident in the months after 9/11, when there was, in addition to the proliferation of photojournalism, a frenzy of amateur picture taking in New York, and an obsession with looking at images.[8] It has thus been referred to as one of the most photographed events in history, producing an "iconomania" of images.[9] This emphasis made clear that both taking and viewing images had a kind of cathartic effect. Initially, the site of Ground Zero was considered to be taboo for photographing and, as Hirsch writes, police told people to "show respect" by putting their cameras away.[10] Thus, in the moment of crisis, photography was seen as a suspect activity.[11] Yet, even in the early weeks, rescue workers and volunteers were photographing at the site. By Christmas time, there were several photographic exhibitions that were quickly installed in open storefronts, where anyone could bring their snapshots and videotape. These shows were hugely popular with both tourists and New Yorkers, as if the urge to both take photographs and to look at the images of disaster was a means of assimilating the event. Photographs can serve to inspire awe and voyeurism through the spectacular, but they can also make catastrophe feel containable. Much of the effect of these exhibitions was a sense of the visceral role the images could play, a catharsis not only in seeing closeup images of Ground Zero, a place still off limits, but also in seeing snapshot images of the events of that day, which seemed to have a more raw and spontaneous quality than the news images.

Among the many images that circulated in the streets of New York in those first few months, and which have continued to populate lower Manhattan ever since, were images of the twin towers themselves. Formerly maligned as objects of banal modernism, the towers acquired a poignancy in their destruction that would have been unimaginable as they stood. Yet, once rendered absent, they were the subject of an extraordinary mourning. Souvenir shops were immediately emptied of World Trade

Center postcards, and photographs of them were placed strategically at viewpoints where they had once been visible. These attempts to insert them into views from which they were missing were a kind of vernacular intervention into the now "empty" skyline. As central areas of the city, such as Grand Central and Penn Stations, were filled with tributes to the dead, the proliferation of images included children's drawings that reimagined the two towers as the "twin brothers," still standing in the skyline. In March 2002, a group of artists created a temporary memorial near Ground Zero, *Tribute in Light*, which consisted of two blue streams of light beamed into the sky.[12] Although it was intended to pay tribute to the dead, it also powerfully evoked the now-missing towers.

It can thus be said that the space of Ground Zero is constantly haunted by the absence of the twin towers. Indeed, the idea that the towers should be mourned as lost buildings is so taken-for-granted in the debate over how to rethink Ground Zero that few have attempted to question it. Yet, this means, in a certain sense, that lower Manhattan is constantly conceived as a space of absence, not only where the dead were lost (and many never found) but also a place that will always seem to be lacking the towers no matter what is built. The proliferation of images of the towers, not only in photographs but also in tourist souvenirs and innumerable coffee table books, forms a kind of mourning, an attempt to fill the space at Ground Zero with images, to imagine it as replenished rather than empty.

Photographing the Pile

Initially the site of the World Trade Center's collapse was a place of emergency, which was quickly cordoned off from public view and restricted from entry. Yet, after the New York City Sanitation Department made a huge effort to clean the streets of the dust that lay everywhere like snow, and the New York Stock Exchange opened the following week, Ground Zero became increasingly a site of fascination.

After the rescue operation had been transformed into a recovery operation, with the recognition that there would be no more survivors, the site was recoded as a construction and engineering puzzle, a huge excavating task, which construction companies and crews had to undertake to "unbuild." In the nine months from September 2001 to May 2002, Ground Zero was essentially a demolition site. In his book *American Ground: Unbuilding the World Trade Center*, William Langewiesche writes that "At the heart of it, under the skeletal walls rising to 150 feet above the street, the debris spread across seventeen acres in smoldering mounds. It was dangerous ground, of course. Workers at the site called it simply, 'the pile.'"[13] Langewiesche's book describes the ways that the various groups of the recovery operation—the firefighters, the police, and the construction workers and engineers—fought constantly over the meaning of the pile and how it should be treated.

Very few people were given access to the pile, and it remained both a dangerous and, to a certain extent, secretive place about which stories were told. People could stand at the periphery and look over the barriers at the piles of debris that stood several stories high, but there was not yet a place for viewing. Yet, in this highly restricted context, several iconic images were produced. The first was an image by photojournalist Thomas Franklin of three firefighters raising a flag on the afternoon of September 11 in the smoking ruins at Ground Zero. Effectively a remake of the famous image of soldiers raising a flag at Iwo Jima, the image was quickly christened as an icon of 9/11 and has been widely circulated since. In its reiteration of that image of heroic triumph in the face of conflict, the firefighter image has operated effectively as a resurrection.[14] In addition, in the months that followed, photographer Joel Meyerowitz, who has spent years photographing the World Trade Center towers from the roof of his building further uptown, was granted access through efforts of the Museum of the City of New York to photograph the site in the months in which the debris was cleared. Meyerowitz states,

> When I heard that there was no photography allowed in there, I got the call in some way to make an archive. I understood that this was something that was being overlooked by the administration, and I thought, this is what I have to give, I know how to make an archive. . . . The first impression for me was the wild chaos of the fall. . . . The complex, jumbled steely wiry, cabley, metallic mess of it. . . . There was no sense of escape. You looked at that pile and just to witness it, to stand up against it, this looming five-, six-story tangled mass was something that no one has ever seen. It was modern disaster.[15]

Meyerowitz's photographs are stunning images. In them, the massive piles of debris are rendered beautiful under the bright spotlights of the demolition crews. Although he photographed many of the recovery operation personnel, who are often formally posed before the camera, it is the chaotic, jagged debris of the buildings that is rendered most startlingly in the images, at once abstract and awesome. Meyerowitz works with a large-format camera, and the images are printed large, thirty by forty inches, so that they have a lush, luminescent quality. Meyerowitz has had a number of exhibitions of the photographs; he published a large number of them in a massive coffee-table book, *Aftermath: World Trade Center Archive*, in 2006, and the book has quite a number of foldout images that emphasize the immensity of the scale of the debris.[16]

Meyerowitz's images are not simply works that document what happened in the clearing of Ground Zero. They are aesthetic objects, with an artistic visual power. As such, they have an effect that is both intimate and spectacular, what Liam Kennedy has called "an epic quality and scale" that lends an aura and weightiness to them.[17] It is likely for these reasons that twenty-eight of the Meyerowitz images (including images of the pile and of rescue personnel at Ground Zero) were selected by the U.S. State Department in 2002 for an exhibition that traveled around the world for two years, to targeted areas in North Africa and the Middle East, Dar es Salaam, Istanbul, Kuwait, and Islamabad as well as numerous sites in South America, Asia, and Europe, as a form of cultural diplomacy.

The easy deployment of Meyerowitz's images as public diplomacy, in which they were exhibited with quotes from President Bush, Secretary of State Colin Powell, and former New York Mayor Rudolph Giuliani, raises questions about how their aesthetics function. As Kennedy points out, Meyerowitz's emphasis on the role of the images as an archive was also a means to downplay their acknowledged beauty, yet it was precisely their visual beauty that made them potential cultural messengers of the administration's attempt to justify its response to 9/11, the War on Iraq. The rhetoric of the texts in the exhibition makes this connection clear. As the statement from Assistant Secretary of State Patricia Harrison reads, "The exhibition will convey to foreign audiences the physical and human dimensions of the recovery effort, images that are less well known overseas than those of the destruction of September 11. Joel Meyerowitz captures the resilience and the spirit of Americans and of freedom-loving people everywhere."[18]

The exhibition contextualized these images as a means to convey a generalized image of suffering and resilience, one that was intended to humanize Americans who were increasingly the source of anger outside the United States. State Department officials attempted to make connections at many exhibition sites between the imagery of Ground Zero and local events, with uneven results. At the National Museum in Nairobi, the exhibit was placed next to an exhibit by local photographers of the bombing of the U.S. embassy in 1998, yet the size of Meyerowitz's images overpowered the local images. In Bangladesh, the exhibition was the site of protests.[19]

The Meyerowitz photographs are a compelling example of how images of Ground Zero were deployed for particular political purpose. They demonstrate the way that images of this highly charged site cannot be separated from the complex political context that created it. Like the images of the twin towers that circulate through the cityscape and throughout the nation, they are attempts to find redemption in disaster, to find meaning in death and destruction. Yet, when deployed as a form of cultural diplomacy, with the explicit attempt to create a better image of the United States throughout the world, they are vulnerable to the charge that, as Kennedy puts it, they affirm an exceptionalism about 9/11 "that the United States is the epicenter of the culture of humanity."[20]

It is precisely this exceptionalist discourse that comic book artist Art Spiegelman attempts to deconstruct in his own engagement with image production after 9/11. Spiegelman, who lives in lower Manhattan, spent three years after 9/11 producing a series of full-page comics about his traumatic experience that day.[21] His tortured work evokes the confusion of how to think about 9/11 in the context of the United States-led War on Iraq. In its adept mixing of past and present, including the transformation of Spiegelman and his wife into historical cartoon characters with the burning towers stuck on their heads, *In the Shadow of No Towers* is a portrait of Spiegelman's own damaged psyche, his need to relive the images and feelings of that day: "Many months have passed. It's time to move on. . . . I guess I'm finally up to about September 20 . . . but I'd feel like such a jerk if a new disaster strikes while I'm still chipping away at the last one."

One of the powerful effects of Spiegelman's book is its depiction of the dilemma of the subject who is stuck in the moment of trauma yet who wants to resist the way in which that trauma is exploited politically. His book integrates his own mourning—even his newly found affection for "the rascals" (the missing towers)—with his own conflicted recognition of the ironies of post-9/11 life. The image of the falling towers repeated until it becomes the subject of his own nostalgia ("he's starting to get nostalgic about his near-death experience back in September 01. . . . But why did those provincial American flags have to sprout out of the embers of Ground Zero? Why not . . . a globe?"). *In the Shadow of No Towers* thus demonstrates an engagement with the memory of 9/11 that is ironized and historically contextualized, demanding in a certain sense that it be seen through the eyes of someone whose quotidian experience is saturated with its memory. Yet, the irony that Spiegelman strives for has been overshadowed by a discourse of sacredness that has been applied to both 9/11 the event and Ground Zero the place.

Sacred Tourism

In the days after it became clear that there were few survivors and that many bodies would never be recovered, the ground on which the towers had stood was declared by many to be "sacred." The concept of sacred ground enabled many things at the site, and has been a particularly powerful discourse, both at Ground Zero and in national politics.

What does it mean when sites of violence are declared sacred? The term sacred implies a religious meaning. Yet, even though many religious figures have performed ceremonies at Ground Zero, the notion of sacredness applied there is derived not from the blessings of priests but from the loss of life that took place there. Indeed, this concept of sacredness can be situated in a long tradition in American culture of designating national spaces as secular sacred spaces, of which Gettysburg is the most obvious example. The connections made between Gettysburg and Ground Zero, which have included numerous readings of the Gettysburg Address at the site, explicitly infer patriotic meaning on the site, a move that situates the 9/11 dead (despite the fact that hundreds of them were not U.S. citizens) within the history of the sacrifice of soldiers who have "died for the nation."

The status of Ground Zero as sacred ground is a highly limiting one that has a huge influence on how Ground Zero is understood and its future imagined. A site of sacred ground is charged with meaning; it is a place of ritual and contemplation, where ordinary activities are suspended, if not inappropriate. The notion of sacredness has thus been an ongoing concern for the residents of lower Manhattan, who have been quite vocal in their desire not to "live in a memorial."

The designation of sacred ground has also had a huge impact on how the space of Ground Zero has been divided, with the decision, early on, that the "footprints" of the two towers were sacred sites for memorialization. Former New York governor George Pataki promised the families of the dead that he would not allow buildings to be built on the footprints of the towers, and from the beginning the many different design proposals for the site have treated the footprints of the towers as a special location. Some families of the victims staked out this issue for particular importance, at one point organizing protests to demand that the footprints be seen as sacred "from bedrock to infinity."[22] Both the master plan for the site by architect Daniel Libeskind and the memorial design, *Reflecting Absence,* by Michael Arad fully inscribe this hierarchy of space, with the footprints designated as unique spaces, voids in a public plaza.

It is also the case that the mediatization of Ground Zero has facilitated this fetishizing of the footprints. Innumerable images have circulated, via the Web and in print, which overlay the grids of the footprints onto aerial photographs of the hole at Ground Zero in which no footprints are actually visible. The footprints have been constantly reimagined via computer images onto the remaining empty space, in such a way that they appear to be imprinted on the ground. Ground Zero has thus been remapped through the innumerable computer images that have been created of it as an architectural site.

The discourse of sacred ground at Ground Zero demonstrates the complex ways in which memorialization and history making intersect with tourism. At first, as I have noted, Lower Manhattan was a restricted area, blocked off from view, in which looking was discouraged. By December, the police had become more accommodating because, as one told me, "people have the right to look." In January 2002, the Lower Manhattan Development Corporation (LMDC), which had been created to oversee the area, commissioned a viewing ramp near St. Paul's Chapel. By the spring, the *New York Times* and other publications were running travel features on where to eat downtown after visiting Ground Zero, effectively constructing the site as a tourist destination. In response to the large numbers of people, in the tens of thousands, who go there every day, the Port Authority of New York and New Jersey, which owned the World Trade Center and continues to own the land where it stood, has placed several outdoor exhibitions on the fence that surrounds the periphery of the site; one explains the history of the neighborhood, the construction of the towers, and a timeline of what happened on September 11 from 6:23 AM until 11:30 PM, others include dramatic photographs of 9/11. These displays effectively turn the construction site itself into an exhibition.

Lower Manhattan is not new to tourism, of course. The World Trade Center towers were a prime tourist destination, although almost exclusively for people taking elevators to its observation deck. Ground Zero is now a place where trinkets, souvenirs, and commodities are sold on the street, the majority by immigrant street merchants who work the area in the complex informal economy of street vending in New York. The proliferation of commodities includes FDNY hats and T-shirts, NYPD dolls, and crystal replicas of the twin towers, the vast majority "made in China," and innumerable photographs of the twin towers. Yet, ironically, the space of Ground Zero is, unlike the World Trade Center, an unphotogenic space. Tourists patrol its perimeter with cameras in hand, yet it is rendered in photographs as a kind of banal space of emptiness, which resembles a construction site rather than a space of meaning. This may be why the photographs and postcards that proliferate there are almost exclusively of the now-lost and now-mourned World Trade Center, rather than images of Ground Zero itself. The act of purchasing such an image—a postcard of a place one can no longer visit—would in most contexts seem to be an odd one. Yet here, the ubiquitousness of these images, and the sense that the towers are forever absent there, seems to normalize this activity.

The transformation of Ground Zero from a place of emergency to a place of tourism is not necessarily in conflict with the desire to see it as sacred ground. Tourist locations, like sacred sites, are places people make pilgrimages to. When people visit the site, they participate in practices of both mourning and tourism—they look in contemplation, they read the exhibits, and they take photographs. This tourism of terrorism is about experiencing some connection to the violence of that day by looking at the remains—about searching for a sense of "authenticity" in relation to urban trauma. Ironically, this increase of tourism, which promises to transform the landscape of this part of the city permanently, dovetails with the economic shifts that were already taking place in the neighborhood, in which the effects of postindustrialization have replaced the earlier urban demands of density in office space. Enabled by new technologies (and prompted to have spaces for information storage outside of Manhattan after the 1993 World Trade Center bombing), the financial firms of downtown had already regionalized by the time the towers were destroyed and office space in lower Manhattan had a high percentage of vacancies even before 9/11. Whereas the rebuilding and design process has focused on the so-called "need" to rebuild all of the office space that the towers once housed, it is most likely that the rebuilding of Ground Zero will create another glut of downtown office space not unlike that created by the World Trade Center when it was built.[23]

Imagining Memorialization

Although few would initially admit it, especially in the first year after 9/11, the fact that a larger area in a major metropolitan city was destroyed created an "opportunity" for architectural design and urban planning. The site of Ground Zero has been the object of an extraordinary number of architectural proposals and memorial designs. Although initially, many architects and citizen groups called for rebuilding the twin towers, in the years since 9/11 a massive effort has been made to rethink the space at Ground Zero, a significant amount of it outside of official channels. As high-profile architects began to produce proposals, both spontaneous and commissioned, for the site, they were accused by a few critics of turning Ground Zero into an "architectural beauty contest." In a 2002 debate with Libeskind, Leon Wieseltier, of *The New Republic*, declared, "There is something a little grotesque in the interpretation of ground zero as a lucky break for art. Lower Manhattan must not be transformed into a vast mausoleum, obviously, but neither must it be transformed into a theme park for advanced architectural taste."[24] Wieseltier's views are echoed in many of the statements that have been made by the families of the dead, for whom any aesthetization of the site has been read as counter to its sacred status as the final burial place of their loved ones.

Yet, one can also see in many of the architectural and memorial proposals a kind of mourning, not only for the buildings, as they stand in for the dead, but also a desire to fill up the empty space because its emptiness haunts the city. However, at the same time, the design proposals that are reimagining lower Manhattan, have also been strangely caught in a time warp, many of them unable to reimagine this part of the city in new terms, unable to consider what renewal of the neighborhood, in a way that would recognize its changing economic terrain, could mean.

The architectural reimagination of the space of Ground Zero began almost immediately, when the *New York Times* interviewed prominent architects within two weeks of the tower's destruction, and many of them declared that the towers should be rebuilt, in the words of Bernard Tschumi, dean of Columbia's School of Architecture, "bigger and better."[25] Only architects Elizabeth Diller and Ricardo Scofidio were willing to talk ironically in that moment, stating, "Let's not build something that would mend the skyline, it is more powerful to leave it void. We believe it would be tragic to erase the erasure." It is worth noting that the skyline that Diller and Scofidio are calling "void" was still populated with numerous skyscrapers.

The architectural community began to informally and formally reimagine the space of Ground Zero within a few months. In January 2002, Max Protetch Gallery held a show, "The New World Trade Center," of quickly conceived proposals for Ground Zero produced by a number of architects that Protetch had asked to reimagine the space downtown.[26] As architecture critic Philip Nobel writes, so soon after September 11, at a time when reports of dead were still coming from Ground Zero, the flippant tone of many of the entries range with dissonance, and "to scan the offerings from this grand, eclectic assembly of poobahs, insurgents, and unknowns . . . was to witness the fracturing of architecture as a profession and the limits of architecture as a communication medium."[27]

The proposals in the Protetch exhibition ran the gamut from fanciful imaginings of strangely organic-shaped towers wrapped together over the site, to green proposals for the landscape. Nobel notes that many felt that this exhibition itself was too early, that its freewheeling rethinking of the space seemed too soon, too callous, when Ground Zero was still, essentially, a graveyard. He writes, "Was it—could it ever be—too early for form?" Yet, in its reimagining of the space of Ground Zero, the exhibition also revealed the ways that architectural design was also functioning as a response to loss, an attempt to virtually fill up the empty space of Ground Zero and to imagine it whole. Tokyo architect Shigeru Ban submitted to the show a small model, called "A Departure from the Ego," of which he wrote, "I designed this temporary World Trade Center Memorial immediately after September 11, without being asked by anyone. Maybe I was motivated because of my experience of building the 'Paper Church' after the Kobe earthquake of 1995."[28]

In the years since the 2002 Protetch show, there have been hundreds of design proposals for how to rebuild Ground Zero, produced by amateurs and professional architects, as well as several competitions for a master plan of the site. It is striking that in a preponderance of these proposals, the shadow of the twin towers was a constant presence, one that ultimately demonstrates that designers are haunted by their presence. Can design be divorced from memorialization? Nowhere was this more evident than in the master plan of Daniel Libeskind, "Memory Foundations," which was chosen from the competition in February 2003. The design was initially popular precisely because Libeskind presented it in terms of memorialization rather than urban renewal. Indeed, Libeskind can be said to have won the design competition precisely because of his ability to negotiate the fraught terrain of design and memory, aesthetics and mourning. Libeskind paid tribute to the experience of Ground Zero in his initial design by leaving part of the "slurry wall" of the pit exposed. Libeskind also gave symbolic names throughout, such as "The Park of Heroes" and "Edge of Hope" and created a "Wedge of Light," a triangular plaza where the sun will reach from 8:46 to 10:28 AM each year on September 11. The key feature of his original design was a 1,776-foot high tower, quickly named the "Freedom Tower" by Governor George Pataki, which was intended to echo the Statue of Liberty (the name has been quietly retired as real estate interests make clear that One World Trade Center is likely to attract more tenants).

It was precisely because of the plan's emphasis on memory, and Libeskind's situation of himself within that discourse (as both a former Jewish refugee and the designer of the Jewish Museum in Berlin), that made the plan popular with politicians and the families of the dead, who can be said in retrospect to have already conceived the space already completely as a site of memory. Nevertheless, the plan was at the center of a controversy about aesthetics before it was chosen. *New York Times* architecture critic Herbert Muschamp wrote a now notorious attack on the design, condemning it as an "astonishingly tasteless" and "emotionally manipulative" design that was bland and smacked of "kitsch."[29]

Very little of Libeskind's master plan will be realized at Ground Zero as it has been whittled away by the political and development interests at work at the site, which have produced not only a highly fortified and uninspired design for the Freedom Tower (now One World Trade Center), a triad of hastily designed office towers by Norman Foster, Richard Rogers, and Fumihiko Maki, which may not be built because of financial concerns, and a hugely expensive transit station by Santiago Calatrava. As New York's architectural community has looked on in increased despair, as costs escalate and as the developers increasingly usurp any chance for public interest, it is clear that the rebuilding of the space of Ground Zero is an opportunity lost. Yet, whatever is eventually built there, Ground Zero remains a space onto which innumerable images have been projected. Just as the photographs of the World Trade Center had populated the site, and the images of 9/11 have defined it, the design proposals for rebuilding lower Manhattan have created an imaginary at Ground Zero. It is, in effect, already a virtual place, which has increasingly been imagined through computer simulations of designed spaces. The proliferation of computer-simulated designs of a rebuilt Ground Zero has thus had the effect of making it appear realized.

This virtual reimagining has also taken place in relation to the design of not only the architectural proposals but also the memorial for the site. In late 2003, the LMDC held an open competition for a memorial design, for which over five thousand entries were submitted from around the world.[30] The competition has been heavily criticized for rushing the process and for producing a bland set of finalists, but it did produce an extraordinary set of reimaginings of the site, which ran the gamut from tasteful to absurd. In its chaotic range of approaches, the contest revealed the ways that design was providing a cathartic response to trauma.

Whereas many could be characterized as timid, almost corporate designs, others were wildly inappropriate yet fascinating for what they seemed to demonstrate about how immediate the trauma still was. One design consisted of an oversized question mark, another featured two airplanes in a park, and another a glowing apple on top of a spire.[31] Reportedly, the jurors were astonished by what they considered to be the "tastelessness" of some of the entries.[32]

The final design, *Reflecting Absence*, by Michael Arad, consists of an open plaza of trees into which the two footprints of the twin towers are imagined as two "voids" with reflecting pools.[33] Its primary aesthetic is thus an emphasis on emptiness and voids, and much of the criticism of the design has fixed on this quality, calling it "void of honor, truth, emotion and dignity."[34] Clearly, the "voids" that demarcate the footprints of the towers in the memorial design replay the presence/absence of the twin towers.

Yet, it is the computer imaging of both the architectural proposals and the memorial design that seem to bring them alive and create a virtual experience of an imagined Ground Zero. These computer images have the effect of making the space seem not only real, but also realized. Several times when I have given talks about these designs and shown the computer-generated images of them, some audience members (who perhaps have only minimally been paying attention) get confused and think that I am discussing spaces that have already been built and memorials that have already been constructed. A key reason is that the computer renderings are highly realistic and include computer-inserted digital images of actual people to make them look photographic. The designers who create these computer images work to create this high level of realism, actually photographing people on the street and digitally inserting them in order to give the designs a sense of being inhabited and experienced by actual people.[35]

The memorial design, which was timid to begin with, has been essentially eviscerated by the demands of politicians and a vocal group of family members, and it is now largely considered to be a "remarkable banality after two years of intense thinking," as *New York Times* architecture critic Nicolai Ouroussoff has written.[36] In addition, the vast area that has been given over to the memorial as voids rather than public space indicates a huge failure in reimagining the space of Ground Zero, one that also equates a large amount of space with an idea of exceptionalism. The most successful memorials are those that create intimate spaces, and many do this with a very small amount of space. One has only to look at those cities that were destroyed in times of war to see what an aberration it is to turn over such an enormous area of the city to memorialization. With plans focused on a large memorial center under the site, the overdetermination of memory at Ground Zero is even more evident.

The constant mediation of Ground Zero has been a key factor in this overdetermination. It is not simply an empty hole in the ground. It is a place onto which images have been constantly projected, a place that is always generating images and objects, a source of endless imaginings, fantasies, and fears. Ground Zero thus exists not simply in its materiality, but as a place of imagining, of photographs, of virtual images, of constant mediatization. Ironically, this means that when Ground Zero is gone, and something stands in its place, it will itself, like the twin towers, be mourned.

Notes

1 According to Michael Tomasky, the first use of the term in print was by Associated Press reporter Larry McShane in the evening of 11 September, in which he wrote, "Shortly after 7 PM, crews began heading into ground zero of the terrorist attack to search for survivors and recover bodies." Michael Tomasky, "Battleground Zero," *New York Review of Books*, 1 May 2003, 18.

2 Amy Kaplan, "Homeland Insecurities: Transformations of Language and Space," in *September 11 in History: A Watershed Moment?*, ed. Mary L. Dudziak (Durham, N.C.: Duke University Press, 2003), 56.

3 Seth Schiesel and Saul Hansell, "A Flood of Anxious Phone Calls Clog Lines, and TV Channels Go Off the Air," *New York Times*, 12 September 2001, A8. When the World Trade Center was built, the broadcasting masts were moved there from the Empire State Building when there were concerns about the buildings blocking broadcast signals. See Angus Kress Gillespie, *Twin Towers: The Life of New York City's World Trade Center* (New York: New American Library, [1999] 2002), 139.

4 In the mid-1980s, I took a video camera up on the observation deck of the World Trade Center. The power of the antenna (which was on the other tower) was such that it completely distorted the video and audio signals when one stood at that end of the deck.

5 Henry Lowood, "Death in the City: Computer Games and the Urban Battlefield," paper presented at the Urban Trauma and the Metropolitan Imagination conference, Stanford University, 6 May 2005. According to Lowood, Microsoft delayed the release of the 2002 version of the game in order to change the New York skyline, and offered users a software patch in order to erase the offending comments. After September 11, reporters used the 2000 version of the game to learn to fly jetliners into the twin towers, and after the release of the 2002 version, players created their own patch to reinsert the "towers back *into* the default scenery."

6 Slavoj Žižek, *Welcome to the Desert of the Real!* (New York: Verso, 2002), 11.

7 Marianne Hirsch, "I Took Pictures: September 2001 and Beyond," in *Trauma at Home: After 9/11*, ed. Judith Greenberg (Lincoln: University of Nebraska Press, 2003), 73.

8 On the changes that 9/11 produced in photojournalism and newspaper layout of images, see Barbie Zelizer, "Photography, Journalism, and Trauma," in *Journalism After September 11*, ed. Barbie Zelizer and Stuart Allan, 48–68 (New York: Routledge, 2002).

9 See Kari Andén-Papadopoulus, "The Trauma of Representation: Visual Culture, Photojournalism and the September 11 Terrorist Attack," *Nordicon Review* 24 (2003): 89–104, http://www.nordicom.gu.se/common/publ_pdf/32_089-104 .pdf.

10 Hirsch, "I Took Pictures," 69.

11 See Barbara Kirshenblatt-Gimblett, "Kodak Moments, Flashbulb Memories: Reflections on 9/11," *The Drama Review* 47, no. 1 (Spring 2003), 14.

12 The project was produced by two architects, John Bennett and Gustavo Bonevardi, and two artists, Paul Myoda and Julian LaVerdiere. They were later joined by architect Richard Nash Gould and lighting designer Paul Marantz. It was produced by the Municipal Art Society and Creative Time. See http://www.creativetime.org/towers/main.html.

13 William Langewiesche, *American Ground: Unbuilding the World Trade Center* (New York: North Point Press, 2002), 11.

14 See Andén-Papadopoulus, "The Trauma of Representation," 98.

15 Interview with Joel Meyerowitz, *Frontline* Web site, http://www.pbs.org/wgbh/pages/frontline/shows/faith/interviews/meyerowitz.html.

16 Joel Meyerowitz, *Aftermath: World Trade Center Archive* (New York: Phaidon, 2006).

17 Liam Kennedy, "Remembering September 11: Photography as Cultural Diplomacy," *International Affairs* 79, no. 2 (2003), 320.

18 The exhibition is available at http://www.911exhibit.state.gov.

19 Kennedy, "Remembering September 11," 325.

20 Ibid., 326.

21 Art Spiegelman, *In the Shadow of No Towers* (New York: Pantheon, 2004).

22 Philip Nobel, *Sixteen Acres: Architecture and the Outrageous Struggle for the Future of Ground Zero* (New York: Metropolitan Books, 2005), 246.

23 Developer Larry Silverstein, who purchased the lease for the towers in the month before they fell, has had an extraordinary, and ultimately destructive, impact on the rebuilding process by insisting that the terms of his lease demand that an equal amount of commercial space be rebuilt. Silverstein's obstinacy has been aided by unvisionary incompetence on the part of city and Port Authority officials and by the complex politics of the ownership of the site, which is technically owned by the Port Authority of New York and New Jersey, which puts it under the jurisdiction of the governors of those two states,

rather than the city government of New York City, in which it stands. The inability of Silverstein and all of the officials involved to take into account the changing context of the New York housing market, with its shift from industrial and business spaces to a demand for residential spaces and a postindustrial regionalization of office space, in particular after the economic collapse of 2008, remains quite stunningly anachronistic. See Paul Goldberger, *Up From Zero: Politics, Architecture, and the Rebuilding of New York* (New York: Random House, 2004).

24 Sarah Boxer, "Debating Ground Zero Architecture and the Value of the Void," *New York Times*, 30 September 2002, B1.
25 "To Rebuild or Not: Architects Respond," *New York Times Magazine*, 23 September 2001, 81.
26 Max Protetch, *A New World Trade Center: Design Proposals From Leading Architects Worldwide* (New York: ReganBooks, 2002).
27 Nobel, *Sixteen Acres*, 82.
28 Protetch, *A New World Trade Center*, 25.
29 Herbert Muschamp, "Balancing Reason and Emotion in Twin Towers Void, *New York Times*, 6 February 2003, E1.
30 The designs are all posted at http://www.wtcsitememorial.org.
31 David W. Dunlap, "5,201 Ideas for 9/11 Memorial, From the Sublime to the Less So," *New York Times*, 20 February 2004, A1.
32 Glenn Collins and David W. Dunlap, "Unveiling of the Trade Center Memorial Reveals an Abundance of New Details," *New York Times*, 15 January 2004, A26.
33 Glenn Collins and David W. Dunlap, "The 9/11 Memorial: How Pluribus Became Unum," *New York Times*, 19 January 2004, A1, A18.
34 Joan Molinaro, "Letter to the Editor," *New York Times*, 20 January 2004, A18.
35 Matthew Bannister, "Urban Apparitions and Ethereal Graffiti," presentation at the Urban Trauma and the Metropolitan Imagination conference, Stanford University, 6 May 2005.
36 Nicolai Ouroussoff, "The Ground Zero Memorial, Revised But Not Improved," *New York Times*, 22 June 2006, E5.

12

Shunya Yoshimi

Tokyo: Between Global Flux and Neonationalism

During the last decade of the twentieth century, the fiercely fluid movements of the new cross-border networks of capital, information, and
people have been rapidly transforming the centripetal power of the large
Japanese cities from within. After World War II, forms of electronic communication—from television to videos to cell phones to the Internet—
have turned our sense of place inside out, extending but also significantly
transforming previous modes of mobility, migration, and sociocultural
networks made possible by earlier forms of transportation and telecommunications. Paradoxically, this tendency toward global flux is accompanied by the rise of a form of nationalism (with accompanying sentiments
of xenophobia) that attempts to rebuild the identity of Japaneseness by
reinvoking the age of prosperity enjoyed by the Japanese state during the
period of high economic growth. These twin tendencies of nationalism
and global flux should not be understood so much as contradictions but
rather as parallel and constitutive parts of the same historical moment in
which nations and electronic networks mutually reconfigure each other.
Tokyo is exemplary in this regard.

Tokyo as a World City?

Tokyo had, since the Meiji period, embodied a certain kind of "internationality," with its brick buildings in the Ginza, modern manners, state institutions, press, and publishing. This "internationality," however, was restricted to the level of ideas, images, and information, and was dependent on the fact that Tokyo was the capital of the Japanese Empire and home to the Emperor. Although it was the undisputed center of the domestic rail network, which bound the entire country to the capital, it had not yet become a nodal point in the global transportation network. After World War I, the trend toward more direct linkage with the global order had been stronger in cities such as Osaka and Kobe, and in the colonial capitals, than it had been in Tokyo.

After World War II, however, with the process of reconstruction to create a more "purified" nation-state, Tokyo has come to enjoy a virtual monopoly of the channels linking Japan with the "world." This is true on all levels, including those of information, capital, and people. This process of recentralization, and Tokyo's dominance in the area of global relations, were symbolized by the Tokyo Olympics in 1964. It was also around then that foreign travel came within the reach of the general population. Port cities, like Kobe and Yokohama, have experienced no reduction in the quantity of goods they handle, but the importance of sea transportation has decreased proportionately as a result of the development of air transportation and telecommunications.

Before the war, airplanes had been restricted largely to military uses, and in that age before international telephony and telexes, sea routes had been of overwhelming importance as the conduits for the cross-border flow of goods, people, and information. After the war, this central importance of sea routes was taken over by air transportation networks, and by the media systems, beginning with satellite television relays, and later satellite broadcasting and the electronic media. In all these new fields, Tokyo possessed distinct advantages and quickly attained dominance.

The tendency toward unilateral concentration on Tokyo, which occurred during the first stage of globalization in the contemporary sense in the 1980s, was an extension of the already established postwar system. Hence, when we look back on what was said about the "global city Tokyo" during the boom years of the bubble economy, the future could only be conceived as an extension of the past. For example, one of the most frequently discussed visions of the future was the idea that "Tokyo is about to become a global city in the same league as New York or London." As the capital of the world's biggest creditor nation, Tokyo would attract industries, personnel, information, and money. People thought that Tokyo was about to become a core global city forming one of the poles in the envisioned three-polar world economy of the twenty-first century.

Underlying such optimism was the assumption that the position of the Japanese state in the world economy would be reflected directly in the international centrality of its capital city. There was much discussion about how Tokyo should be "internationalized" in order to make it into a "world city," but at the same time such discussion was still paradoxically very much focused on the framework of the nation-state. For example, recognizing that competition between cities was beginning to take place on a world scale, it was argued that there should be a base for advanced communications in Tokyo, and that offshore markets and convention facilities should be developed, and an international business center established. Tokyo, it was proposed, had to set an example as a model of internationalization for regional centers. The Marunouchi and Yaesu business districts in central Tokyo were already being seen as centers of world finance just like Wall Street, and there was a view that Tokyo was bifurcating into an international information city, on the one hand, and a domestic residential city, on the other. In all these discussions, the internationalization of Tokyo was pursued inseparably from the internationalization of Japan, and the strengthening of Japan's international competitive power.

The Information Landscape

The new network mediated by air transportation and electronic communications has a whole dimension that renders it structurally different from the earlier network based on sea routes. The worldwide airway network has social implications quite different from those of the older network based on railways, stations, ships, and sea routes. Although railways and steamships allowed people to travel much faster than they had previously by horse-drawn carriages and walking, the distance covered remained a function of the time spent traveling. However, the speed of air travel makes any such proportionality irrelevant. The concept of "movement" has been entirely transformed, as has the very meaning of geographical space. These days, air travel feels as though it is "movement without movement, that is, a direct connection between one point and another, without anything in between."

Thus, the cities now seem to be only a place for temporary transit, one point on a synaptic trajectory path, something like an old fortress on a sloping bank, a ridgeway, a borderline, where how fast things move and the way of looking at them is unified like a machine. To return to the subject of airports, airplane routes do not simply provide high-speed connections between cities. Rather, air transport has transformed cities themselves from places of settled living to spheres of almost incessant motion.[1] Modern cities are founded on almost incessant movement. Furthermore, this has given rise to a worldwide simultaneousness, which practically nullifies any spatial sense of area or distance.[2] This change in the existential basis of cities should be of crucial importance when considering what Tokyo's being a "world city" meant in the 1980s.

Indeed, as Uchida Ryuzo suggests, from the beginning of the bubble period, Tokyo was starting to experience a serious "feeling of uncertainty about its own foundations." This was not caused by Tokyo's limitless expansion, but by its aimless fluidity. For this reason, the renewed expansion of Tokyo into suburban areas and around the bay are not so much an expression of a tense relationship with those surrounding areas, or of the loss of boundaries. It represents instead a contortion and denial of the existing order of Tokyo as a result of new social forms emerging from within Tokyo itself. It could also be described as a process of "self-differentiation."

In other words, in developing into a world city, Tokyo had not simply expanded outward. Rather, as globalization progressed, the city was nurturing internally a new self-image that negated what Tokyo had been until then. This tendency toward a divided identity is gradually deepening. Uchida calls this process Tokyo's "hyper-urbanization." For the same reason, it could equally well be called "hyper-Tokyofication." In the Tokyo undergoing "hyper-Tokyofication," the speed of capital far outstrips the rate of spatial change. Even the explosive rise in land prices and wave of redevelopment that occurred in the 1980s could no longer keep up with this speed of capital. Nowadays, "things of the city" are distributed and consumed before they can be spatialized. The thing with the closest relationship to such capital is the concept of "information." In other words, the "hyper-Tokyofication" of Tokyo implies also that it is undergoing a process of "informationization" (*johoka*). Of course, in this context, "informationization" refers to something quite different from what it means in theories of the information society. On the contrary, the main thrust of this argument concerns the post-spatialization of Tokyo, that is, the situation in which the city divorces itself from its geographical context, and permeates outward as part of the global flow. This urban flow naturally involves many different intersecting dimensions.

We can find many instances of this hyper-spatialization of Tokyo in the urban landscape that has become familiar since the 1980s. On the one hand, there are the flat themed environments, ranging from Tokyo Disneyland, which has lost any sense of spatial depth and breadth and become like a collage projected on a three-dimensional screen, and extending to the artificial cities built on the shores of Tokyo Bay, where futuristic postmodernity coexists with a desolate landscape of depopulated ruins, besides the kitsch streets of Tama New Town, and the vast suburban shopping malls. On the other hand, hyper-spatialization is also manifested in the highly fragmented phenomenon of "things in the Tokyo style." This overflows far beyond the so-called geographical boundaries. Here we may include, for example, television dramas, animation programs, and fashion made in Tokyo. Just as we understand the global flow of visual images as the distribution of "things in the Hollywood style," we would propose that these subcultural images be understood not as the "Japanization" of culture, but as the deterritorialized flow of "Tokyo style."

A city that has been transformed into a flow is a city of mobile networks. In other words, it is not the case that cities preexist as fixed spaces and are then linked into a network. A city is something that is always in a state of motion. In a city transformed by networks of information and capital, reality moves from monitor screen to memory bank, to video disk, and to networks of imagination. The model for such a city is neither Bentham's panopticon, nor the shining city of Le Corbusier. Rather, it appears as the nonlinear vision of a computer matrix full of ruptures, discontinuities, and disconnections.[3]

This is no mere metaphor. Here, we are not using cyberspace simply as a metaphor to depict the modern-day city. The discontinuous and symbolic landscapes of the cities of today are inseparable from the constantly moving communication mediated by the pagers and mobile phones of young people. This has become even more fully a reality than envisioned by Robert Venturi in his discussion of Las Vegas.[4] It would be a mistake to think that the concrete form of the city will continue to be bounded by durable buildings and stable patterns of permanent residence. The spatiality of today's cities is clearly beginning to diverge from this older type of spatiality. As an "information landscape" rather than a bounded "imagined community," Tokyo, and indeed Japan as a whole, have overflowed from their previous boundaries and now float in the time–space of global capital and information.

The Cross-Border Network City

The global fluidization of capital and the resulting changes in the city are also accompanied by the formation of cross-border networks of people. As scholars such as David Morley, Kevin Robins, Asu Aksoy, Marie Gillespie, and Tajima Junko have argued, people make use of the international telephone network, videos, and various forms of ethnic media to cross borders and take up residence in foreign cities where they live their daily lives with a perception of distance quite different from before.[5] Their perception of distance is constructed intersubjectively within their respective social networks, which do not necessarily coincide with the global spatial order formed by capital. Thus, in "hyper-Tokyofied" Tokyo, numerous networks, each containing a diversity of elements, have proliferated in a far from uniform way among the various nonnative populations.

Tajima Junko and others have been conducting ongoing research among the Asian immigrants who have settled in inner areas of Tokyo such as Ikebukuro and Shinjuku. These studies vividly depict the networks proliferating among people who have crossed borders. It is interesting to compare the studies conducted by Okuda Michihiro and Junko in Ikebukuro in 1988 and 1989; their study of Shinjuku in 1992; and the studies Tajima made in these two areas in the middle of the 1990s. The cross-border networks, whose existence could be only faintly discerned at the end of the 1980s, have gradually become more visible and have come to exert an extremely dynamic influence on the city and region. More than just an artifact created by the deepening perceptiveness of the researchers involved, this attests to the rapid maturation of the networks of foreigners currently residing in Tokyo during the past ten years.

One of the clearest indications of this is the flourishing of ethnic businesses based in these areas. During the first stage of the influx of foreigners from Asia in the 1980s, cross-border networks formed as those already settled in the country brought over their families, relatives, friends and acquaintances. In the second stage, the concentrations of newcomers began to develop distinctive subcultural worlds of their own. The transition between these two stages occurred in the 1990s, altering the lifeworld of Asian immigrants in places like Ikebukuro and Shinjuku. As influx changed to settlement, and the lives of these people in Tokyo began to show signs of being long-term, a new pattern of demand for information and culture from their home countries arose. Clusters of ethnic businesses appeared. Native-language newspapers and magazines were started by immigrants themselves. Native-language video rental stores also appeared, as well as restaurants, beauty salons, and the like, which have come to act as meeting places. These are all catalysts for the rediscovery of ties with the native country, and the reorganization of ethnic networks.

Tajima demonstrates through her studies that the number of entrepreneurs establishing ethnic businesses in Ikebukuro and Shinjuku increased rapidly from the beginning of the 1990s. Many of these were set up by people who had come to Japan in the 1980s. In contrast to the Japanese economy as a whole, which fell into long-term recession after the speculative bubble of the 1980s burst, Tokyo's ethnic businesses have experienced a boom. H Media, for example, began as a book-lending business in Ikebukuro. Then, in response to the needs of Chinese immigrants, it expanded its business in several directions, including the travel agency business, visa consulting, newspaper publishing, restaurants, real estate, ethnic groceries, and videos. It even opened a trade office in Shanghai, and a book purchasing agency in Hong Kong, where the owner of the business had family connections. What is interesting is that one of the reporters from the newspaper run by H Media went on to establish his own Chinese language newspaper, and another person from that newspaper in turn became independent and established yet another newspaper in Shinjuku. In this way, the Chinese media in Japan compete among themselves, while diversifying.

While introducing many such examples, Tajima emphasizes the way in which these ethnic businesses do not simply create changes in one particular local area, but give rise to new networks, by bringing together people from different areas, besides linking them to the home country. Ethnic businesses serve not only to maintain the links with the native country and the bonds between compatriots. Rather, they operate in such a way as to constantly reorder the life-worlds of immigrants so that they straddle simultaneously the place where they have come to live and their native country. Deterritorialized networks of a kind that could never have existed in the past are being created and multiplied through the media and spaces of ethnic businesses, such as newspapers, video stores, restaurants, bars, and beauty salons. Boundaries are forever being brought into question by the people who cross them. Furthermore, this new state of affairs has been made possible by the global expansion of communication networks, and a transport system that makes mobility incomparably easier than before.

At the same time, the networks of immigrants in Japan that are strengthening such cross-border ties have a dimension not seen by most Japanese. To a certain extent, the presence of these networks has become manifested in local society in visible forms, such as restaurants, grocery stores, and religious establishments. In areas where many foreigners live, the points of contact between them and other residents of the area are increasing. However, such areas are limited to places like Shin-Okubo in Tokyo, and the cross-border networks of immigrants have not yet come to alter the underlying reality of the city. On the level of Tokyo as a whole, the cross-border networks of capital and information have had far more of an impact since the 1990s, and the importance of the ethnic dimension has not yet been widely recognized.

The Inversion of the "Global City"

Nevertheless, it would be a mistake to think that these cross-border networks of people are in a dichotomous, contradictory relationship with the cross-border capital and information mentioned earlier. As may be clearly seen from the examples of London, New York, and Los Angeles, where the development of ethnic businesses is considerably more advanced than it is in Tokyo, network-type businesses run by foreigners, far from being in conflict with global capital networks, are actually an important part of them. Thus, in today's global city of Tokyo, a loosely interconnected whole is gradually emerging from the confluence of the different cross-border networks of capital, information, commodities, and people. In this process, the very identity of the city is fundamentally placed in question.

This is a completely different process from that envisioned in the discussions about "Tokyo as a global city" in the 1980s. The assumptions then taken for granted are being overturned. As we have already seen, the debate about the internationalization of Tokyo and its transformation into a global city in the 1980s was predicated on the idea of Tokyo being at the center of Japan's national economic strength. It was assumed that this center of identity would go on to play a central role in the flow of capital, information, and people in the global economy as well. There was no doubt that the nation of Japan had already spilled over its territorial boundaries, and Tokyo too was experiencing such expansion. Nevertheless, this expansion was understood as an additional stage within an ongoing narrative of identity, according to which the "imperial capital," having become a "national metropolis," would then develop into a "global city."

However, the basis for this narrative underlying the identity of Tokyo has been torn apart, both internally and externally, since the 1990s. Furthermore, this change seems to have occurred in advance of a more general shakeup in the national identity of Japan. One wonders how well the people of Tokyo—in particular, the middle mass of Japanese who form the majority—will be able to cope with this reversal in the international dimension of their city. To what extent will they respond positively to the transformation of Tokyo from a fixed place with clear boundaries to a fluid complex whose boundaries are forever being called into question?

Shunya Yoshimi

As far as concerns the immediate future, our answer to such questions has to be negative. Just as Tokyo clung to the ideology of the "imperial capital," with the emperor's place of residence as its imaginary focus during the prewar era, and clung to the ideology of the "national metropolis" as the model for "development" during the era of high economic growth, Tokyo now seems to be fastening its grip on an ideology that seeks to retrieve its identity as a "world city" in this age of globalization. Many people in Tokyo will probably continue to see the present internationalization of their city not as something threatening its identity, but simply as a further stage in the internationalization that began in the period of high economic growth—in other words, as an expansion of the city's identity as a capital from the nation to the world at large.

At present, the imaginary basis for this mildly global city is provided by the image of postwar Japan in the 1950s and 1960s, when it began to "stretch its wings toward the world." Many present-day Japanese seek refuge from uncertainty not in the *exterior* of modernity by trying to return to a native identity thought to have existed before globalization and modernization, but rather in the *interior* of modernity, by returning to that age during the Cold War when Japan was most strongly subject to American influence.

Three Times Triumphant

It is perhaps no coincidence that Ishihara Shintaro, one of the leading representatives of this retronationalism, should become, since his election as governor in 1998, the new face of the global city, Tokyo. Indeed, the career of Ishihara Shintaro is not unrelated to contemporary reactionary nationalist tendencies. Ishihara Shintaro has three major triumphs to his name. The first was in 1955, when he made his brilliant literary debut, as author of the novel *Taiyo no kisetsu (Season of the Sun)*.[6] The second triumph came in 1968, when he stood for election to the upper house of parliament and came in at the top of the polls, gaining more than three million votes in a nationwide constituency. During his thirty-year parliamentary career, he was conspicuous for little more than his repeated hardline statements, and can hardly be said to have distinguished himself as a politician. Then, having just resigned his parliamentary seat, he made a surprise move by becoming a candidate in the election for Tokyo governor, in which he won a handsome victory with over 1,660,000 votes (about 30 percent of the valid vote count). Once again, he had succeeded in becoming a focal point for common people's hopes and fears.

The timing of Ishihara's three triumphs is highly significant. The years of 1955 and 1968, and the end of the 1990s were all important times of transition in Japan's modern history. On the occasion of the second triumph, Eto Jun, a close friend of Ishihara, made the following observation: "There seems no doubt that he [Ishihara] is a forerunner of things to come."[7] If this is true, why then did this trickster figure reemerge in the 1990s? When he first entered the limelight in 1955, he was greeted as a symbol of the new hedonism of the Shonan area. In 1968, he became an emblem of the spirit of Japanese "progress" during the period of rapid economic growth. Against a background of nostalgic popular feeling for his brother Yujiro (a movie actor, now deceased), what was it that enabled him to find common cause with the Japanese masses of the end of the century?

It is clear that Ishihara's third triumph cannot only be attributed to any widespread sympathy for his brand of nationalism. It would be more accurate to say that the electorate saw in him an answer to their deep-seated dissatisfaction with the existing political parties and bureaucratic elites. However, in order to understand how such a "nationalist" could come to occupy the top position in a global city, we must look beyond such immediate causes. Symbolically at least, there must be some structurally convoluted linkage between the present popular consciousness in Tokyo and Ishihara's nationalist rhetoric.

Reports in the American press on the day after the gubernatorial election gave prominence to the fact that Ishihara was the joint author of the book *The Japan That Can Say No*, labeling him as an anti-American with a declared electoral promise to secure return of the American base in Yokota.[8] However, these reports seemed to have forgotten entirely that Ishihara was once, around the time of his first triumph in 1955, an advocate for a certain form of "Americanism," openly affirming the pursuit of materialistic desires. In an interview given to the weekly journal *Shukan Asahi* immediately after he won the Akutagawa Prize for literary achievement, he stated that he watched "nothing but American movies" and had a "special liking" for *High Noon* and *Champion*. He went on to give jazz as his musical preference, and cited Hemingway as the author he particularly respected. Admittedly, what Ishihara admired in America was not so much its "affluence" as its materialism and sense of speed. Nevertheless, his writing and behavior were from the very beginning entirely lacking in local color, and tended to be American in style.

It is as well to think back to the 1950s, the period during which *Taiyo no Kisetsu* first appeared. This was the very same age that saw James Dean in *Rebel Without a Cause* attain mythic hero status among the young, Elvis Presley's popularity reach its peak, and the worldwide boom sparked by the film *Blackboard Jungle*, with its open promotion of rock and roll. Young people donned skintight trousers and became ecstatic about the mambo. Ishihara Shintaro, and his brother Yujiro, were soon to become models for such youth. It was also during this period that household appliances came to be widely available, and there was already a foretaste of the coming age of high economic growth and its all-out affirmation of personal desires. As I have argued elsewhere, the symbolic changes in the images of domestic electric appliances began in the mid 1950s, and was reflected in the expression of *Sanshu no Jingi* (three sacred treasures), which referred to the washing machine, the refrigerator, and the black and white TV. Even though quite expensive for most families at that time, they rapidly became popular in Japanese homes so that by 1960 45 percent of Japanese homes had washing machines, 54 percent had TVs, and 15 percent had refrigerators. By the 1970s, the figures for all these appliances exceeded 90 percent. Meanwhile, by the late 1960s, a new holy trinity of treasures—a car, an air conditioner, and a color TV—emerged.[9] This consumer frenzy took place at a time of heightened cathexis on the image of America as both a space of desire (for material goods, youth culture movie icons such as James Dean and Elvis Presley, and a whole set of media and advertising images), and as a space of violence (with, for example, Japanese protests over U.S. occupation at military bases in the 1950s).[10] In every sense, the popularity of *Taiyo no Kisetsu*, and of Ishihara Yujiro following his debut in the film *Kurutta Kajitsu* (Crazy Fruit), belonged to this same era, and coincided with the worldwide popularity of James Dean and Elvis Presley. But the Ishihara of the 1990s stirring up nationalist consciousness among the public is not the product of some "conversion of faith." Instead, today's resurgence of faith is grounded in nostalgia for the "modern" Japan promised in the cold war past. In this sense, it is also not surprising that we now see a wave of nostalgic sentiment surrounding the figure of Ishihara Shintaro's deceased brother Yujiro, a popular movie actor in the 1950s and 60s.

An examination of past history shows that there have been many instances so far when contemporary responses to globalization have sought to ground themselves in the globalization of the immediately preceding era. Modernity feels unease at the further progression of modernity. A distinctive feature of the neonationalist mood prevalent in Japan since the 1990s is that the basis to which this politics of identity appeals is imaginary, extremely vague, and cannot exist without contradiction. In the case of Ishihara, the object of his aspirations may be the Japan that colonized Asia and formed its own empire in resistance to those of the Western powers. However, the masses of people who support him are less interested in such a direct return to prewar times than in the Cold War period during which the postwar Japanese identity was rebuilt under the American umbrella.

In fact, the "Golden Age" to which the populist nationalism represented by Ishihara is trying to return can no longer exist as an imaginary place either. As Tokyo enters more and more into a state of flux, any sense of it being a core "world city" expanding globally along with the identity of Japan is being lost. In such a situation, there is a nostalgic reevocation of the 1950s and 60s, when, like a set of concentric circles centered on Tokyo, the nation of Japan "spread its wings toward the world." As a "favorite son" of that age of Americanism, who made such a brilliant debut back then, it is hardly surprising that Ishihara should reappear as the man most suited to represent its reevocation. There is therefore a sense in which Ishihara's anti-American nationalism finds its basis paradoxically in the "internal colonialism" of Americanism, in spite of his right-wing rhetoric.

Like a thick blanket of cloud, America had enveloped Japan with an enormous protective membrane preserving its postwar time–space. As mentioned previously, Ishihara was a splendid embodiment of this "America's Japan." A situation is clearly developing here that seems paradoxical, but is not in fact necessarily contradictory. The paradox is that the populist nationalism of post-Cold War Japan has grounded itself in the period when the Cold War was at its height. The identity formed in the Cold War period has been carried over into the post-Cold War period, altering its positional meaning and giving rise to new political consequences.

The Politics of Hatred

Since becoming governor, Ishihara has courted pubic opinion by giving vent to a popular sense of fear. This can be clearly seen in how he promotes his own brand of exclusionary nationalism, as was witnessed in a speech he gave at a ceremony of the Self Defense Forces on 9 April 2000. In that speech he made the following statement: "If you look at Tokyo today you can see that very vicious crimes are repeatedly being committed by many *sangokujin* ["third country people"], foreigners, who enter the country illegally. The nature of crime in Tokyo is already different from in the past." The comments evoked instant criticism from a wide range of politicians and public commentators. The main focus of these criticisms was Ishihara's use of the word "*sangokujin*," a term that is generally understood as a discriminatory reference to resident Koreans and Taiwanese permanent residents in Japan. Ishihara's response was not so much retraction as counterattack. He accused certain media outlets of misleading the public by failing to quote his words accurately and in full (particularly for citing the word "*sangokujin*" without quoting the words "who have entered the country illegally").

In this extremely problematic speech, Ishihara's loudly declaimed proposal to mobilize the Self Defense Forces for the maintenance of public order and his threatening attitude toward globalization are two sides of the same coin. His point of view is founded on the assumption that globalization is an inevitable process, and that society will become more and more heterogeneous as the influx of immigrants continues. The status and safety of the "pure Japanese" will almost certainly be threatened by seditious "foreigners." Such "bad others" will then have to be excluded by force. Thus, a complementary relationship can be discerned between the neoliberal immigration policies on the one hand, and Ishihara's heavy-handed approach to "illegal" immigrants on the other.

It is surprising how little negative public reaction there has been to the violent, racist, and fascistic thought underlying Ishihara's use of the term "*Sangokujin*." To the contrary, a majority (61 percent) of telephone calls and faxes made to the Tokyo Municipal Government Office immediately after he made the statement were supportive, while only 36 percent were critical. Despite intense media criticism, the "Ishihara brand" has lost none of its value. Public opinion has continued to lend its support to the "strong leader" image being played out by Ishihara. A comment characterized Ishihara as a politician who uses "hatred" as a means to mobilize the populace. This politics of "hatred" is related to the feeling of uncertainty experienced by many Japanese people in the 1990s.

The "hatred" expressed by Ishihara as leader of Tokyo has taken numerous concrete forms: a "hatred of bureaucracy" expressed in the swinging wage cuts imposed on staff; a "hatred of banks" through the sudden introduction of a new bank tax; a "hatred of China's rising status" in his statements negating the very existence of the Chinese state. All these synchronize with the "hatreds" felt by members of the public. That a governor who makes statements such as that quoted earlier could gain such a degree of popular support is a reflection of the depth of public hatred toward illegal immigrants and toward the intrusion of globalization into the landscape of everyday life.

There is a fatal flaw in Ishihara's discourse, with its appeal to an imagined nationalistic "purity" using as a springboard popular hatred of the "other." As already emphasized, cooperative and competitive places no longer connected to one fixed place are constantly forming and proliferating in the context of the diasporic networks of the global city, and the cross-border flow of information, capital, and people. Such changes may not yet be easily visible to many people. Nevertheless, the paradigms of identity, place, and social status are undergoing corrosive change. As Doreen Massey suggests, we should no longer think of place in terms of a closed space with a fixed center and boundaries.[11] The concepts of place, identity, space, and city are amenable to deconstruction. According to such a deconstruction, the exterior would already be present in the interior, the interior open to the exterior, and complex identities would arise amid heterogeneity. So there is a wide gap between the reality of the transnational networks taking shape in today's Tokyo and the imaginary threat posed by the *"sangokujin"* so feared by Ishihara. With the development of new media and transportation networks, global cities are becoming places not just for cross-border interaction among people of different nationalities, but also for populist politics of "hatred" based on the popular sentiment to protect themselves against the global flux.

Notes

1 For discussion of airports and their relation to cities see David Pascoe, *Airspaces* (London: Reaktion Books, 2001).

2 For a general discussion of cities, the loss of spatiality, and the effects of telecommunications see David Harvey, *The Condition of Postmodernity: An Enquiry into the Origins of Cultural Change* (London: Basil Blackwell, 1989), Chapter 17; Paul Virilio, *Speed and Politics* (1977, reprint; New York: Semiotext(e), 2007); Paul Virilio, "The Overexposed City," in *Rethinking Architecture: A Reader in Cultural Theory*, ed. Neil Leach, 380–90 (London: Routledge, 1997).

3 For more on cities and communication networks see Saskia Sassen, *Global Networks, Linked Cities* (New York: Routledge, 2002); Saskia Sassen, *The Global City: New York, London, Tokyo* (Princeton: Princeton University Press, 2001); M. Christine Boyer, *Cybercities: Visual Perception in the Age of Electronic Communication* (Princeton: Princeton Architectural Press, 1996).

4 Robert Venturi, *Learning from Las Vegas: The Forgotten Symbolism of Architectural Form* (Cambridge, Mass.: MIT Press, 1977).

5 In addition to Morley's and Askoy and Robins's chapters in this volume see David Morley and Kevin Robins, *Spaces of Identity: Global Media, Electronic Landscapes, and Cultural Boundaries* (London: Routledge, 1995); David Morley, *Home Territories: Media, Mobility, and Identity* (London: Routledge, 2000): Marie Gillespie, *Television, Ethnicity and Cultural Change* (London: Routledge,1995).

6 Original reprinted in Ishihara Shintaro, *Ishihara Shintaro tanpen zenshu*, Vol. 1 (2 volumes; Tokyo: Shinchosha, 1973), 46–81. The story is available in translation under the title "Season of Violence" in Shintaro Ishihara, *Season of Violence*, trans. John G. Mills, Toshie Takahama, and Ken Tremayne (Rutland, Vt.: Charles E. Tuttle Co., 1966).

7 Eto, 1968.

8 Ishihara Shintaro and Morita Akio, "NO" to ieru Nihon (Tokyo: Kobunsha, 1989), followed by three other books. An English language selection of material appeared as Shintaro Ishihara, *The Japan that Can Say No: Why Japan Will Be First Among Equals* (New York: Simon and Schuster, 1991).

9 Shunya Yoshimi, "'Made in Japan': The Cultural Politics of 'Home Electrification' in Postwar Japan." *Media, Culture & Society* 21 (1999): 155.

10 For more on this see Shunya Yoshimi, "America as Desire and Violence: Americanization in Postwar Japan and Asia during the Cold War," trans. Davis Buist, *Inter-Asia Cultural Studies* 4, no.3 (2003): 433–51.

11 Doreen Massey, *Space, Place, and Gender* (Minneapolis: University of Minnesota Press, 1994).

Contributors

ASU AKSOY works in the Department of Cultural Management at Istanbul Bilgi University, Istanbul. She is a visiting researcher at Goldsmiths College, University of London.

CHRIS BERRY is professor of film and television studies in the Department of Media and Communication at Goldsmiths, University of London. His research focuses on Chinese screen-based media, and his publications include *China on Screen: Cinema and Nation* (with Mary Farquhar) and *Postsocialist Cinema in Post-Mao China: The Cultural Revolution after the Cultural Revolution*.

CHARLOTTE BRUNSDON is professor of film and television studies at the University of Warwick. She is author of, most recently, *London in Cinema* (2007) and *Law and Order* (2010).

RATIBA HADJ-MOUSSA is associate professor of sociology of culture at York University in Toronto, Canada. Her research areas include new media in the Maghreb, Algerian cinema, and forgetting and history in the North African context. Among her publications are *The Mediterranean Reconsidered* (edited with Mauro Peressini) and *Suffering in Art* (with Michael Nijhawan, forthcoming).

SOYOUNG KIM is professor of cinema studies in the School of Film and Multimedia at Korean National University of Arts. She is author of *Specters of Modernity* and *Cinema: Blue Flower in the Land of Technology*. Her documentary *Women's History Trilogy* can be found at www.seoulselection.com. Her essays have been translated into Japanese, Spanish, Chinese, English, and Italian.

TAMAR LIEBES-PLESNER is the Karl and Matilda Newhouse Professor in the Communications Department at the Hebrew University of Jerusalem. Among her books are *American Dreams, Hebrew Titles: Globalization from the Receiving End; Reporting the Arab–Israeli Conflict: How Hegemony Works;* and (with Elihu Katz) *The Export of Meaning: Cross-Cultural Readings of Dallas*.

DAVID MORLEY is professor of communication in the Department of Media and Communication, Goldsmiths College, University of London. He is author of *Spaces of Identity* (with Kevin Robins); *Home Territories;* and *Media, Modernity, and Technology: The Geography of the New*.

LISA NAKAMURA is director of the Asian American Studies Program and a professor of media and cinema studies at the University of Illinois, Champaign-Urbana. She is author of *Digitizing Race: Visual Cultures of the Internet* (Minnesota, 2007), *Cybertypes: Race, Ethnicity, and Identity on the Internet* (2002), and coeditor of *Race in Cyberspace* (2000).

ARVIND RAJAGOPAL teaches at New York University and is author of *Politics after Television: Hindu Nationalism and the Reshaping of the Public in India* (2001), among other publications. This book received the Ananda K. Coomaraswamy Prize from the Association of Asian Studies in 2003. Most recently he has edited *The Indian Public Sphere: Readings in Media History* (2009). His new book, *After Decolonization: Transformations of Political Authority in a Globalizing Age,* is forthcoming.

KEVIN ROBINS is a visiting fellow at Goldsmiths College, University of London, and a visiting professor at Istanbul Bilgi University. He is author of *The Challenge of Transcultural Diversities: Cultural Policy and Cultural Diversity*.

JEFFREY SCONCE is associate professor in the Screen Cultures program at Northwestern University. He is author of *Haunted Media: Electronic Presence from Telegraphy to Television* and editor of *Sleaze Artists: Cinema at the Margins of Taste, Style, and Financing*.

LYNN SPIGEL is the Frances E. Willard Professor of Screen Cultures at Northwestern University. She is author of *TV by Design, Welcome to the Dreamhouse,* and *Make Room for TV*. She has edited numerous anthologies, including *Television after TV,* and is editor of the Console-ing Passions book series.

MARITA STURKEN is professor in the Department of Media, Culture, and Communication at New York University. She is the author of several books, including *Tangled Memories: The Vietnam War, the AIDS Epidemic, and the Politics of Remembering; Practices of Looking: An Introduction to Visual Culture* (with Lisa Cartwright); and *Tourists of History: Memory, Kitsch, and Consumerism from Oklahoma City to Ground Zero.*

SHUNYA YOSHIMI is professor of information studies at the University of Tokyo. He specializes in sociology, cultural studies, and media studies. Among his many books in Japanese are *Tokyo Studies: A New Critical Guidebook for Tokyo* and *Expo Syndrome: Postwar Politics and Cultural Struggle in Contemporary Japan.* Several of his essays have been translated into English.

Index

British Museum Zoological Department, 39

Broadband House, 56, 72, 75, 84

Brockes, Emma, 14n21

Brooks, Rodney, 92n80

Brook, Timothy, 114n28

Bruno, Giuliana, xviii, xxvin44

Brunsdon, Charlotte, xxi–xxii, 132, 135n41, 220n4

Bukatman, Scott, 21, 31n2

Bumming in Beijing: The Last Dreamers (Liulang Beijing), 100–101

Burke, Catherine, 76, 91n65, 91n66

Burnett, Robert, 25, 27, 31n17

Burns, Lewis J., 85n1

Bush, George W., 30, 232

Butler, Judith, xvi

Cable Street Gallery, 203

Calatrava, Santiago, 239

Calder, Angus, 222n39

Caldwell, John T., xviii, xxviin50

Calhoun, Craig, 104, 114n27

Canada, 37

Carbine, Mary, x, xxivn11

Cardiff, David, 154n23

Care Bears, 18, 20

Carlier, Omar, 123–124, 134n20

"Carolina Moon," 38

Carrington, Hereward, 37, 52n6, 52n11

Carrousel of Progress, 85n8

Cartwright, Lisa, 23, 31n10, 32n26, 32n28

Caruso, Denise, 90n56

Casanova, Jose, 170n8

CCTV (China Central Television), 98, 100, 102, 106

Centre for the Study of Developing Societies, 163

Chadwick, Alexander, 224n55

Chairman Mao, 98

Chamberlain, Heath B., 104, 114n27

Champion, 254

Chan, Alex, 106, 113n14, 115n35

Chat room, 5

Chatterjee, Partha, 170n16

Cheek, Timothy, 104, 114n27

Cheung, Charles, xxivn9

Chicago, x

Chinese Communist Party Propaganda Department, 105

Chikhaoui, Isabelle Berry, 136n42

China on Screen, xiv

Chua, Geok-lian, xxvin33

Cinema, ix, xviii, 36; American silent, x; Australian, xiv; British, xxi; Chinese, 98; and Hollywood classical film style, x; Egyptian, xiv; French, xiv; and gender and race in early US movie theaters, x; Hollywood, 80; horror genre, 209–10, 218; and maternal melodrama, 81, 83; and nationalism, xiv; and the railway, 199; social realist, 203; and spectatorship, x, 199. *See also* documentary

Cinema and the City: Film and Urban Societies in a Global Context, xviii

Cinematic City, The, xviii

Cinéma vérité, 103

City after Dark, 213, 218

"Civil society," 97, 104–108, 115n30

Clarke, David B., xviii, xxviin47

Cleaver, Joanne, 90n58

CNN (Cable News Network), 186 187

Cohen, Anthony, 174, 191n5

Cohen, Robin, 191n4

Cold War, 58, 61, 253, 256

Collin, Françoise, 136n44

Collins, Glenn, 243n32, 243n33

Colomina, Beatriz, ix, xxiiin8, 67, 88n36

Colony, The, 210

Columbia University, School of Architecture, 237

Compaq, 62

Computer, 24, 26; laptop, 68, 71, 74, 85n3; and family conflicts, 76–77; in households, 74–76